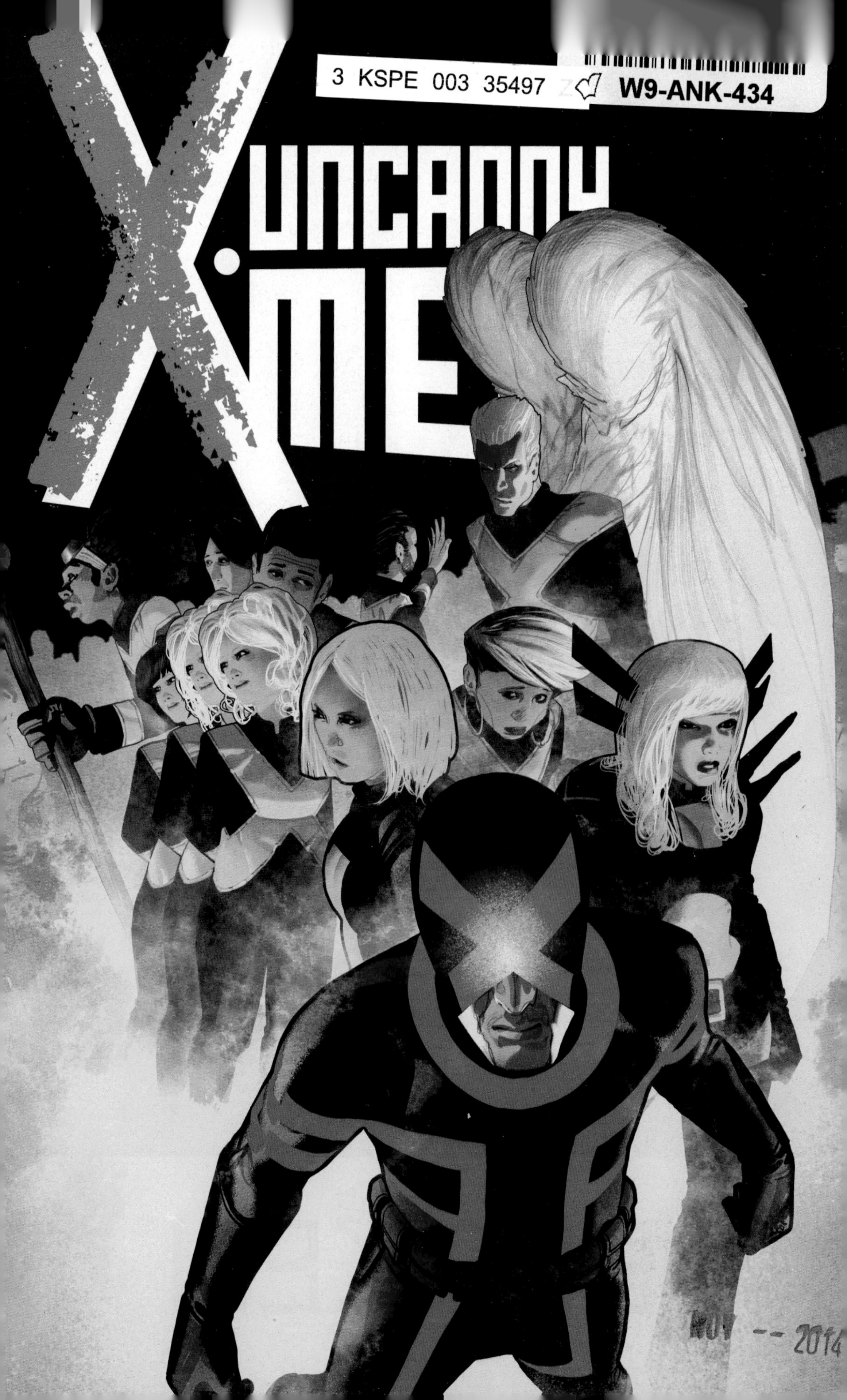
X UNCANNY MEN

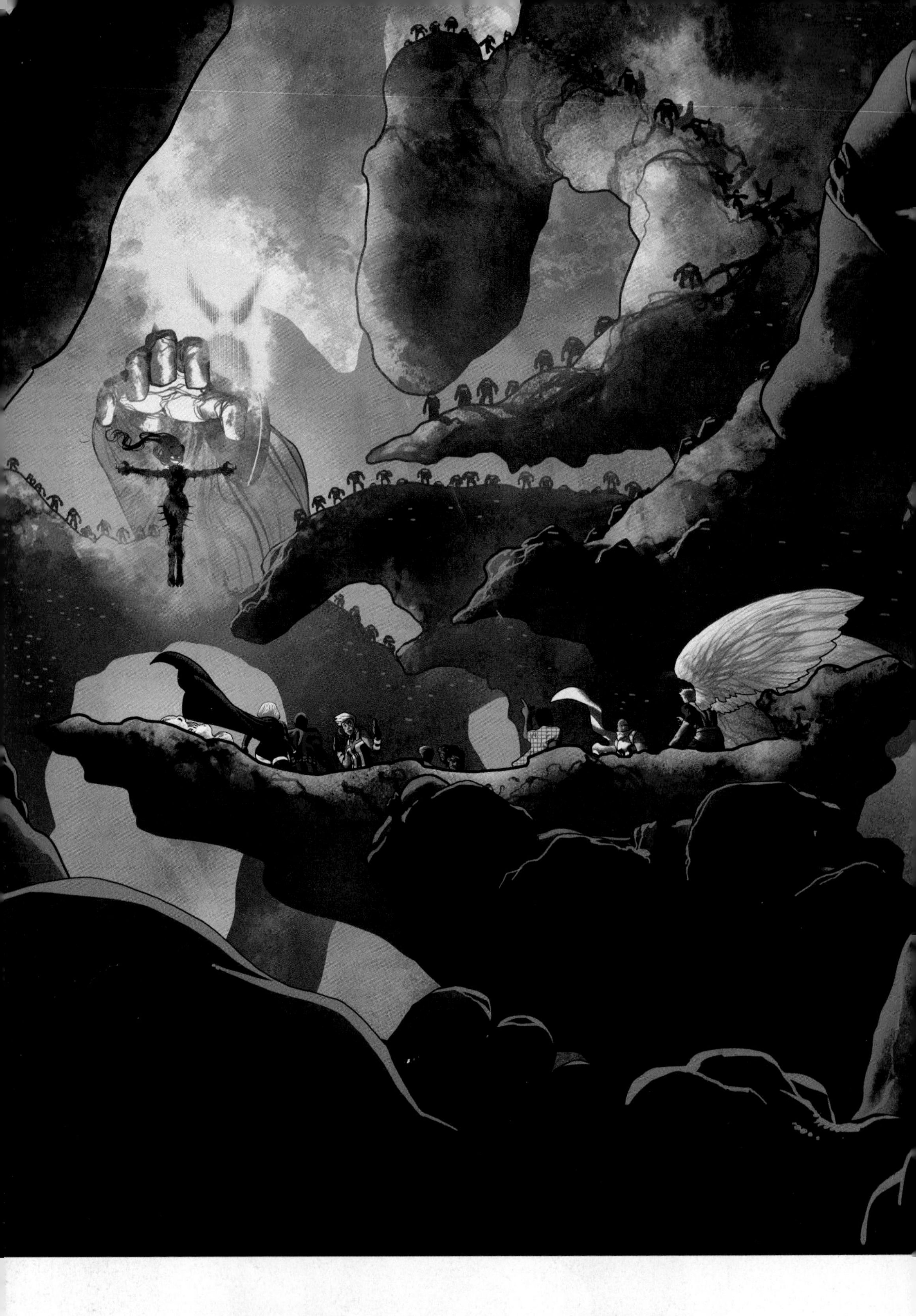

BROKEN

CYCLOPS
SCOTT SUMMERS

EMMA FROST

MAGNETO
ERIK LEHNSHERR

MAGIK
ILLYANA RASPUTIN

TRIAGE
CHRISTOPHER MUSE

TEMPUS
EVA BELL

FABIO MEDIA

BENJAMIN DEEDS

BRIAN MICHAEL
BENDIS
WRITER

FRAZER
IRVING
ARTIST, #6-7 & #10-11
WITH KRIS ANKA (#11)

CHRIS
BACHALO
PENCILER/COLORIST, #8-9

TIM
TOWNSEND
INKER, #8-9
WITH MARK IRWIN,
AL VEY & JAIME MENDOZA (#9)

COVER ART: **FRAZER IRVING (#6-7 & #10), CHRIS BACHALO & TIM TOWNSEND (#8-9) AND PHIL NOTO (#11)**

VC'S JOE
CARAMAGNA
LETTERER

JORDAN D.
WHITE
ASSISTANT EDITOR

NICK
LOWE
EDITOR

COLLECTION EDITOR: **JENNIFER GRÜNWALD**
ASSISTANT EDITOR: **SARAH BRUNSTAD**
ASSOCIATE MANAGING EDITOR: **ALEX STARBUCK**
EDITOR, SPECIAL PROJECTS: **MARK D. BEAZLEY**
SENIOR EDITOR, SPECIAL PROJECTS: **JEFF YOUNGQUIST**
SVP PRINT, SALES & MARKETING: **DAVID GABRIEL**

EDITOR IN CHIEF: **AXEL ALONSO**
CHIEF CREATIVE OFFICER: **JOE QUESADA**
PUBLISHER: **DAN BUCKLEY**
EXECUTIVE PRODUCER: **ALAN FINE**

UNCANNY X-MEN VOL. 2: BROKEN. Contains material originally published in magazine form as UNCANNY X-MEN #6-11. First printing 2014. ISBN# 978-0-7851-6703-7. Published by MARVEL WORLDWIDE, INC., a subsidiary of MARVEL ENTERTAINMENT, LLC. OFFICE OF PUBLICATION: 135 West 50th Street, New York, NY 10020. Copyright © 2013 and 2014 Marvel Characters, Inc. All rights reserved. All characters featured in this issue and the distinctive names and likenesses thereof, and all related indicia are trademarks of Marvel Characters, Inc. No similarity between any of the names, characters, persons, and/or institutions in this magazine with those of any living or dead person or institution is intended, and any such similarity which may exist is purely coincidental. **Printed in the U.S.A.** ALAN FINE, EVP - Office of the President, Marvel Worldwide, Inc. and EVP & CMO Marvel Characters B.V.; DAN BUCKLEY, Publisher & President - Print, Animation & Digital Divisions; JOE QUESADA, Chief Creative Officer; TOM BREVOORT, SVP of Publishing; DAVID BOGART, SVP of Operations & Procurement, Publishing; C.B. CEBULSKI, SVP of Creator & Content Development; DAVID GABRIEL, SVP Print, Sales & Marketing; JIM O'KEEFE, VP of Operations & Logistics; DAN CARR, Executive Director of Publishing Technology; SUSAN CRESPI, Editorial Operations Manager; ALEX MORALES, Publishing Operations Manager; STAN LEE, Chairman Emeritus. For information regarding advertising in Marvel Comics or on Marvel.com, please contact Niza Disla, Director of Marvel Partnerships, at ndisla@marvel.com. For Marvel subscription inquiries, please call 800-217-9158. **Manufactured between 5/9/2014 and 6/16/2014 by R.R. DONNELLEY, INC., SALEM, VA, USA.**
10 9 8 7 6 5 4 3 2 1

Born with genetic mutations that gave them abilities beyond those of normal humans, mutants are the next stage in evolution. As such, they are feared and hated by humanity. A group of mutants known as the X-Men fight for peaceful coexistence between mutants and humankind. But not all mutants see peaceful coextistence as a reality.

UNCANNY X-MEN

Cyclops, one of the original X-Men, and his team are formidable leaders of the new mutant revolution, demanding investigations into the recent series of anti-mutant attacks, and challenging anyone who opposes them. They've also been gathering new mutants as fast as they appear: their new Xavier school is now home to four — very green — students poached from the Jean Grey school.

But behind their public front, the Uncanny X-Men are rattling demons. Magneto's loyalty is in doubt, and each team member's mutant powers have been broken by the rigors of battle. While her teammates are merely handicapped, Magik's powers are tied to a corrupted dimension — Limbo. Making a play for dominance in Limbo, the demon lord Dormammu has forced the X-Men, young and old, into a confrontation they can't handle, and pushed Magik into her demonic Darkchylde persona, which she can barely control.

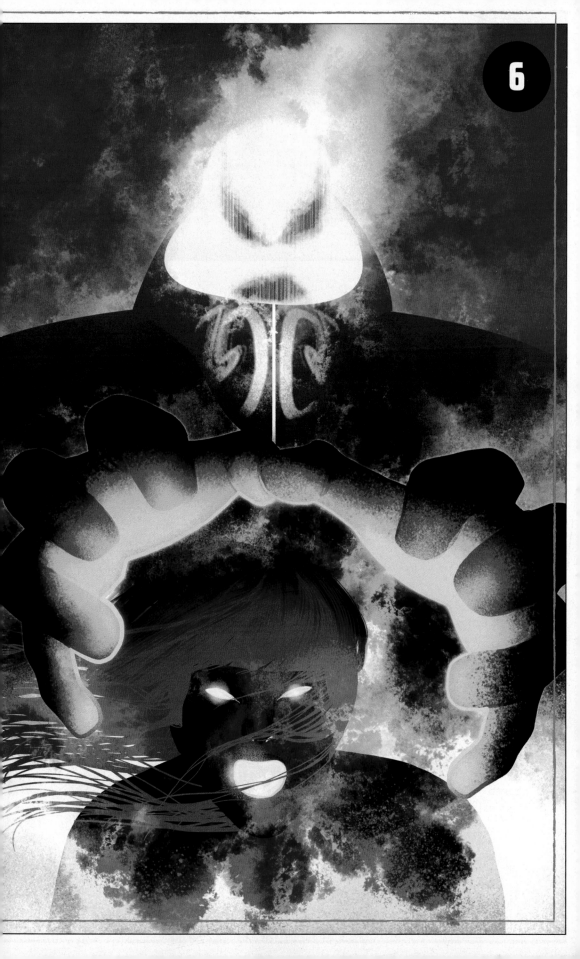

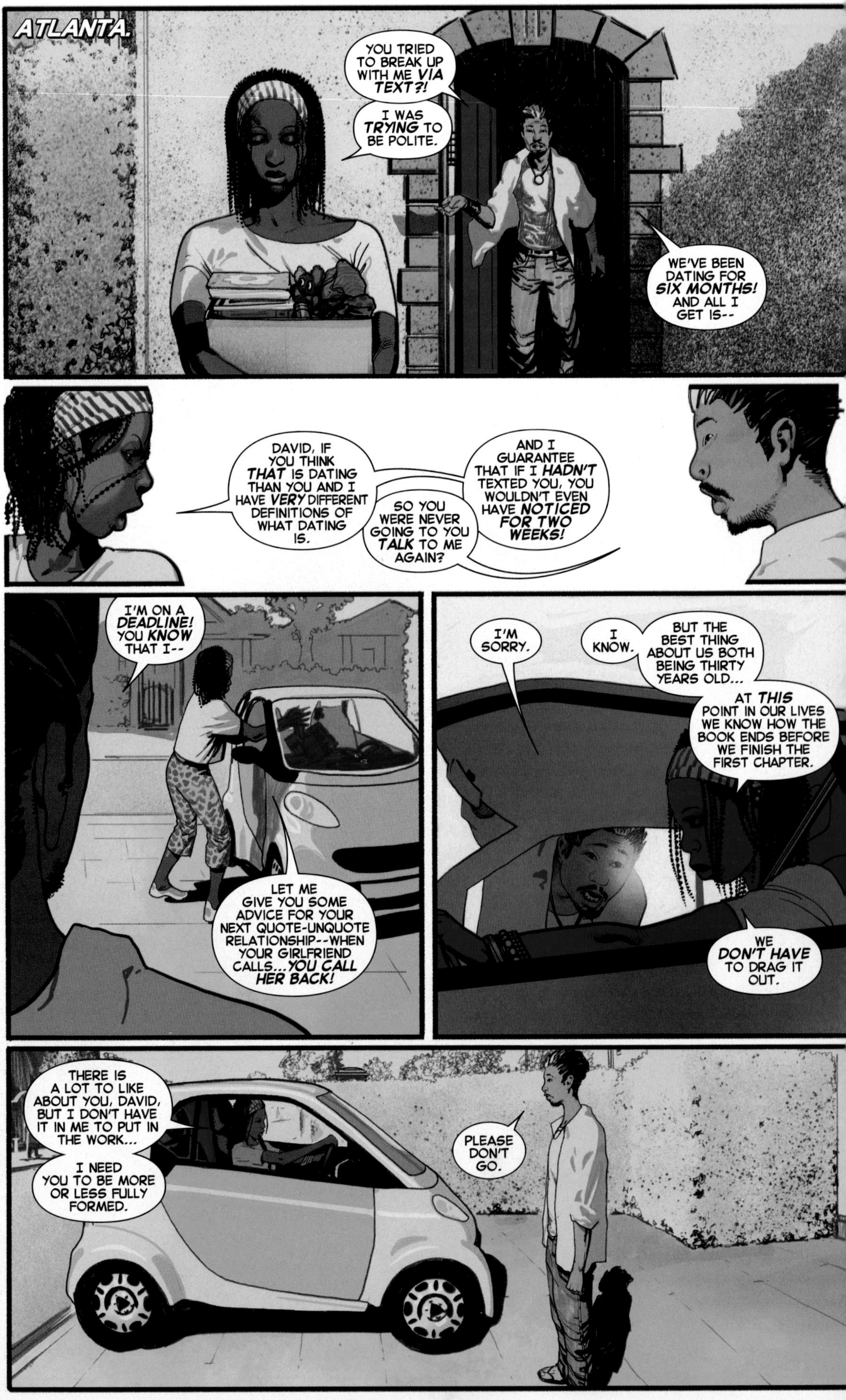
ATLANTA.
YOU TRIED TO BREAK UP WITH ME VIA TEXT?!
I WAS TRYING TO BE POLITE.
WE'VE BEEN DATING FOR SIX MONTHS! AND ALL I GET IS--
DAVID, IF YOU THINK THAT IS DATING THAN YOU AND I HAVE VERY DIFFERENT DEFINITIONS OF WHAT DATING IS.
AND I GUARANTEE THAT IF I HADN'T TEXTED YOU, YOU WOULDN'T EVEN HAVE NOTICED FOR TWO WEEKS!
SO YOU WERE NEVER GOING TO YOU TALK TO ME AGAIN?
I'M ON A DEADLINE! YOU KNOW THAT I--
LET ME GIVE YOU SOME ADVICE FOR YOUR NEXT QUOTE-UNQUOTE RELATIONSHIP--WHEN YOUR GIRLFRIEND CALLS...YOU CALL HER BACK!
I'M SORRY.
I KNOW.
BUT THE BEST THING ABOUT US BOTH BEING THIRTY YEARS OLD...
AT THIS POINT IN OUR LIVES WE KNOW HOW THE BOOK ENDS BEFORE WE FINISH THE FIRST CHAPTER.
WE DON'T HAVE TO DRAG IT OUT.
THERE IS A LOT TO LIKE ABOUT YOU, DAVID, BUT I DON'T HAVE IT IN ME TO PUT IN THE WORK...
I NEED YOU TO BE MORE OR LESS FULLY FORMED.
PLEASE DON'T GO.

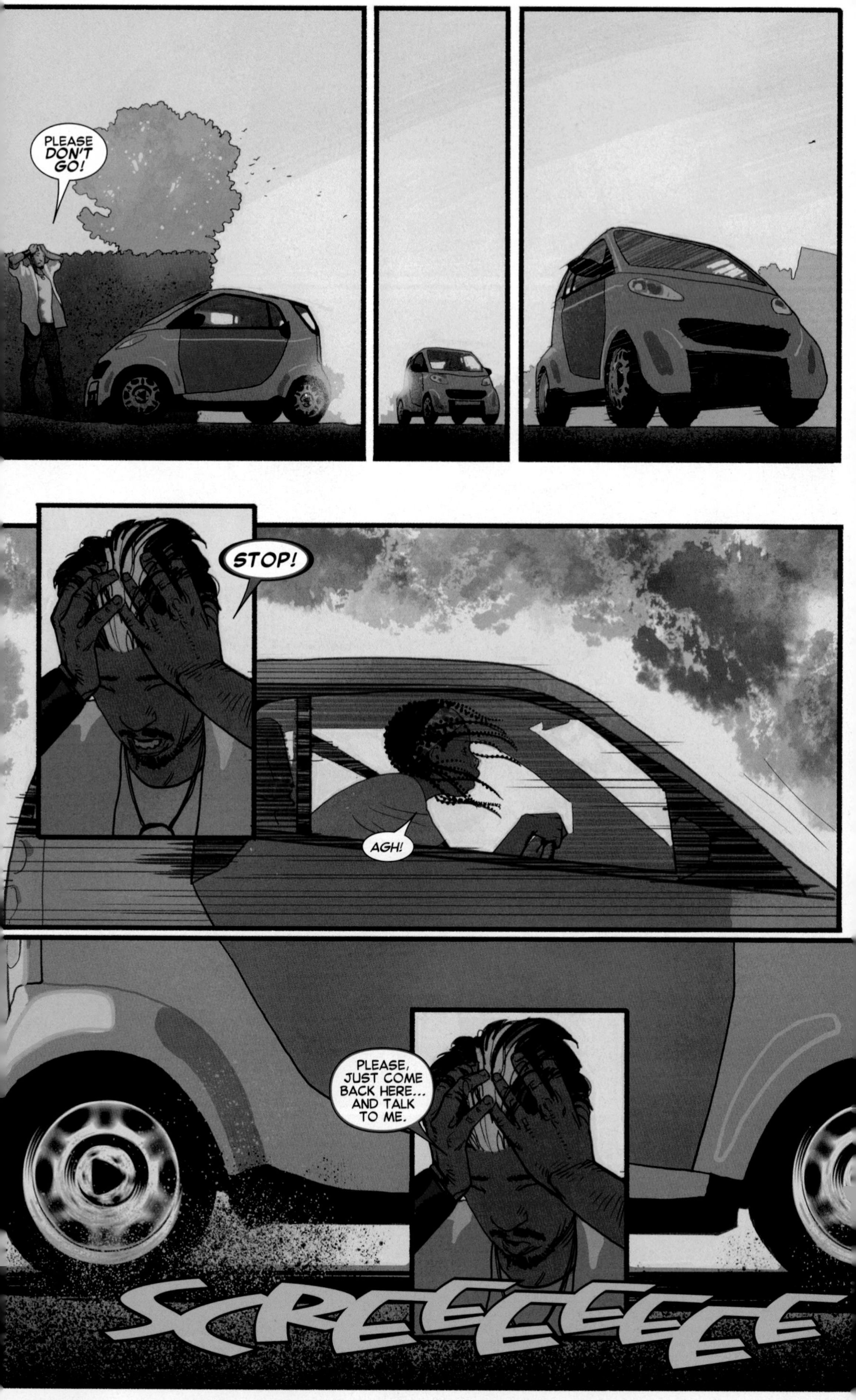
PLEASE DON'T GO!
STOP!
AGH!
PLEASE, JUST COME BACK HERE... AND TALK TO ME.
SCREEEEEEE

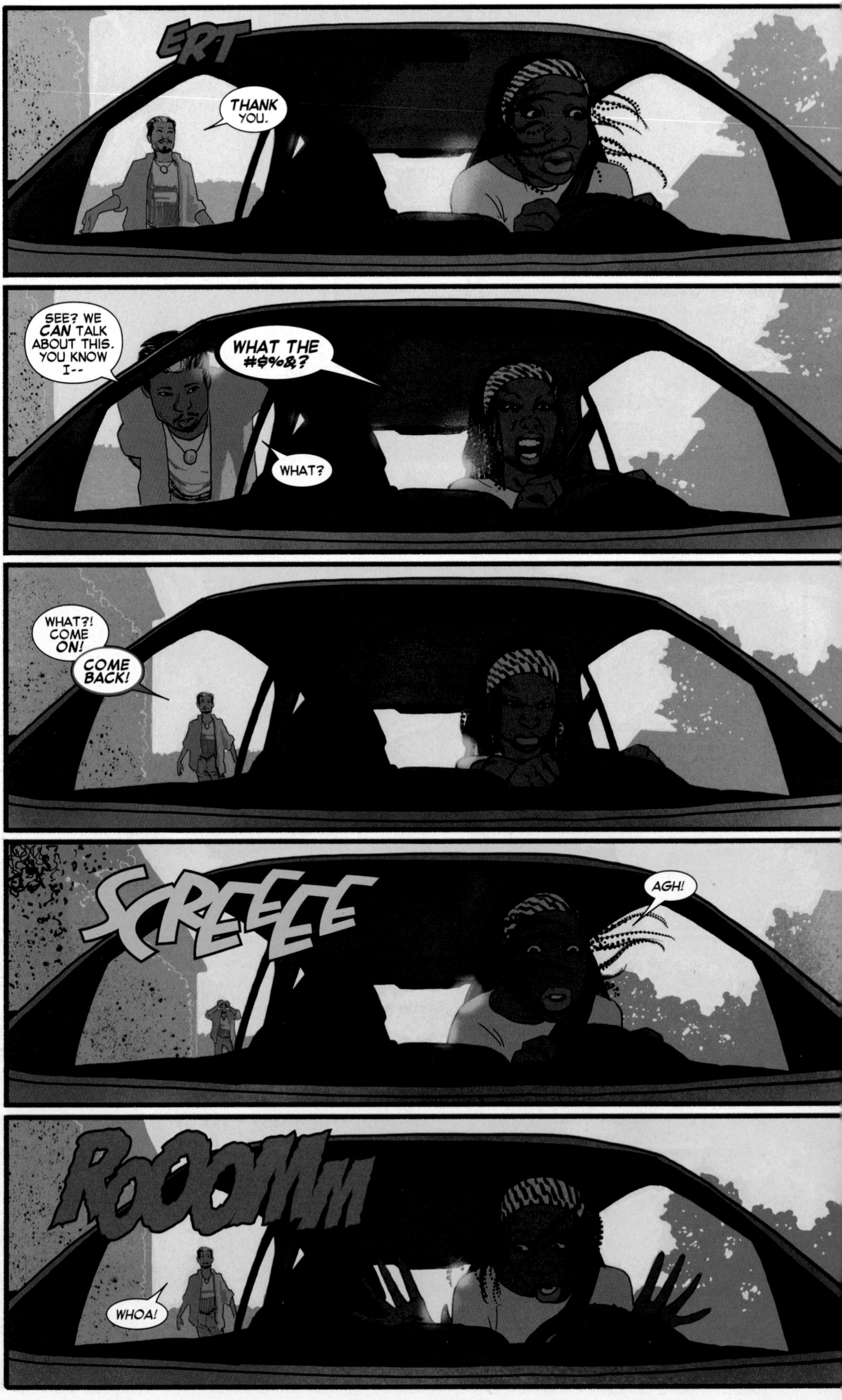
ERT
THANK YOU.
SEE? WE CAN TALK ABOUT THIS. YOU KNOW I--
WHAT THE #$%&?
WHAT?
WHAT?! COME ON!
COME BACK!
SCREEEE
AGH!
ROOOMM
WHOA!

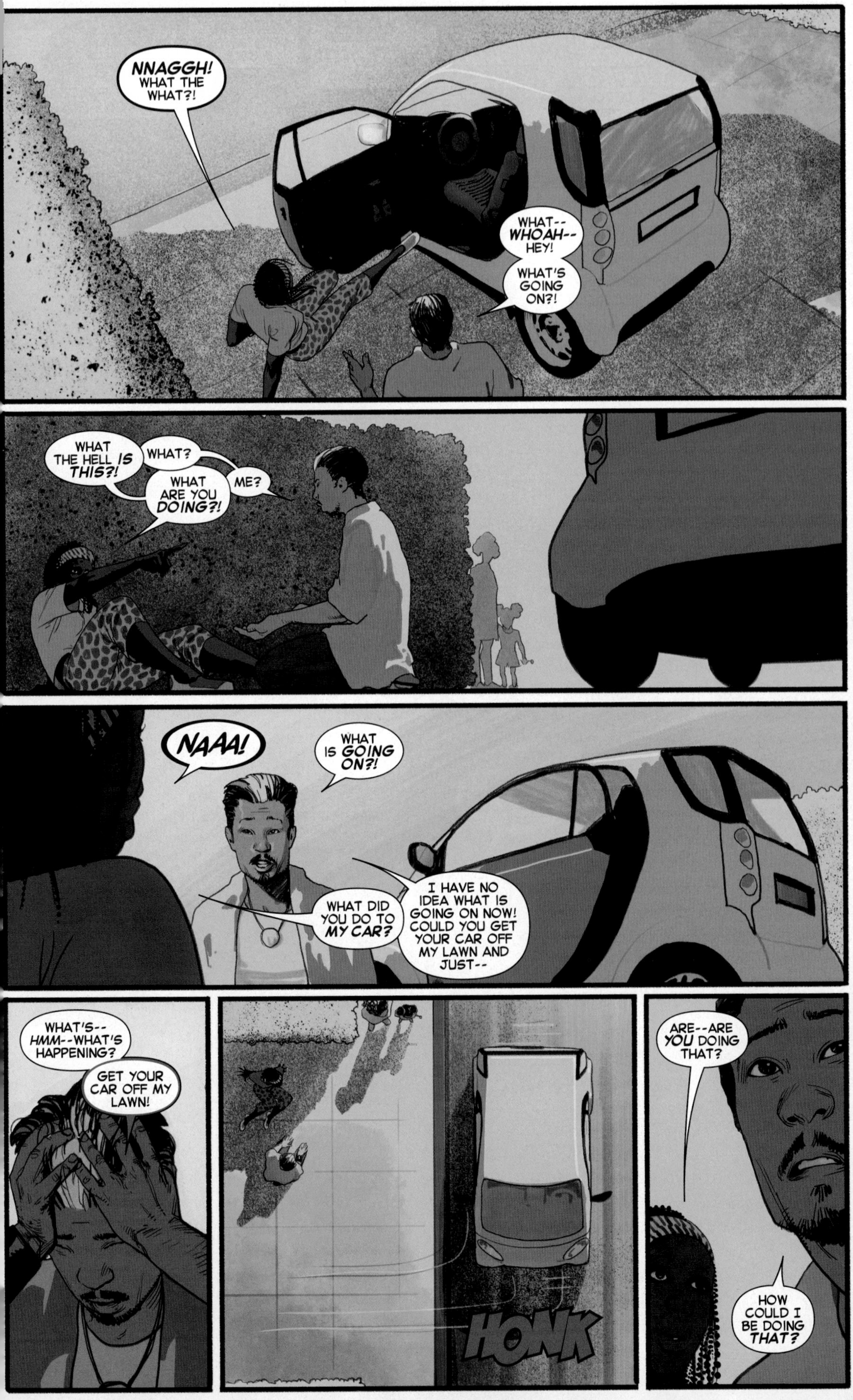
NNAGGH! WHAT THE WHAT?!
WHAT-- WHOAH-- HEY!
WHAT'S GOING ON?!
WHAT THE HELL IS THIS?!
WHAT?
WHAT ARE YOU DOING?!
ME?
NAAA!
WHAT IS GOING ON?!
WHAT DID YOU DO TO MY CAR?
I HAVE NO IDEA WHAT IS GOING ON NOW! COULD YOU GET YOUR CAR OFF MY LAWN AND JUST--
WHAT'S-- HMM--WHAT'S HAPPENING?
GET YOUR CAR OFF MY LAWN!
HONK
ARE--ARE YOU DOING THAT?
HOW COULD I BE DOING THAT?

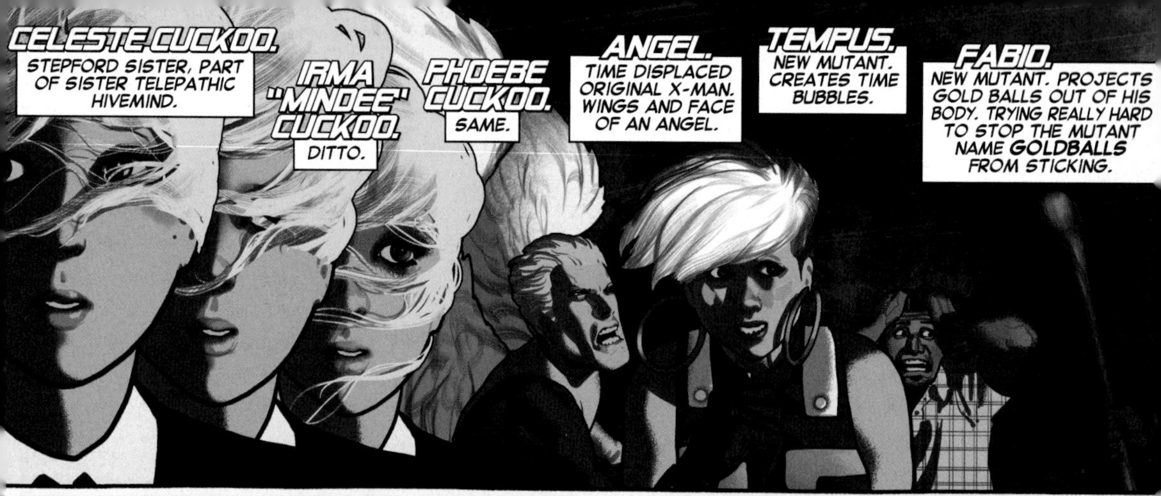
CELESTE CUCKOO.
STEPFORD SISTER, PART OF SISTER TELEPATHIC HIVEMIND.
IRMA "MINDEE" CUCKOO.
DITTO.
PHOEBE CUCKOO.
SAME.
ANGEL.
TIME DISPLACED ORIGINAL X-MAN. WINGS AND FACE OF AN ANGEL.
TEMPUS.
NEW MUTANT. CREATES TIME BUBBLES.
FABIO.
NEW MUTANT. PROJECTS GOLD BALLS OUT OF HIS BODY. TRYING REALLY HARD TO STOP THE MUTANT NAME GOLDBALLS FROM STICKING.

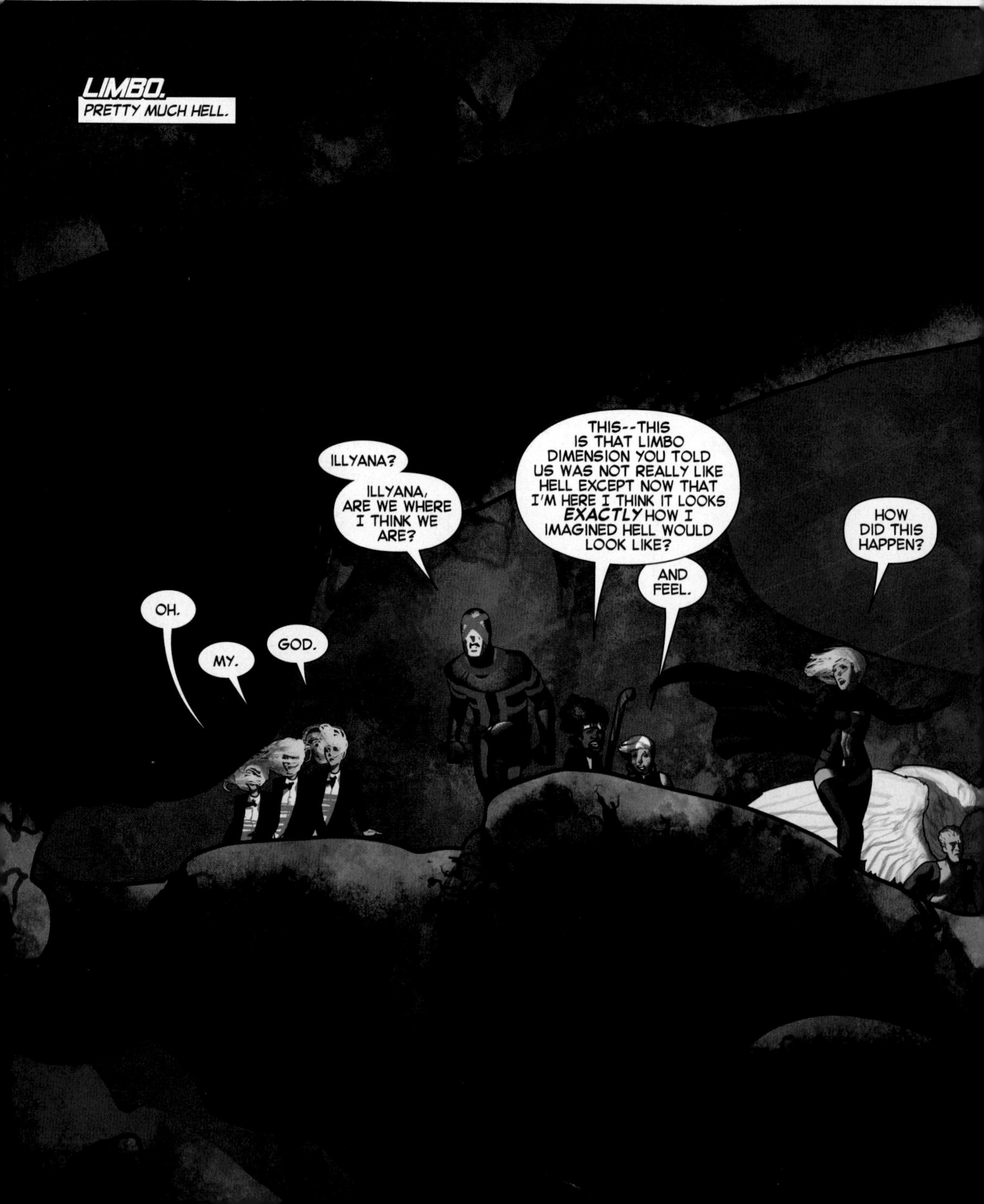
LIMBO.
PRETTY MUCH HELL.
OH.
MY.
GOD.
ILLYANA?
ILLYANA, ARE WE WHERE I THINK WE ARE?
THIS--THIS IS THAT LIMBO DIMENSION YOU TOLD US WAS NOT REALLY LIKE HELL EXCEPT NOW THAT I'M HERE I THINK IT LOOKS EXACTLY HOW I IMAGINED HELL WOULD LOOK LIKE?
AND FEEL.
HOW DID THIS HAPPEN?

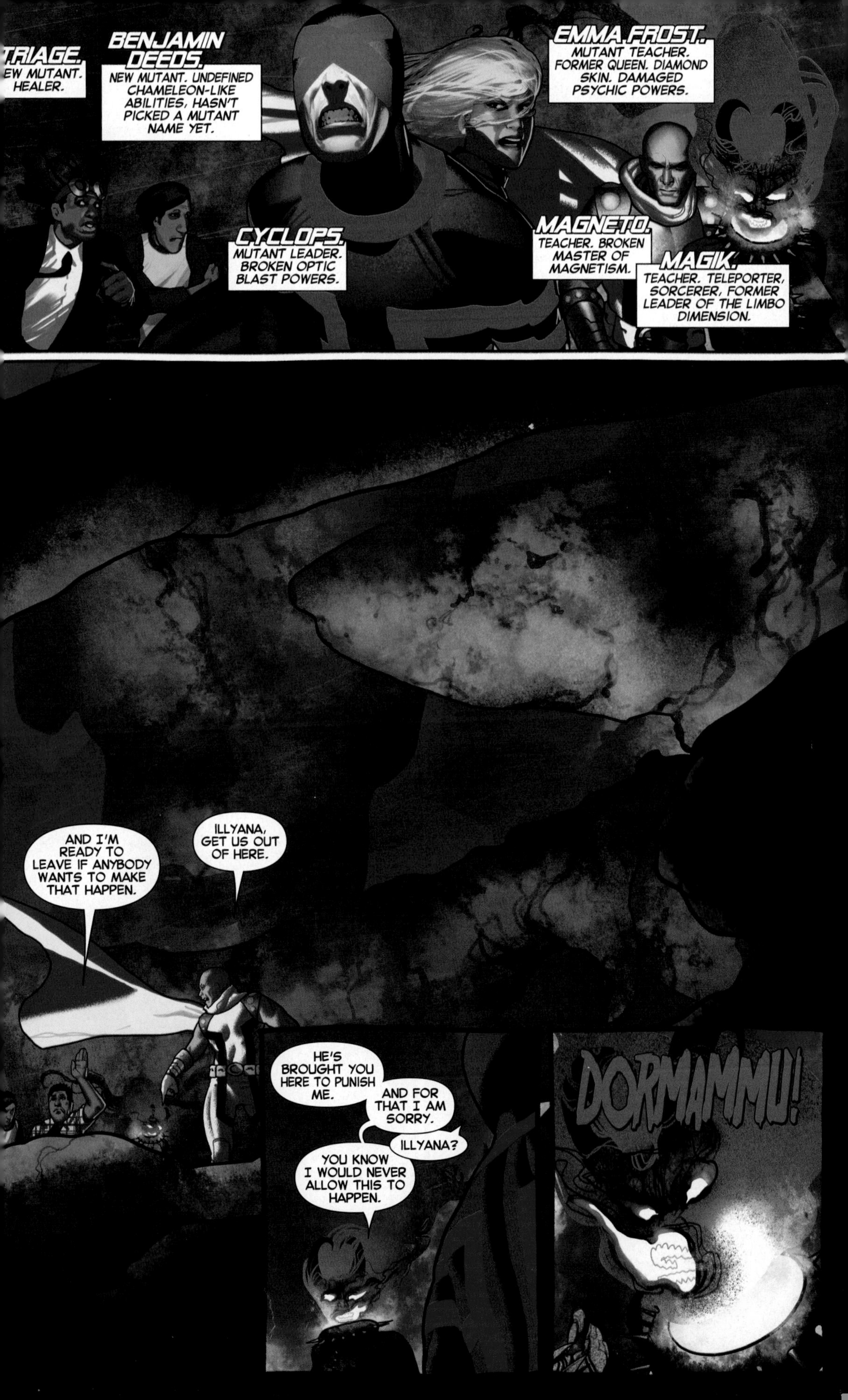

TRIAGE.
EW MUTANT. HEALER.
BENJAMIN DEEDS.
NEW MUTANT. UNDEFINED CHAMELEON-LIKE ABILITIES, HASN'T PICKED A MUTANT NAME YET.
CYCLOPS.
MUTANT LEADER. BROKEN OPTIC BLAST POWERS.
EMMA FROST.
MUTANT TEACHER. FORMER QUEEN. DIAMOND SKIN. DAMAGED PSYCHIC POWERS.
MAGNETO.
TEACHER. BROKEN MASTER OF MAGNETISM.
MAGIK.
TEACHER. TELEPORTER, SORCERER, FORMER LEADER OF THE LIMBO DIMENSION.
ILLYANA, GET US OUT OF HERE.
AND I'M READY TO LEAVE IF ANYBODY WANTS TO MAKE THAT HAPPEN.
HE'S BROUGHT YOU HERE TO PUNISH ME.
AND FOR THAT I AM SORRY.
ILLYANA?
YOU KNOW I WOULD NEVER ALLOW THIS TO HAPPEN.
DORMAMMU!

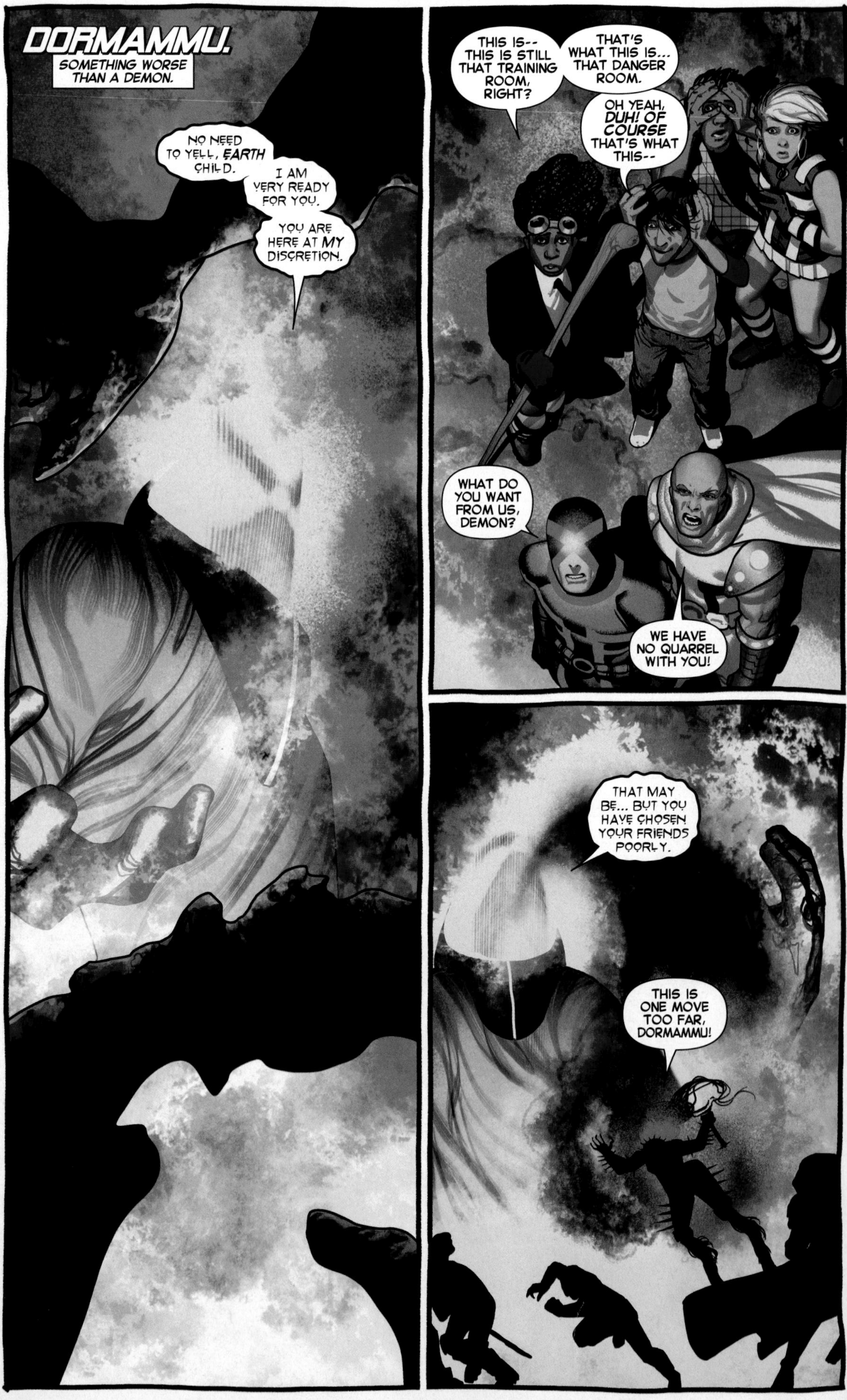
DORMAMMU.
SOMETHING WORSE THAN A DEMON.
NO NEED TO YELL, EARTH CHILD.
I AM VERY READY FOR YOU.
YOU ARE HERE AT MY DISCRETION.
THIS IS-- THIS IS STILL THAT TRAINING ROOM, RIGHT?
THAT'S WHAT THIS IS... THAT DANGER ROOM.
OH YEAH, DUH! OF COURSE THAT'S WHAT THIS--
WHAT DO YOU WANT FROM US, DEMON?
WE HAVE NO QUARREL WITH YOU!
THAT MAY BE... BUT YOU HAVE CHOSEN YOUR FRIENDS POORLY.
THIS IS ONE MOVE TOO FAR, DORMAMMU!

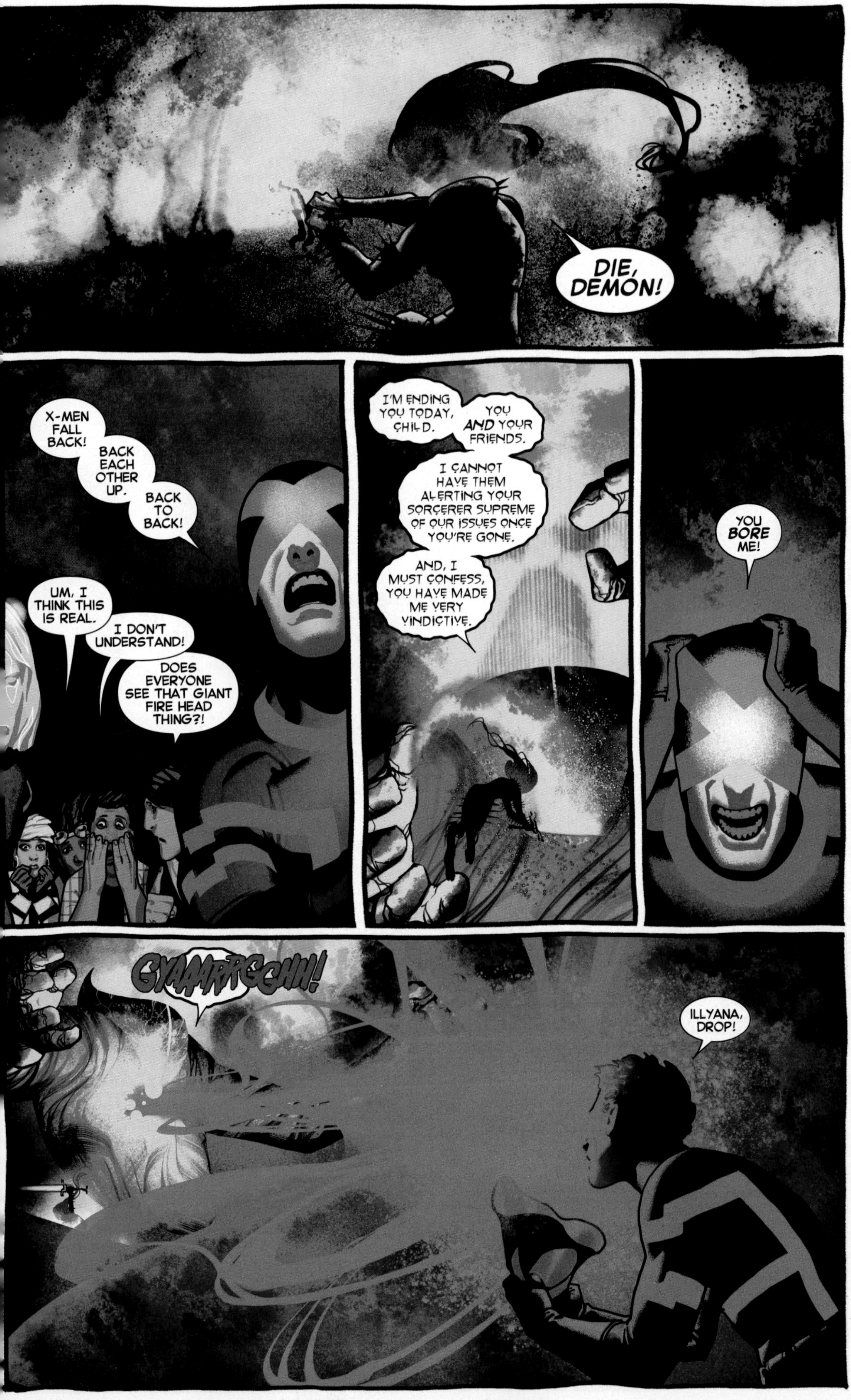
DIE, DEMON!
X-MEN FALL BACK!
BACK EACH OTHER UP.
BACK TO BACK!
UM, I THINK THIS IS REAL.
I DON'T UNDERSTAND!
DOES EVERYONE SEE THAT GIANT FIRE HEAD THING?!
I'M ENDING YOU TODAY, CHILD.
YOU AND YOUR FRIENDS.
I CANNOT HAVE THEM ALERTING YOUR SORCERER SUPREME OF OUR ISSUES ONCE YOU'RE GONE.
AND, I MUST CONFESS, YOU HAVE MADE ME VERY VINDICTIVE.
YOU BORE ME!
GYAAARRGGHH!
ILLYANA, DROP!

AAAAGGHHH!

SCOTT!

WOW.

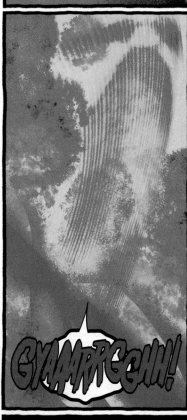

GYAAARRGGHH!

WHOA!

HE'S NOT GOING TO BE ABLE TO DO THAT AGAIN...

NICE!

IT IS TIME TO LEAVE THIS PLACE.

RASPUTIN! GET US OUT OF HERE!

LISTEN CAREFULLY, THIS DEMON HAS POWER OVER ME.

I WILL SEND YOU BACK TO OUR REALM.

CONTACT DR. STEPHEN STRANGE AND TELL HIM CLEARLY THAT *DORMAMMU* IS MAKING A PLAY FOR LIMBO AND IS TRYING TO USE ME AS A--

AGH! DAMN YOU, DEMON!

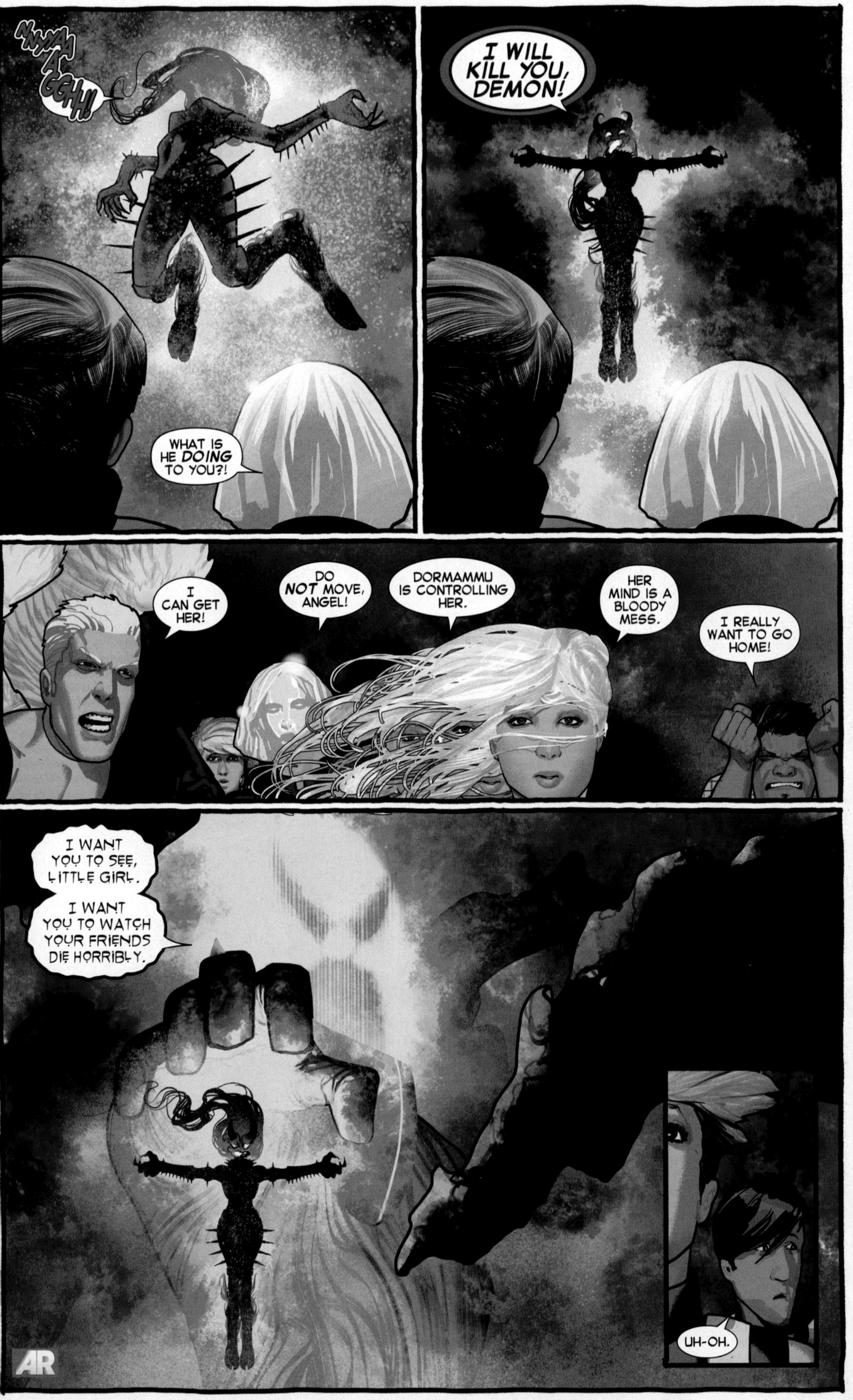
NNYAA AGGHH!
WHAT IS HE DOING TO YOU?!
I WILL KILL YOU, DEMON!
I CAN GET HER!
DO NOT MOVE, ANGEL!
DORMAMMU IS CONTROLLING HER.
HER MIND IS A BLOODY MESS.
I REALLY WANT TO GO HOME!
I WANT YOU TO SEE, LITTLE GIRL.
I WANT YOU TO WATCH YOUR FRIENDS DIE HORRIBLY.
UH-OH.

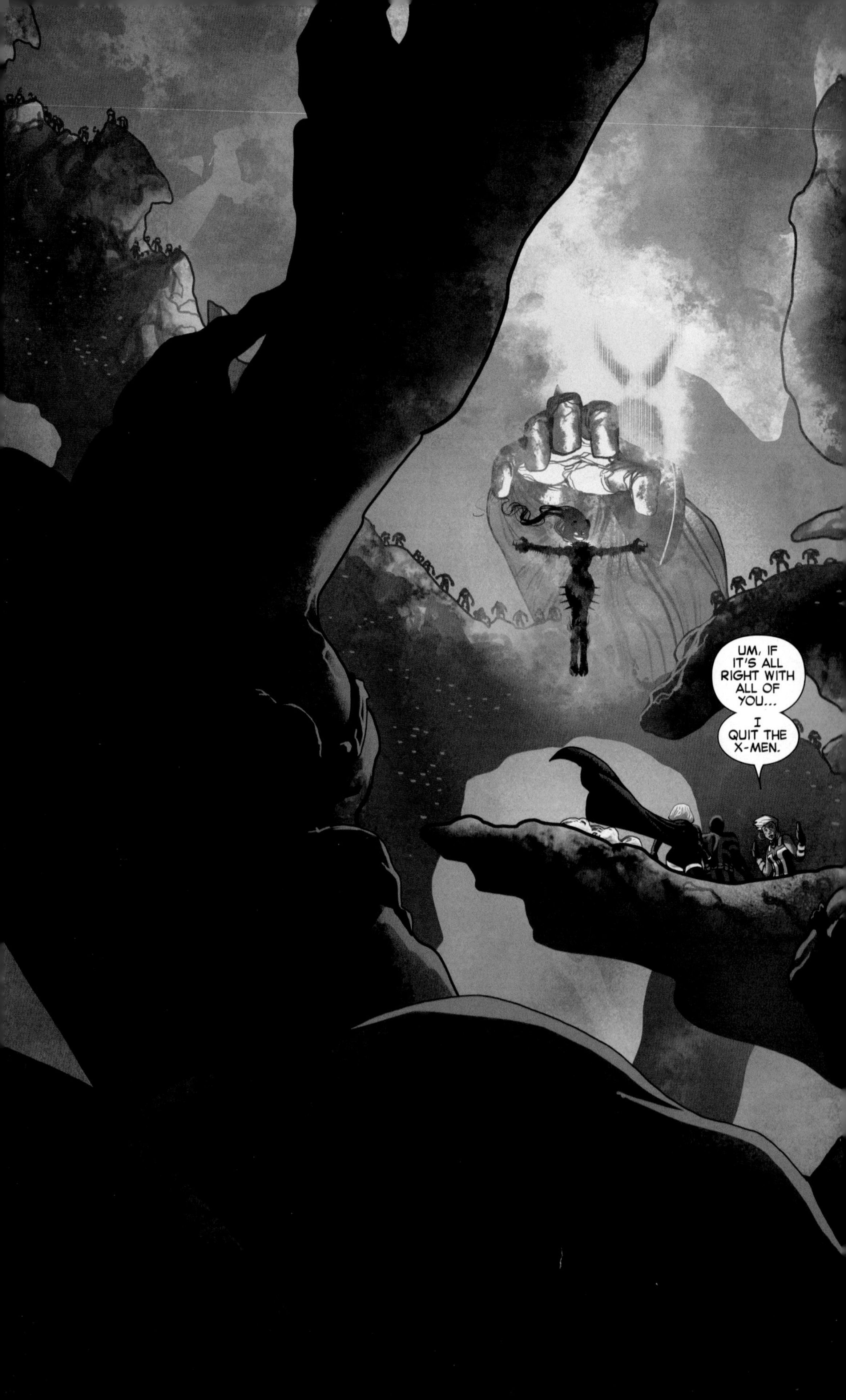
UM, IF IT'S ALL RIGHT WITH ALL OF YOU...
I QUIT THE X-MEN.

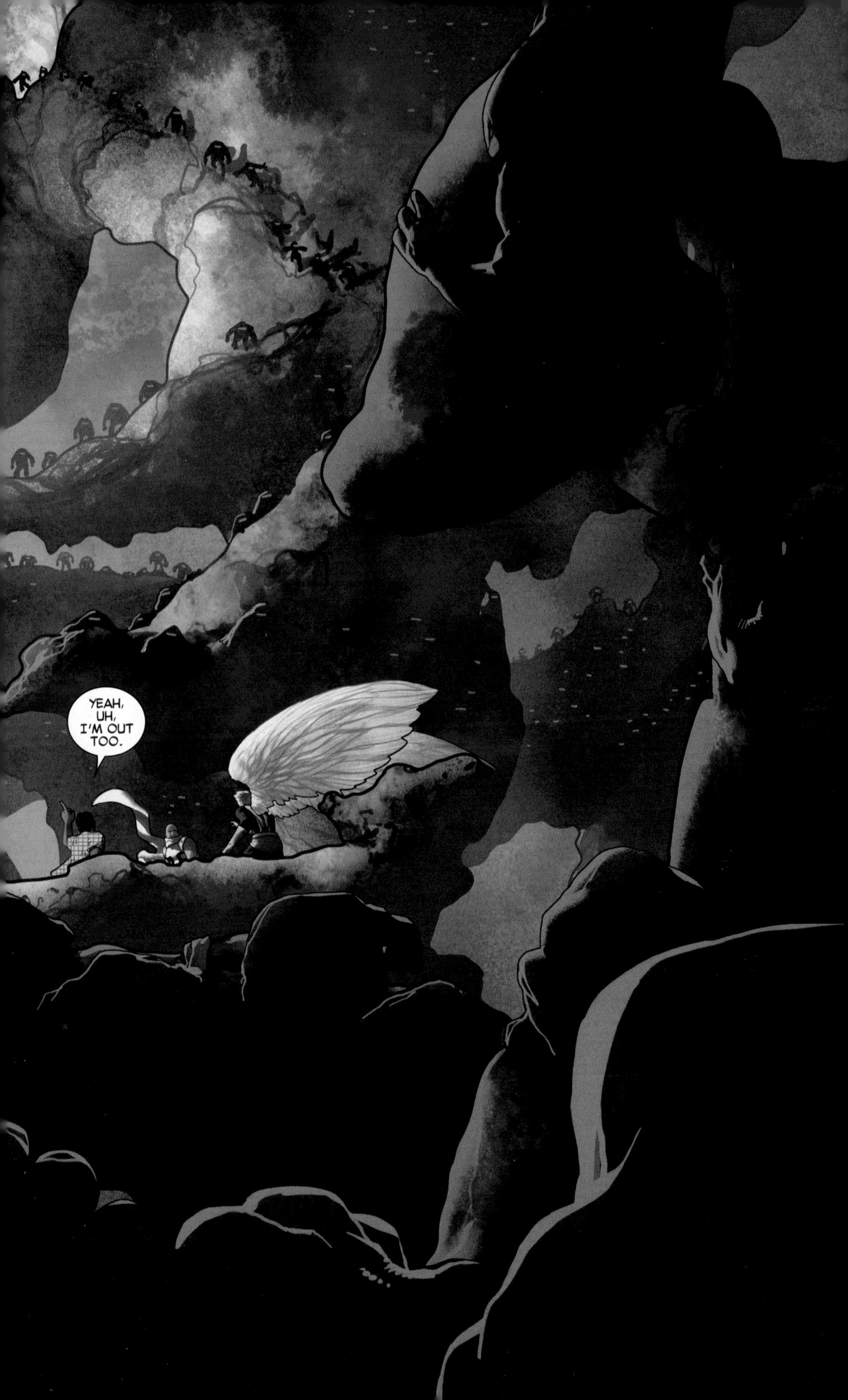
YEAH, UH, I'M OUT TOO.

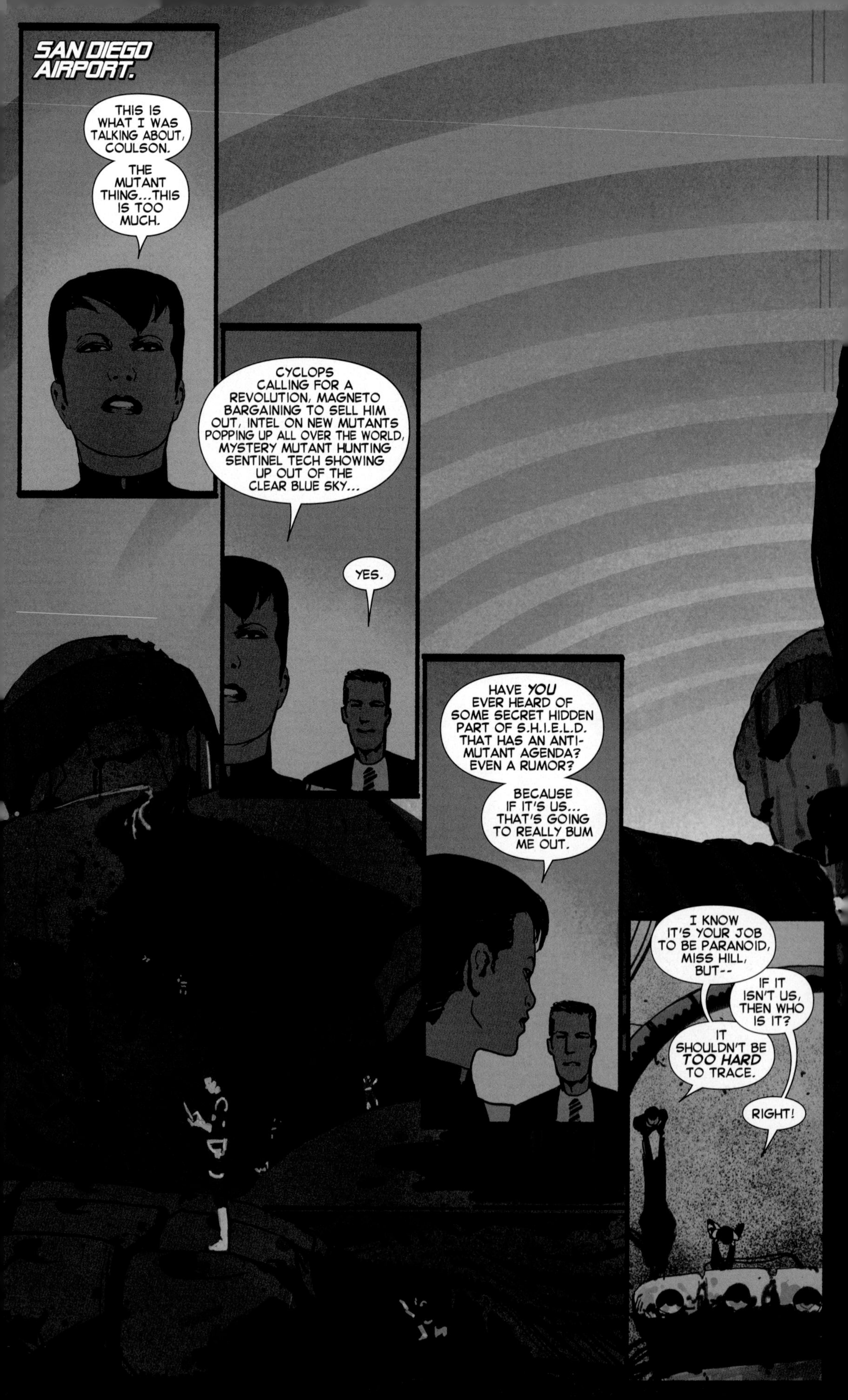
SAN DIEGO AIRPORT.
THIS IS WHAT I WAS TALKING ABOUT, COULSON.
THE MUTANT THING...THIS IS TOO MUCH.
CYCLOPS CALLING FOR A REVOLUTION, MAGNETO BARGAINING TO SELL HIM OUT, INTEL ON NEW MUTANTS POPPING UP ALL OVER THE WORLD, MYSTERY MUTANT HUNTING SENTINEL TECH SHOWING UP OUT OF THE CLEAR BLUE SKY...
YES.
HAVE YOU EVER HEARD OF SOME SECRET HIDDEN PART OF S.H.I.E.L.D. THAT HAS AN ANTI-MUTANT AGENDA? EVEN A RUMOR?
BECAUSE IF IT'S US... THAT'S GOING TO REALLY BUM ME OUT.
I KNOW IT'S YOUR JOB TO BE PARANOID, MISS HILL, BUT--
IF IT ISN'T US, THEN WHO IS IT?
IT SHOULDN'T BE TOO HARD TO TRACE.
RIGHT!

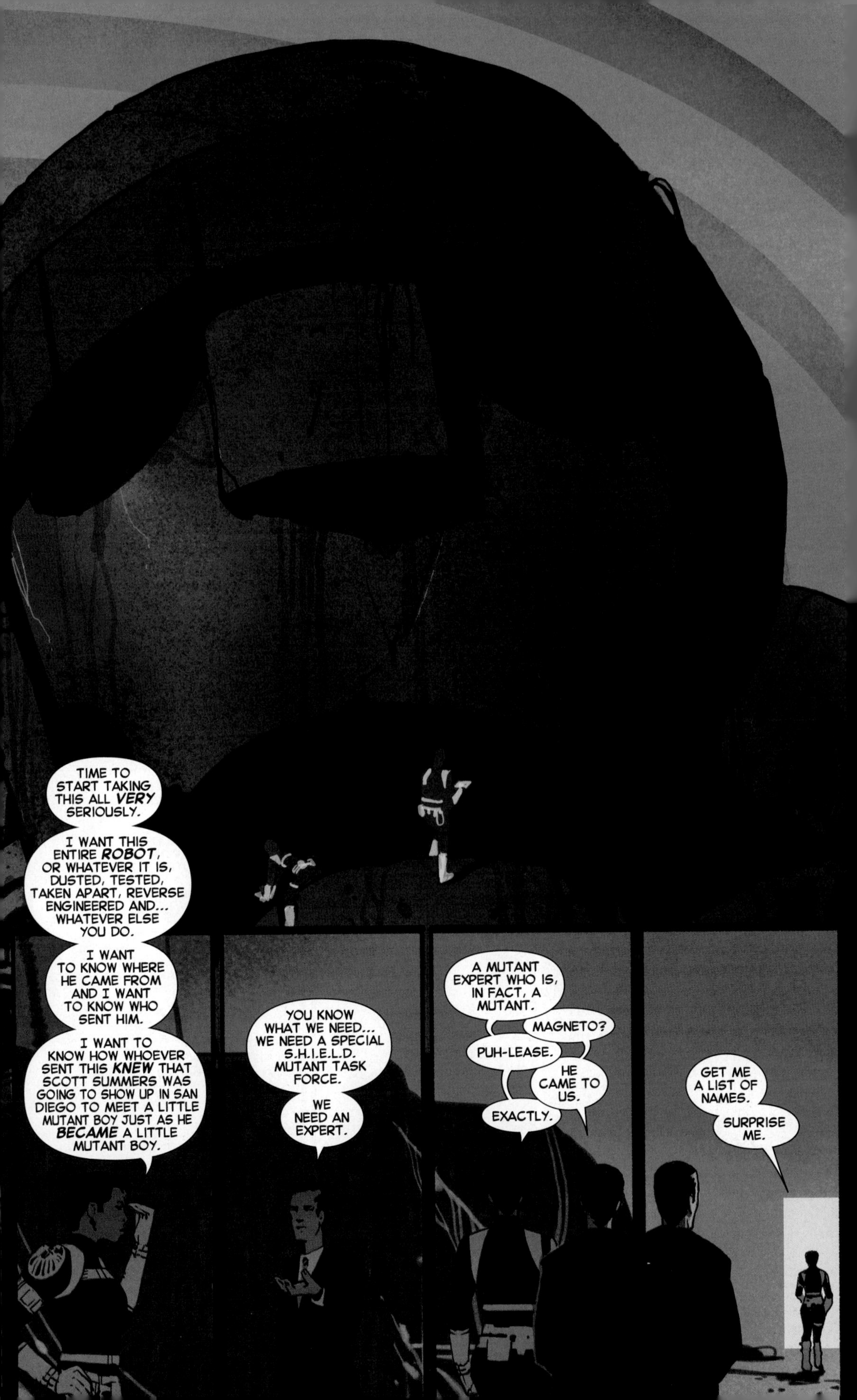
TIME TO START TAKING THIS ALL *VERY* SERIOUSLY.
I WANT THIS ENTIRE *ROBOT*, OR WHATEVER IT IS, DUSTED, TESTED, TAKEN APART, REVERSE ENGINEERED AND... WHATEVER ELSE YOU DO.
I WANT TO KNOW WHERE HE CAME FROM AND I WANT TO KNOW WHO SENT HIM.
I WANT TO KNOW HOW WHOEVER SENT THIS *KNEW* THAT SCOTT SUMMERS WAS GOING TO SHOW UP IN SAN DIEGO TO MEET A LITTLE MUTANT BOY JUST AS HE *BECAME* A LITTLE MUTANT BOY.
YOU KNOW WHAT WE NEED... WE NEED A SPECIAL S.H.I.E.L.D. MUTANT TASK FORCE.
WE NEED AN EXPERT.
A MUTANT EXPERT WHO IS, IN FACT, A MUTANT.
MAGNETO?
PUH-LEASE.
HE CAME TO US.
EXACTLY.
GET ME A LIST OF NAMES.
SURPRISE ME.

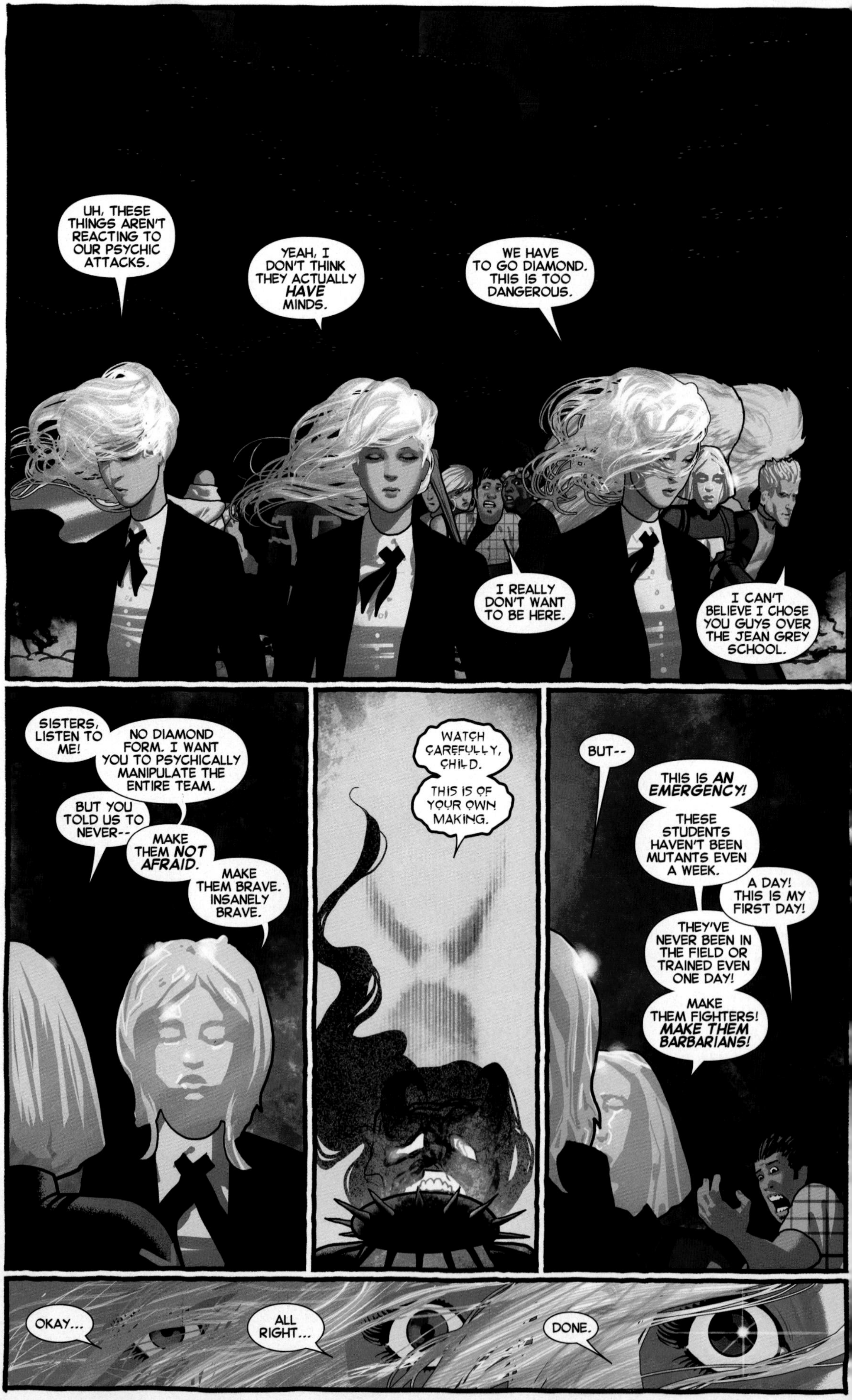
UH, THESE THINGS AREN'T REACTING TO OUR PSYCHIC ATTACKS.
YEAH, I DON'T THINK THEY ACTUALLY HAVE MINDS.
WE HAVE TO GO DIAMOND. THIS IS TOO DANGEROUS.
I REALLY DON'T WANT TO BE HERE.
I CAN'T BELIEVE I CHOSE YOU GUYS OVER THE JEAN GREY SCHOOL.
SISTERS, LISTEN TO ME!
NO DIAMOND FORM. I WANT YOU TO PSYCHICALLY MANIPULATE THE ENTIRE TEAM.
BUT YOU TOLD US TO NEVER--
MAKE THEM NOT AFRAID.
MAKE THEM BRAVE. INSANELY BRAVE.
WATCH CAREFULLY, CHILD.
THIS IS OF YOUR OWN MAKING.
BUT--
THIS IS AN EMERGENCY!
THESE STUDENTS HAVEN'T BEEN MUTANTS EVEN A WEEK.
A DAY! THIS IS MY FIRST DAY!
THEY'VE NEVER BEEN IN THE FIELD OR TRAINED EVEN ONE DAY!
MAKE THEM FIGHTERS! MAKE THEM BARBARIANS!
OKAY...
ALL RIGHT...
DONE.

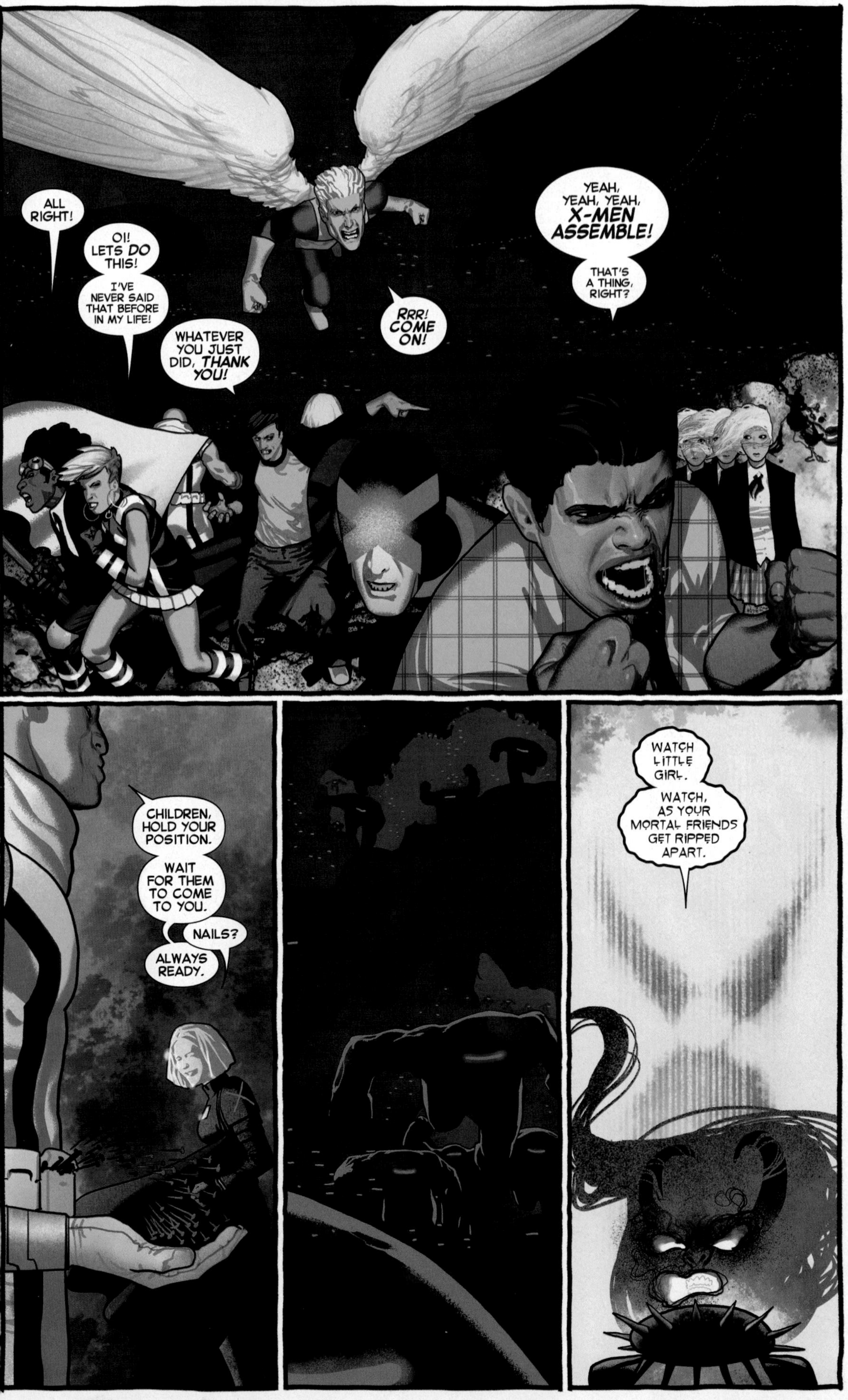
ALL RIGHT!
OI! LETS DO THIS!
I'VE NEVER SAID THAT BEFORE IN MY LIFE!
WHATEVER YOU JUST DID, THANK YOU!
RRR! COME ON!
YEAH, YEAH, YEAH, X-MEN ASSEMBLE!
THAT'S A THING, RIGHT?
CHILDREN, HOLD YOUR POSITION.
WAIT FOR THEM TO COME TO YOU.
NAILS?
ALWAYS READY.
WATCH LITTLE GIRL.
WATCH, AS YOUR MORTAL FRIENDS GET RIPPED APART.

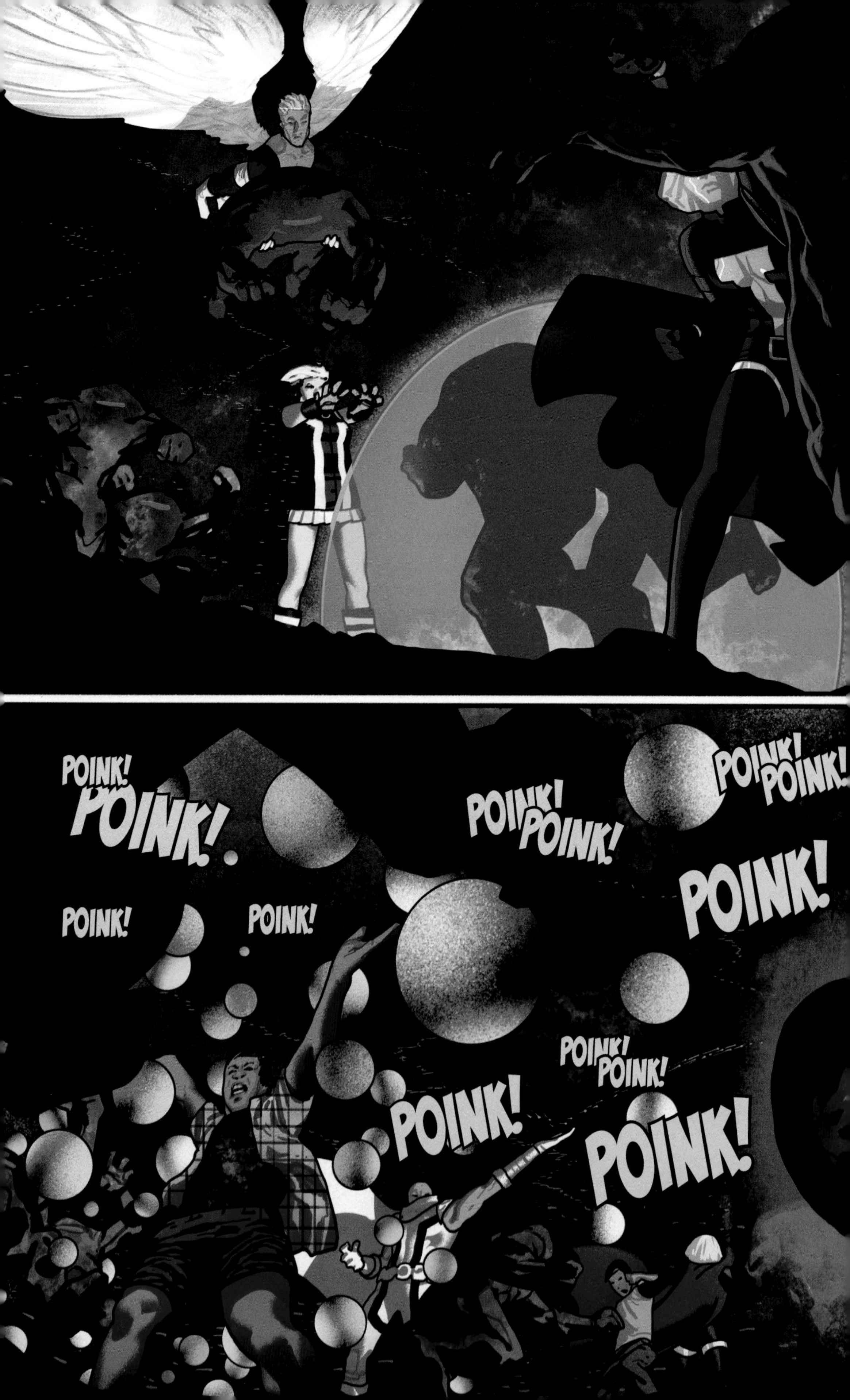
POINK!
POINK!
POINK!
POINK!
POINK!
POINK!
POINK!
POINK!
POINK!
POINK!
POINK!
POINK!
POINK!

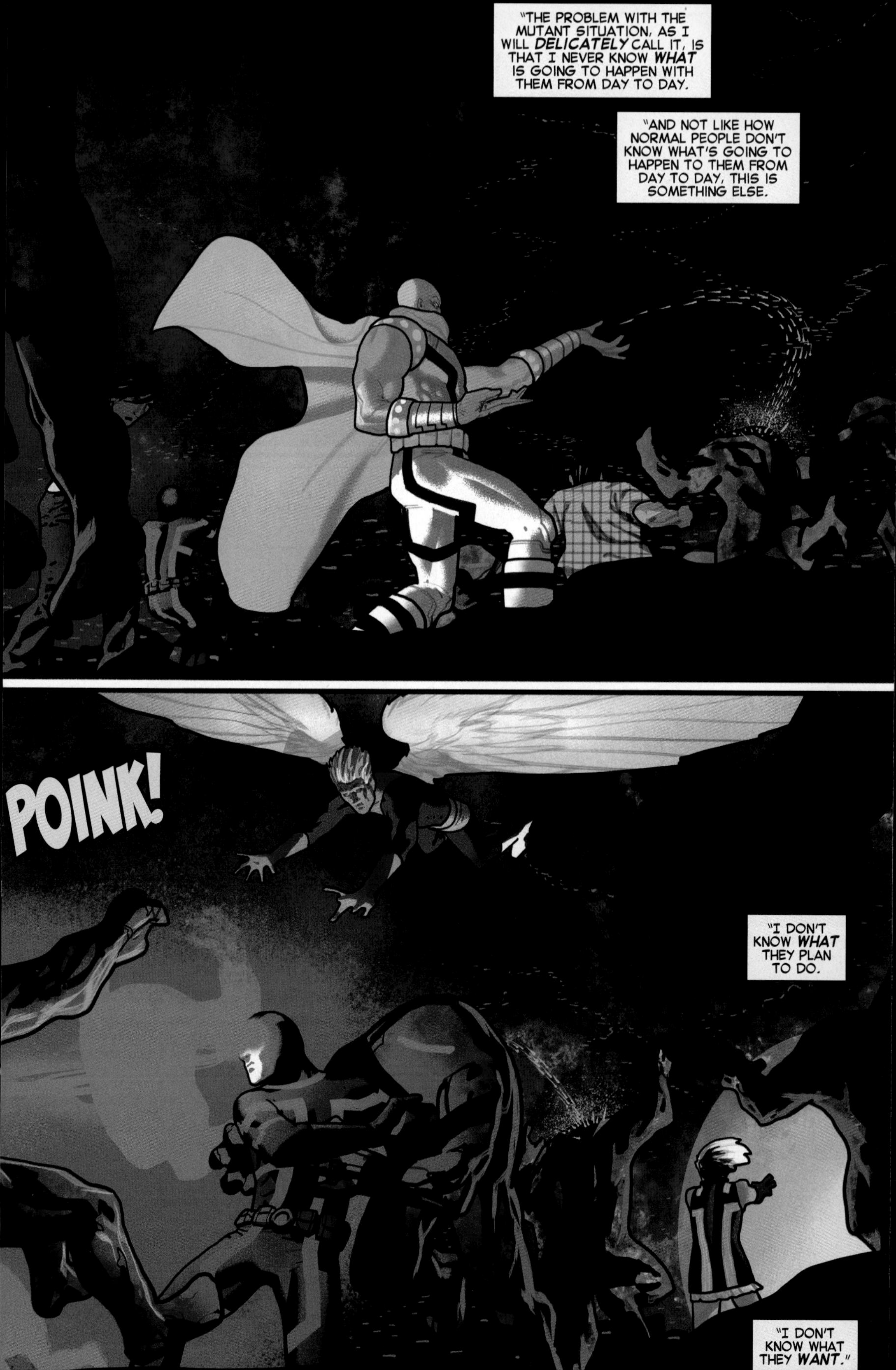
"THE PROBLEM WITH THE MUTANT SITUATION, AS I WILL DELICATELY CALL IT, IS THAT I NEVER KNOW WHAT IS GOING TO HAPPEN WITH THEM FROM DAY TO DAY.
"AND NOT LIKE HOW NORMAL PEOPLE DON'T KNOW WHAT'S GOING TO HAPPEN TO THEM FROM DAY TO DAY, THIS IS SOMETHING ELSE.
POINK!
"I DON'T KNOW WHAT THEY PLAN TO DO.
"I DON'T KNOW WHAT THEY WANT."

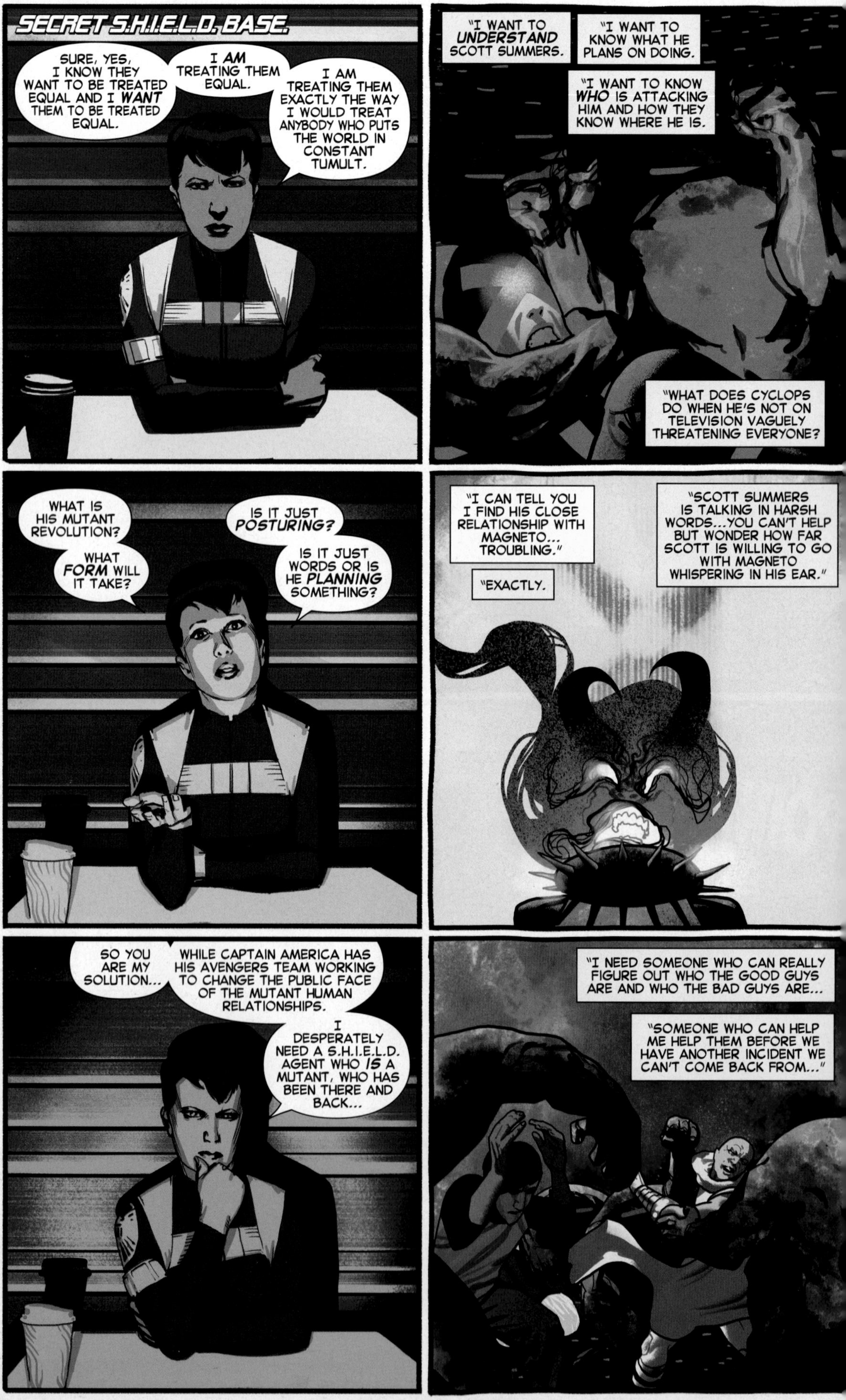

SECRET S.H.I.E.L.D. BASE.
SURE, YES, I KNOW THEY WANT TO BE TREATED EQUAL AND I WANT THEM TO BE TREATED EQUAL.
I AM TREATING THEM EQUAL.
I AM TREATING THEM EXACTLY THE WAY I WOULD TREAT ANYBODY WHO PUTS THE WORLD IN CONSTANT TUMULT.
"I WANT TO UNDERSTAND SCOTT SUMMERS.
"I WANT TO KNOW WHAT HE PLANS ON DOING.
"I WANT TO KNOW WHO IS ATTACKING HIM AND HOW THEY KNOW WHERE HE IS.
"WHAT DOES CYCLOPS DO WHEN HE'S NOT ON TELEVISION VAGUELY THREATENING EVERYONE?
WHAT IS HIS MUTANT REVOLUTION?
WHAT FORM WILL IT TAKE?
IS IT JUST POSTURING?
IS IT JUST WORDS OR IS HE PLANNING SOMETHING?
"I CAN TELL YOU I FIND HIS CLOSE RELATIONSHIP WITH MAGNETO... TROUBLING."
"EXACTLY.
"SCOTT SUMMERS IS TALKING IN HARSH WORDS...YOU CAN'T HELP BUT WONDER HOW FAR SCOTT IS WILLING TO GO WITH MAGNETO WHISPERING IN HIS EAR."
SO YOU ARE MY SOLUTION...
WHILE CAPTAIN AMERICA HAS HIS AVENGERS TEAM WORKING TO CHANGE THE PUBLIC FACE OF THE MUTANT HUMAN RELATIONSHIPS.
I DESPERATELY NEED A S.H.I.E.L.D. AGENT WHO IS A MUTANT, WHO HAS BEEN THERE AND BACK...
"I NEED SOMEONE WHO CAN REALLY FIGURE OUT WHO THE GOOD GUYS ARE AND WHO THE BAD GUYS ARE...
"SOMEONE WHO CAN HELP ME HELP THEM BEFORE WE HAVE ANOTHER INCIDENT WE CAN'T COME BACK FROM..."

WOULD THAT MAKE ME AN AGENT OF S.H.I.E.L.D.?
IF YOU'RE SAYING YES...
YES, IT DOES.
DAZZLER
AGENT OF S.H.I.E.L.D.
YEAH, I COULD DO THAT.
AR

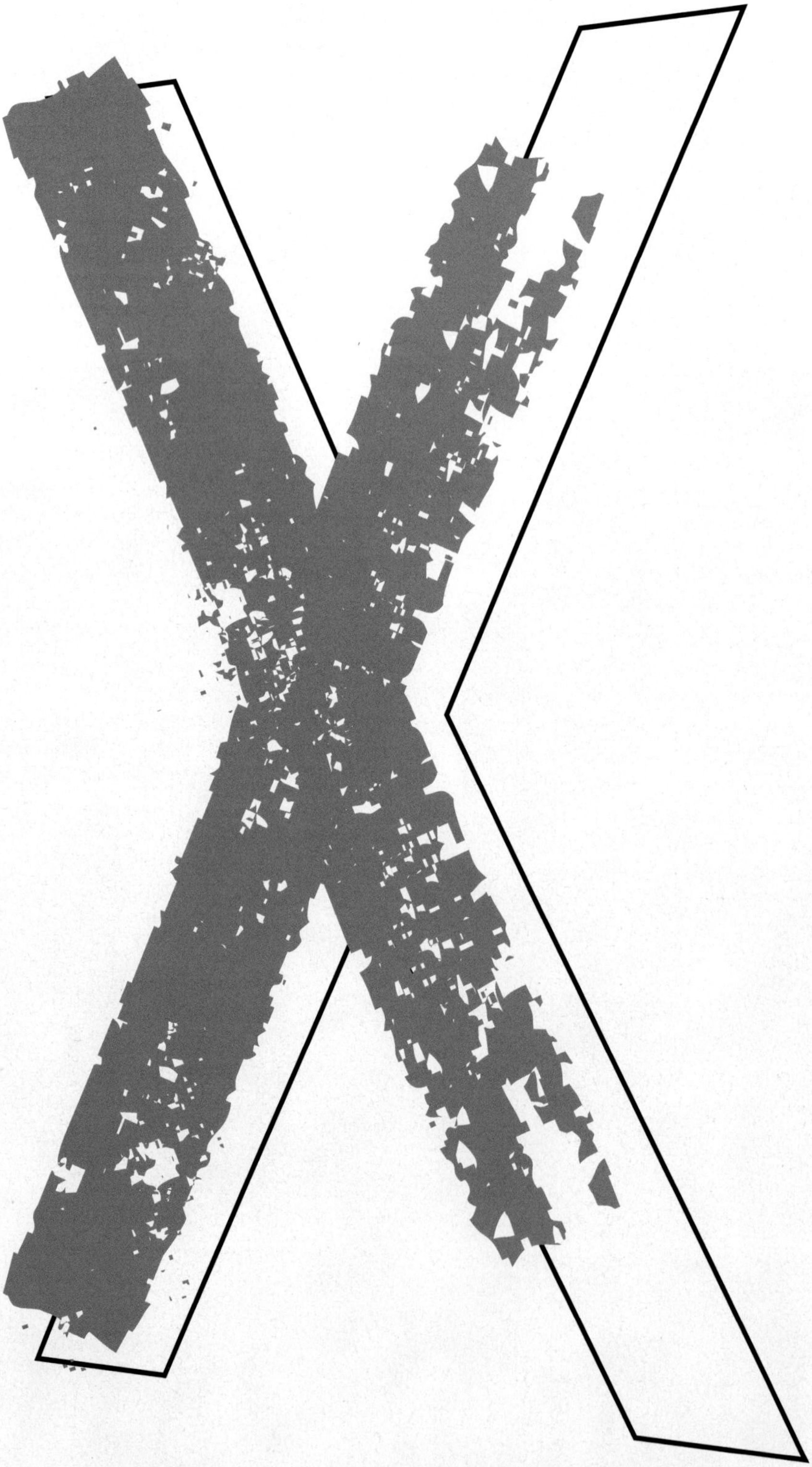

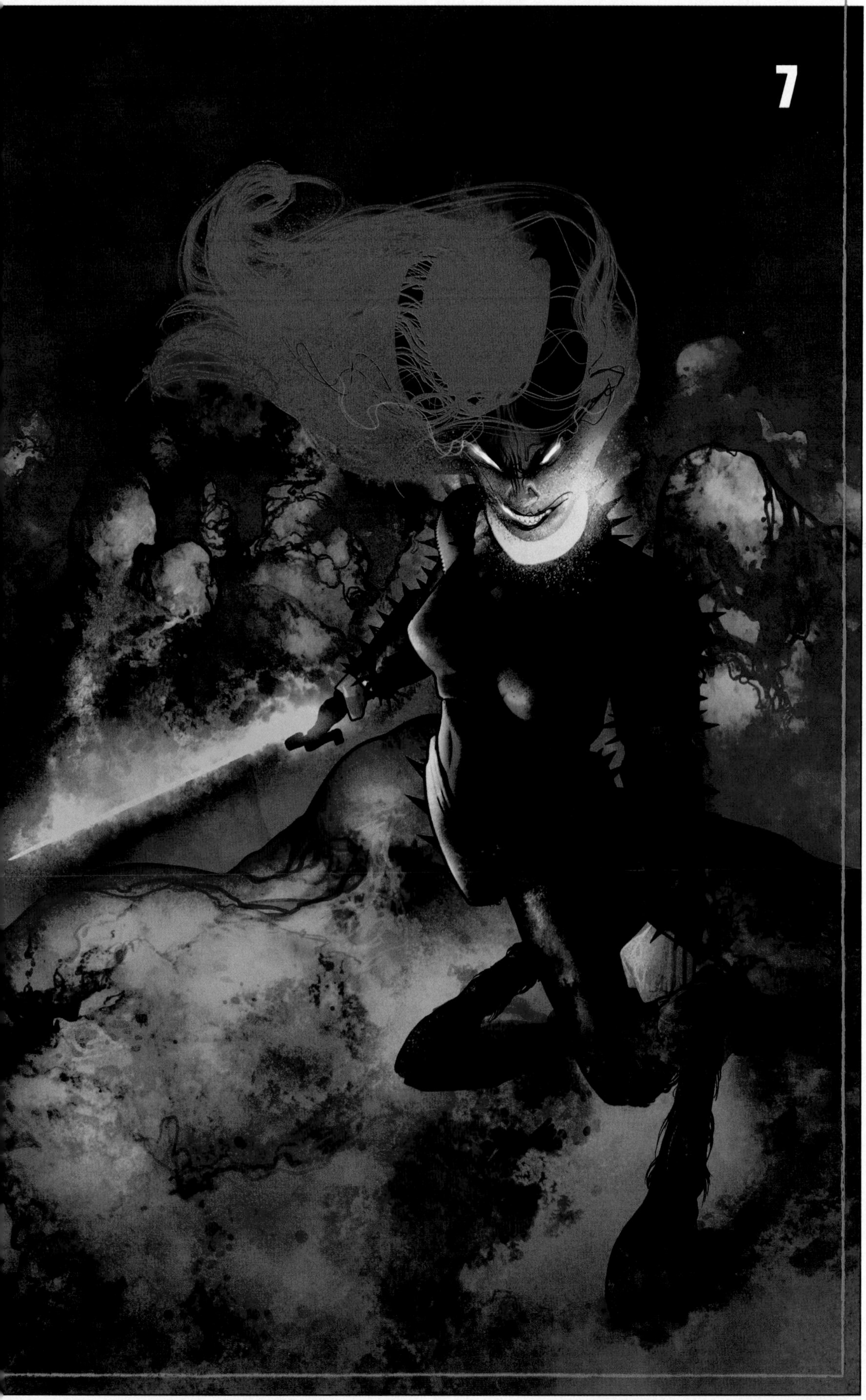
7

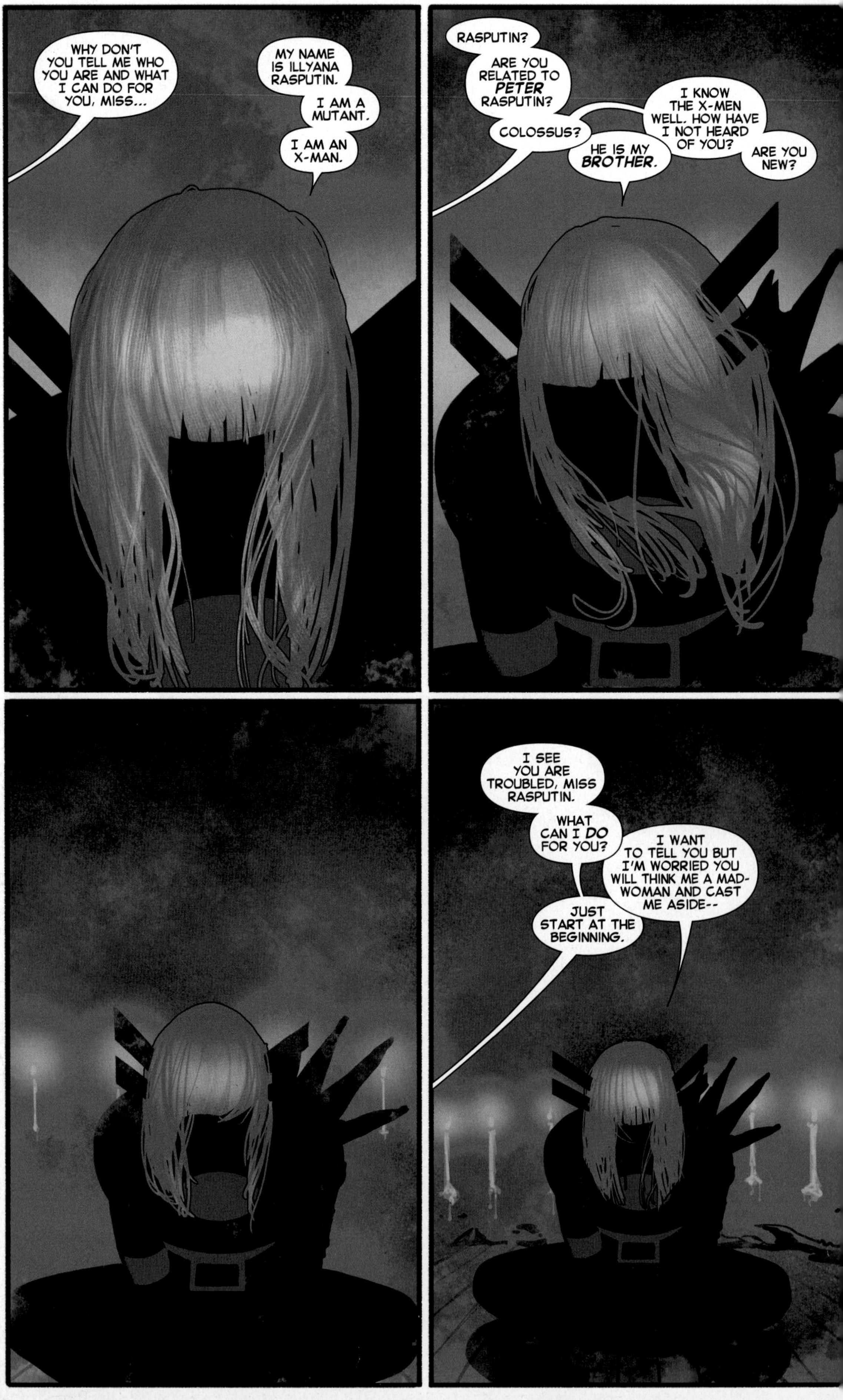
WHY DON'T YOU TELL ME WHO YOU ARE AND WHAT I CAN DO FOR YOU, MISS...
MY NAME IS ILLYANA RASPUTIN.
I AM A MUTANT.
I AM AN X-MAN.
RASPUTIN?
ARE YOU RELATED TO PETER RASPUTIN?
COLOSSUS?
HE IS MY BROTHER.
I KNOW THE X-MEN WELL. HOW HAVE I NOT HEARD OF YOU?
ARE YOU NEW?
I SEE YOU ARE TROUBLED, MISS RASPUTIN.
WHAT CAN I DO FOR YOU?
I WANT TO TELL YOU BUT I'M WORRIED YOU WILL THINK ME A MAD-WOMAN AND CAST ME ASIDE--
JUST START AT THE BEGINNING.

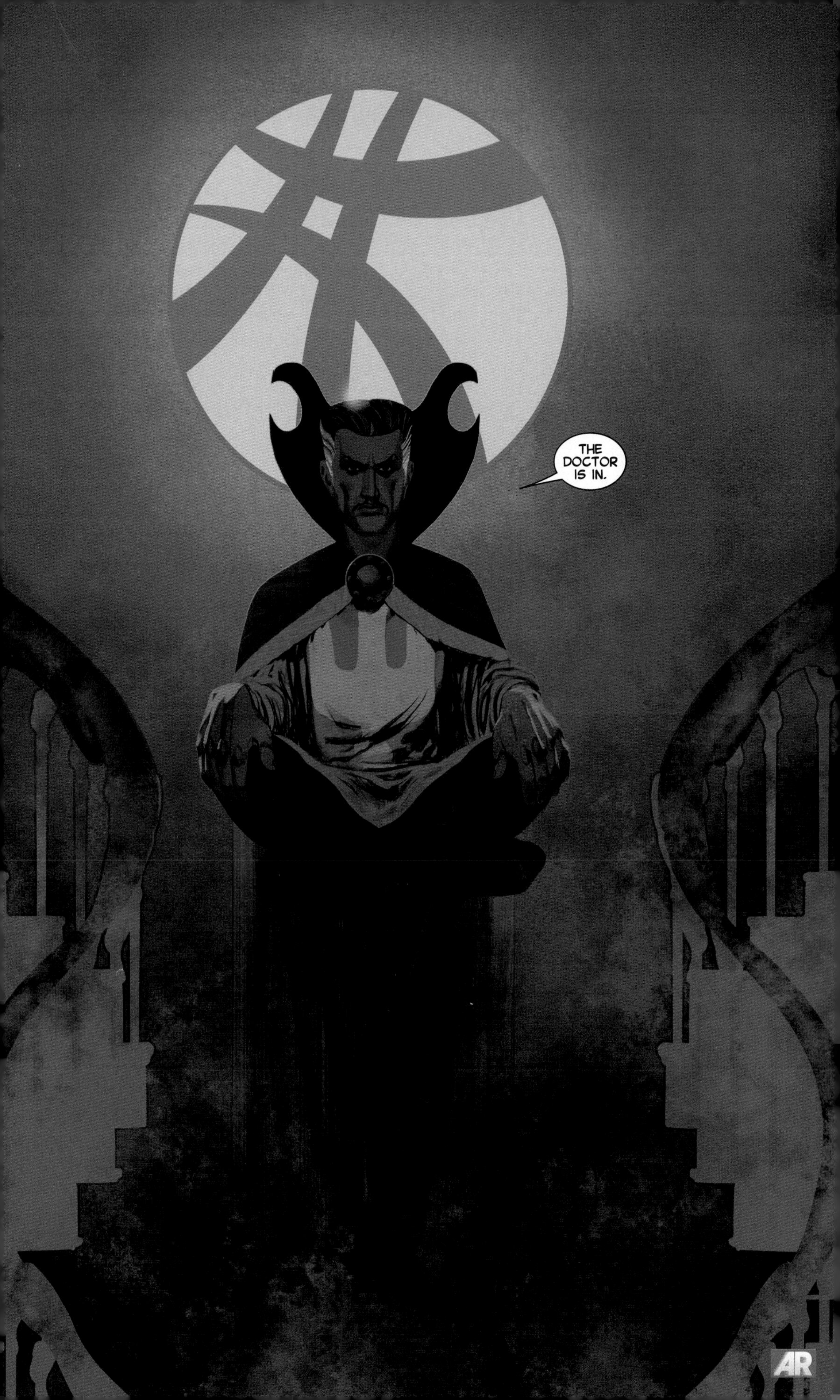
THE DOCTOR IS IN.

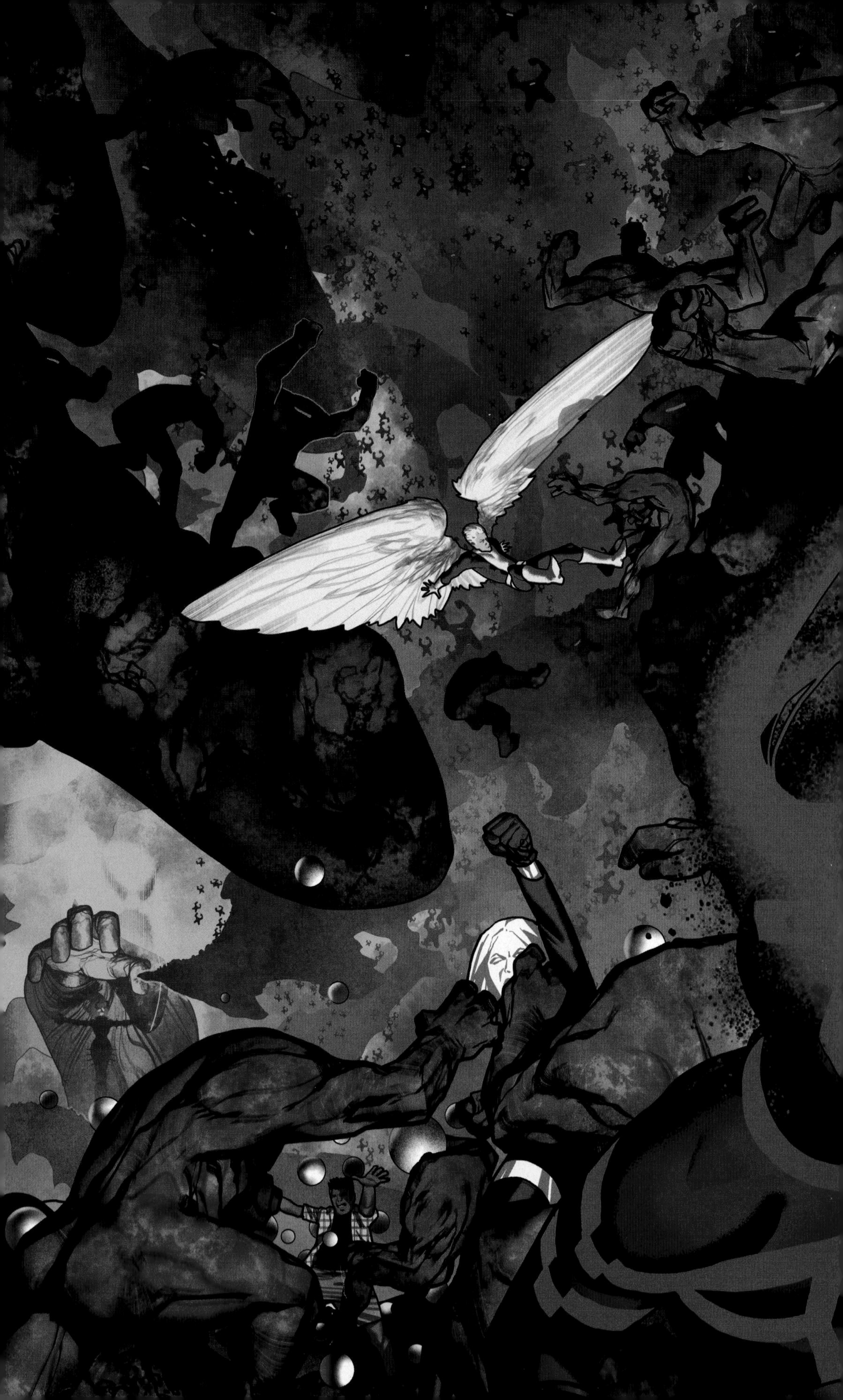

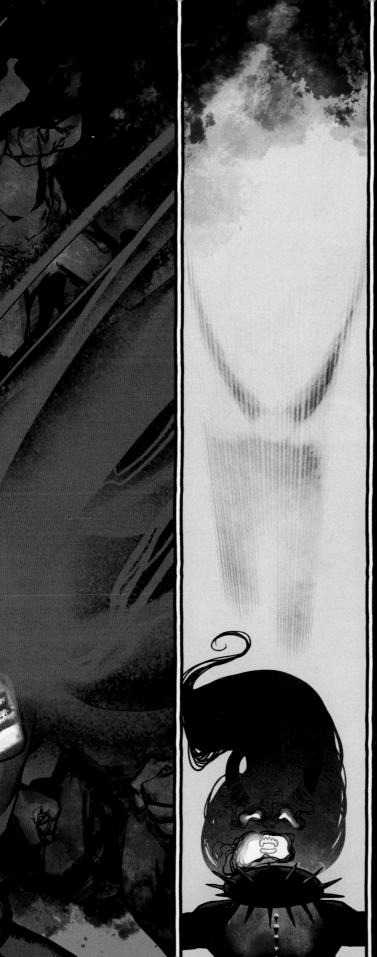

"I KNOW YOU KNOW OF THE LIMBO DIMENSION, AND I KNOW, DOCTOR, YOU KNOW OF THE DREADED *DORMAMMU*."

"BUT DORMAMMU CALLS THE *DARK* DIMENSION HIS HOME. HE NEVER LEAVES IT."

"AND NOW, I AM TELLING YOU, HE WANTS LIMBO AS WELL.

"MAYBE HE WAS OUSTED FROM HIS HOME.

"MAYBE IT LAID THERE ABANDONED AND HE JUST WANTED IT.

"I DON'T KNOW WHAT DRIVES HIM.

"ON THE FARM, WHEN I WAS A LITTLE GIRL IN RUSSIA, MY FATHER WOULD LAUGH AT ME BECAUSE I WOULD OFTEN PROJECT MY MORE COMPLICATED HUMAN EMOTIONS ON THE LITTLE ANIMALS.

"WITH A CREATURE LIKE DORMAMMU I HAVE LEARNED NOT TO REPEAT THAT MISTAKE.

"HE IS JUST A BASE CREATURE-- AN ANIMAL WHO ONLY CARES FOR HIS OWN NEEDS."

"I CAN'T DISAGREE WITH YOU."

"I HAVE ANGERED THIS CREATURE AND HE WAS PUNISHING ME BY MAKING ME WATCH MY FRIENDS FIGHT FOR THEIR LIVES WHILE HE HELD ME CAPTIVE."

"THE OTHER X-MEN?"

"YES. THE STEPFORD SISTERS, THE PSYCHICS ON OUR TEAM, EMPOW- ERED THE NEW STUDENTS TO FIGHT THE GOOD FIGHT. WITHOUT THIS MANIPULATION, I CRINGE TO THINK--"

"ARE THEY OKAY NOW?"

"IT'S--

"IT'S BETTER IF I TELL YOU WHAT HAPPENED..."

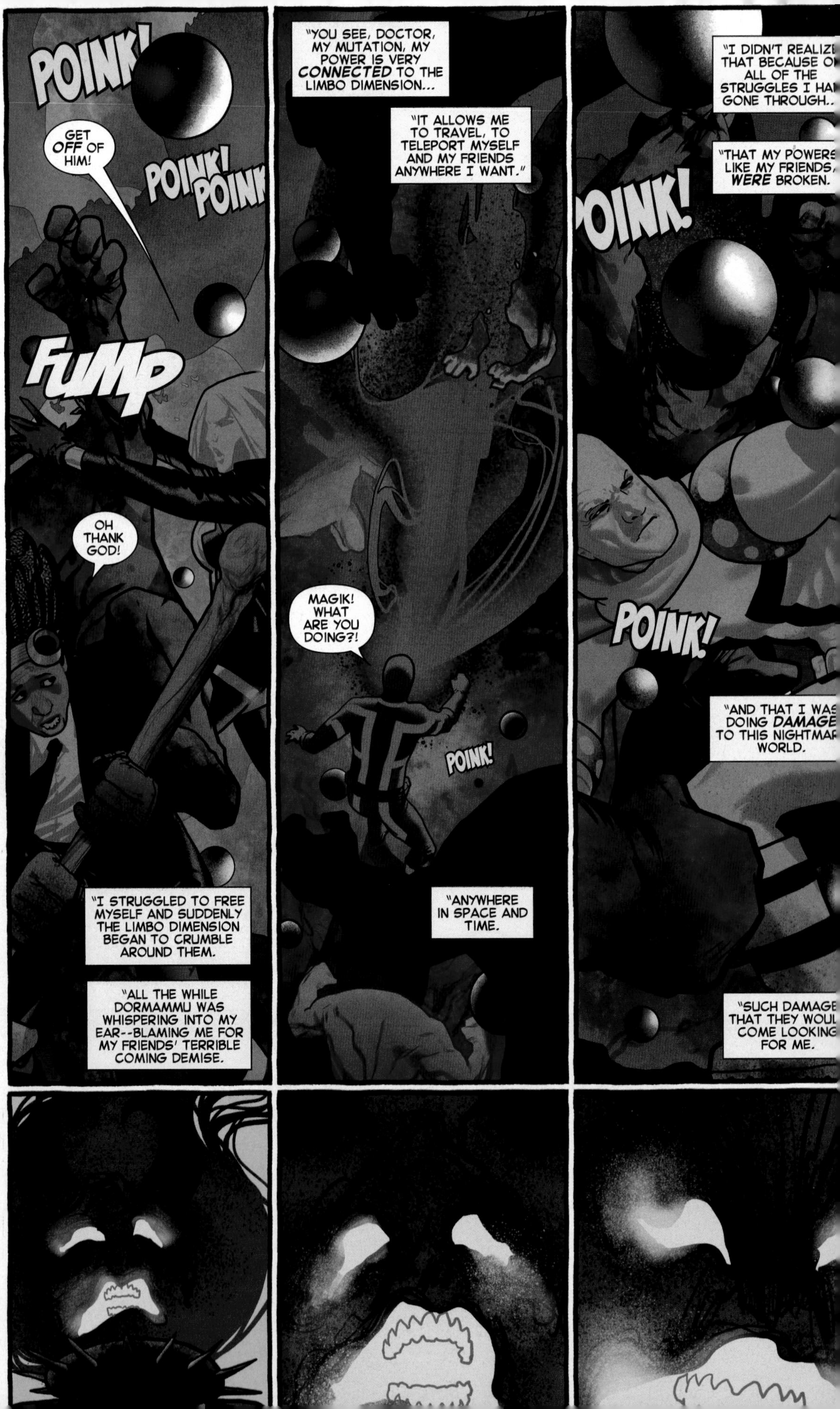
POINK!
GET OFF OF HIM!
POINK! POINK!
FUMP
OH THANK GOD!
"I STRUGGLED TO FREE MYSELF AND SUDDENLY THE LIMBO DIMENSION BEGAN TO CRUMBLE AROUND THEM.
"ALL THE WHILE DORMAMMU WAS WHISPERING INTO MY EAR--BLAMING ME FOR MY FRIENDS' TERRIBLE COMING DEMISE.
"YOU SEE, DOCTOR, MY MUTATION, MY POWER IS VERY CONNECTED TO THE LIMBO DIMENSION...
"IT ALLOWS ME TO TRAVEL, TO TELEPORT MYSELF AND MY FRIENDS ANYWHERE I WANT."
MAGIK! WHAT ARE YOU DOING?!
POINK!
"ANYWHERE IN SPACE AND TIME.
"I DIDN'T REALIZE THAT BECAUSE OF ALL OF THE STRUGGLES I HAD GONE THROUGH...
"THAT MY POWERS, LIKE MY FRIENDS, WERE BROKEN.
POINK!
POINK!
"AND THAT I WAS DOING DAMAGE TO THIS NIGHTMARE WORLD.
"SUCH DAMAGE THAT THEY WOULD COME LOOKING FOR ME.

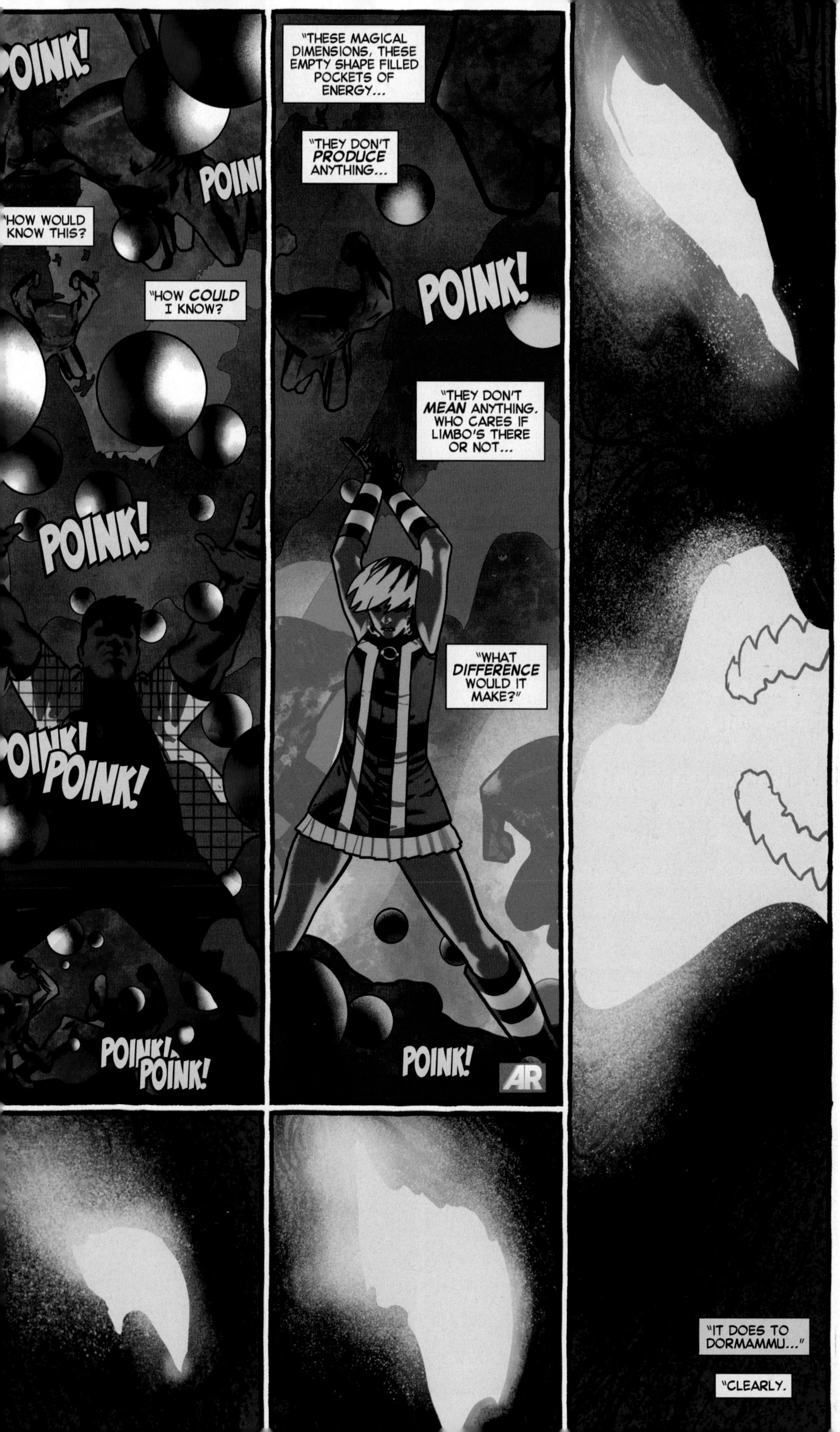

POINK!
POINK
"HOW WOULD KNOW THIS?
"HOW COULD I KNOW?
POINK!
POINK! POINK!
POINK! POINK!
"THESE MAGICAL DIMENSIONS, THESE EMPTY SHAPE FILLED POCKETS OF ENERGY...
"THEY DON'T PRODUCE ANYTHING...
POINK!
"THEY DON'T MEAN ANYTHING. WHO CARES IF LIMBO'S THERE OR NOT...
"WHAT DIFFERENCE WOULD IT MAKE?"
POINK!
AR
"IT DOES TO DORMAMMU..."
"CLEARLY.

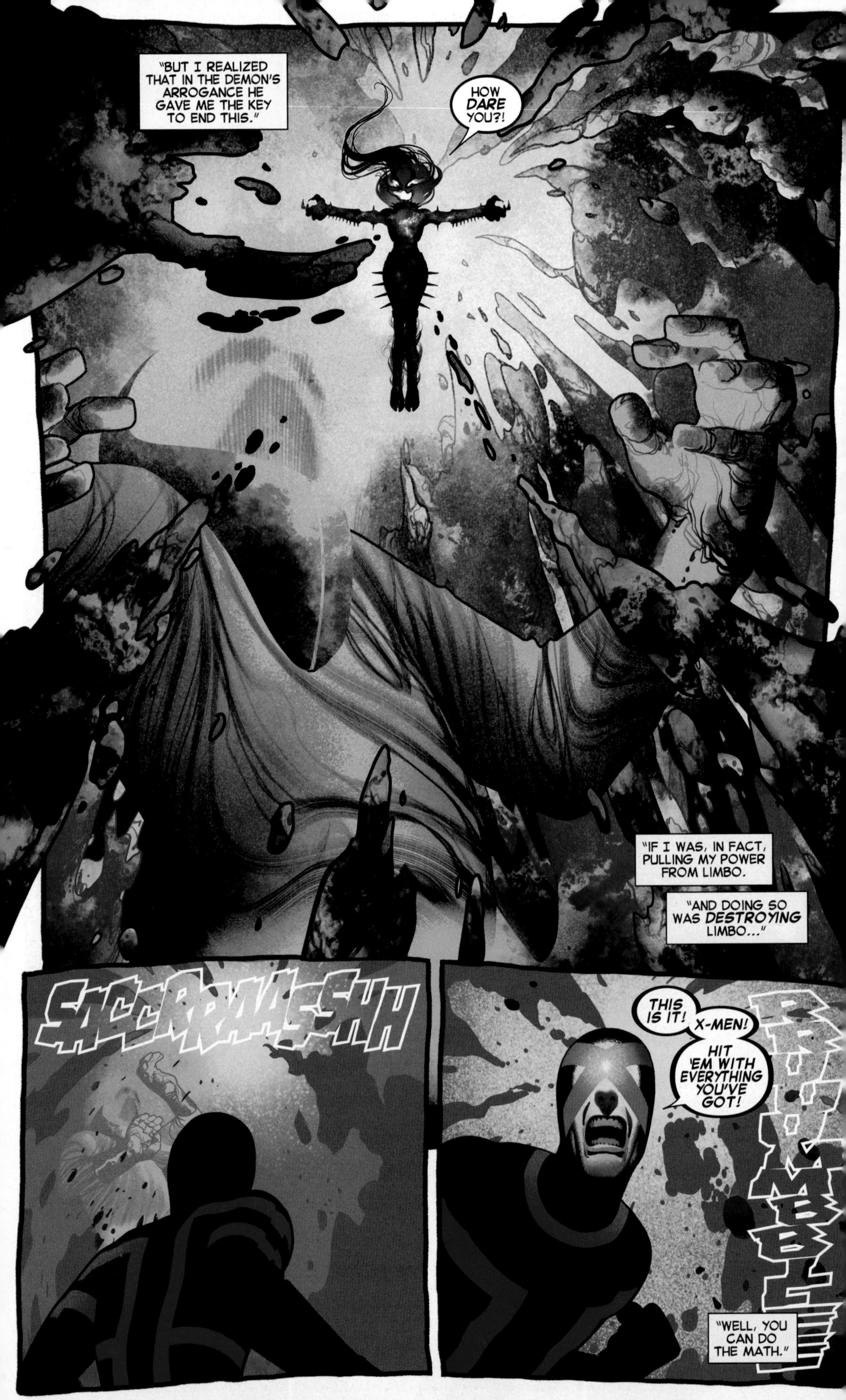
"BUT I REALIZED THAT IN THE DEMON'S ARROGANCE HE GAVE ME THE KEY TO END THIS."
HOW *DARE* YOU?!
"IF I WAS, IN FACT, PULLING MY POWER FROM LIMBO.
"AND DOING SO WAS *DESTROYING* LIMBO..."
THIS IS IT!
X-MEN!
HIT 'EM WITH EVERYTHING YOU'VE GOT!
"WELL, YOU CAN DO THE MATH."

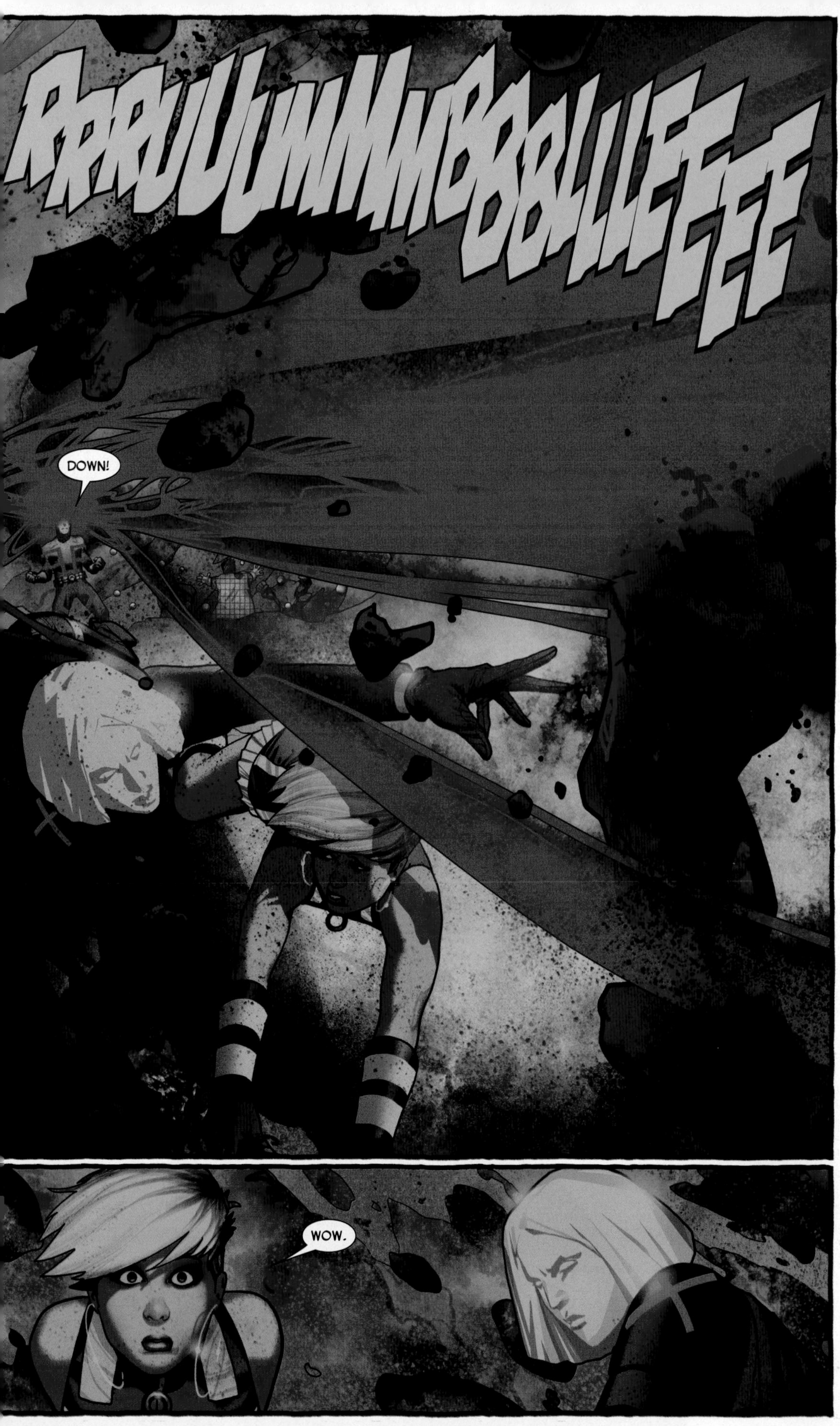
RRRUUMMMBBBLLLEEEE
DOWN!
WOW.

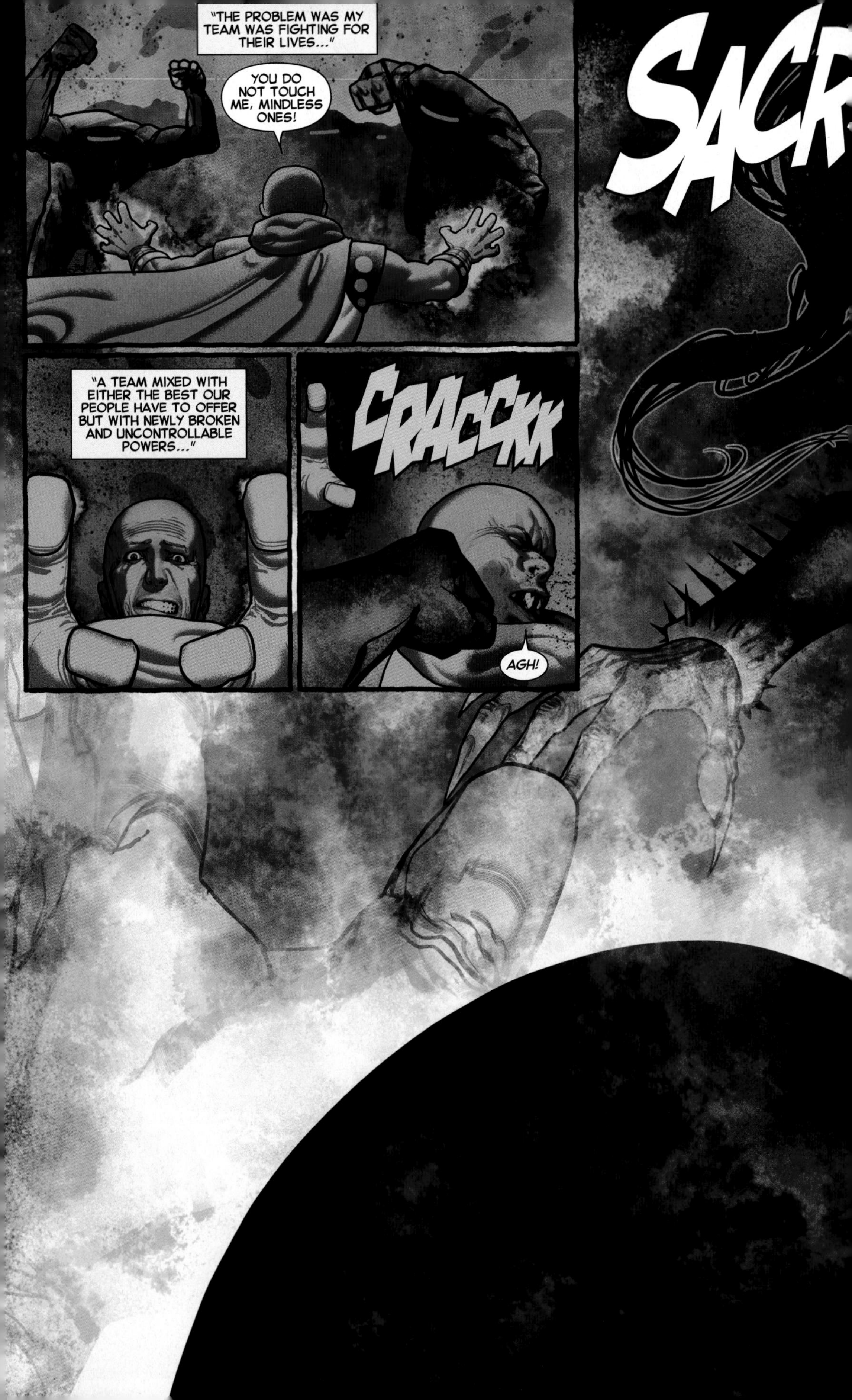
"THE PROBLEM WAS MY TEAM WAS FIGHTING FOR THEIR LIVES..."
YOU DO NOT TOUCH ME, MINDLESS ONES!
"A TEAM MIXED WITH EITHER THE BEST OUR PEOPLE HAVE TO OFFER BUT WITH NEWLY BROKEN AND UNCONTROLLABLE POWERS..."
CRACCKK
AGH!
SACR

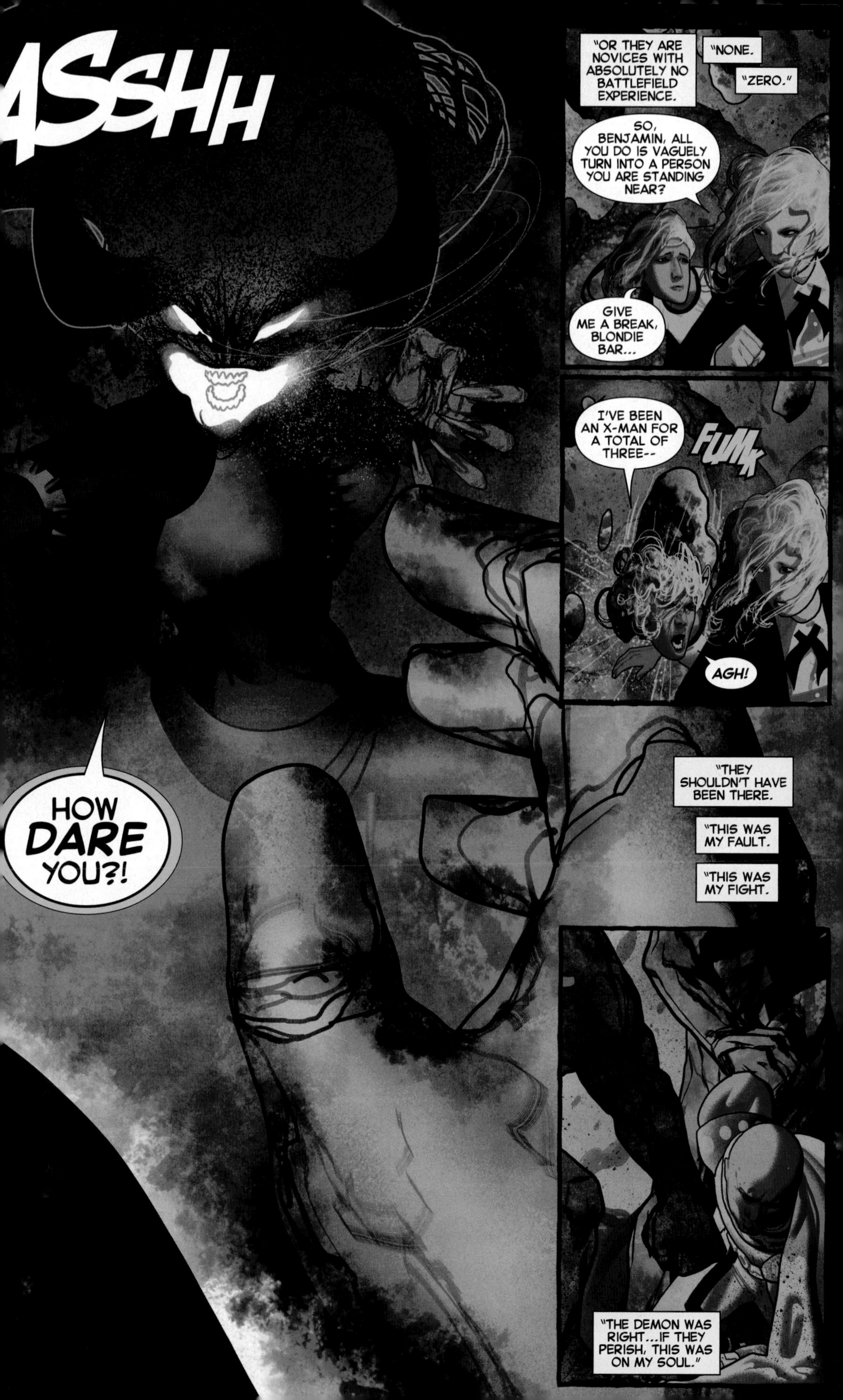

ASSHH
"OR THEY ARE NOVICES WITH ABSOLUTELY NO BATTLEFIELD EXPERIENCE.
"NONE.
"ZERO."
SO, BENJAMIN, ALL YOU DO IS VAGUELY TURN INTO A PERSON YOU ARE STANDING NEAR?
GIVE ME A BREAK, BLONDIE BAR...
I'VE BEEN AN X-MAN FOR A TOTAL OF THREE--
FUMK
AGH!
HOW DARE YOU?!
"THEY SHOULDN'T HAVE BEEN THERE.
"THIS WAS MY FAULT.
"THIS WAS MY FIGHT.
"THE DEMON WAS RIGHT...IF THEY PERISH, THIS WAS ON MY SOUL."

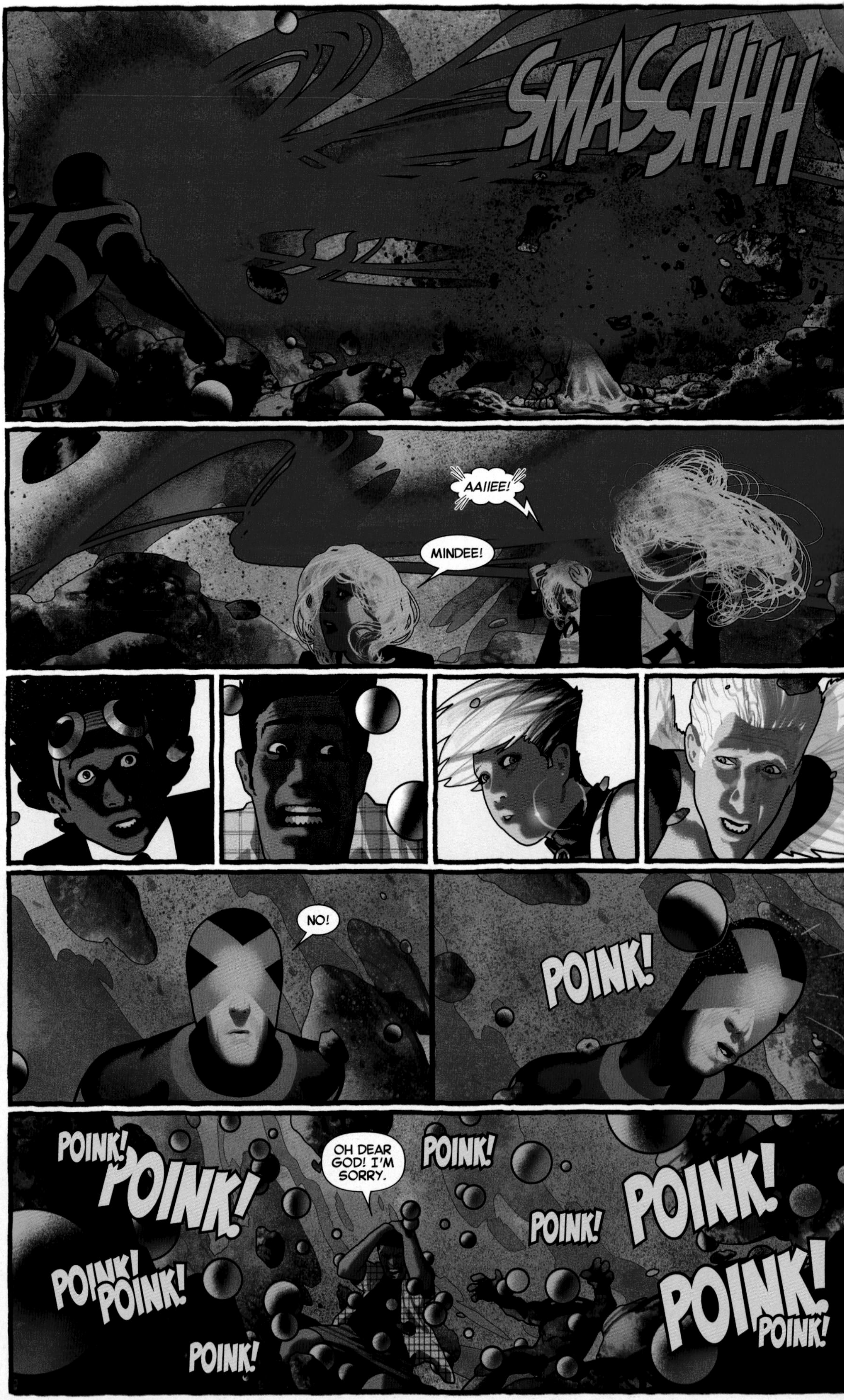
SMASSHHH
AAIIEE!
MINDEE!
NO!
POINK!
POINK!
POINK!
POINK!
POINK!
OH DEAR GOD! I'M SORRY.
POINK!
POINK!
POINK!
POINK!
POINK!
POINK!

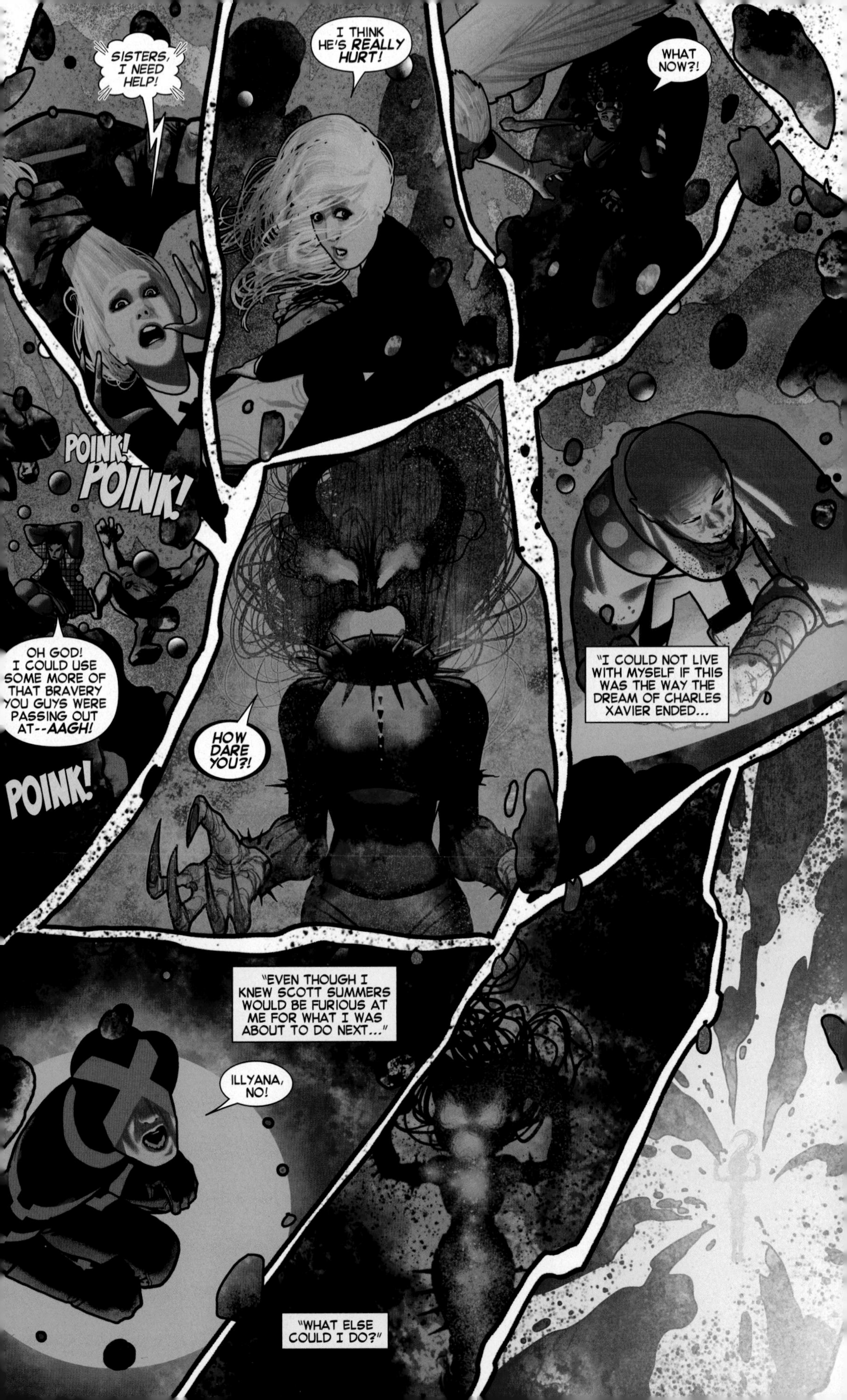

SISTERS, I NEED HELP!
I THINK HE'S REALLY HURT!
WHAT NOW?!
POINK! POINK!
OH GOD! I COULD USE SOME MORE OF THAT BRAVERY YOU GUYS WERE PASSING OUT AT--AAGH!
POINK!
HOW DARE YOU?!
"I COULD NOT LIVE WITH MYSELF IF THIS WAS THE WAY THE DREAM OF CHARLES XAVIER ENDED...
"EVEN THOUGH I KNEW SCOTT SUMMERS WOULD BE FURIOUS AT ME FOR WHAT I WAS ABOUT TO DO NEXT..."
ILLYANA, NO!
"WHAT ELSE COULD I DO?"

"I ENDED
THE LIMBO
DIMENSION.

"I TOOK
IT INSIDE
MYSELF.

"EVERY
PART.

"IT MAY HAVE
BEEN OVERREACHING
BUT SOMETIMES YOU
DON'T KNOW WHAT
YOU CAN DO TILL
YOU TRY."

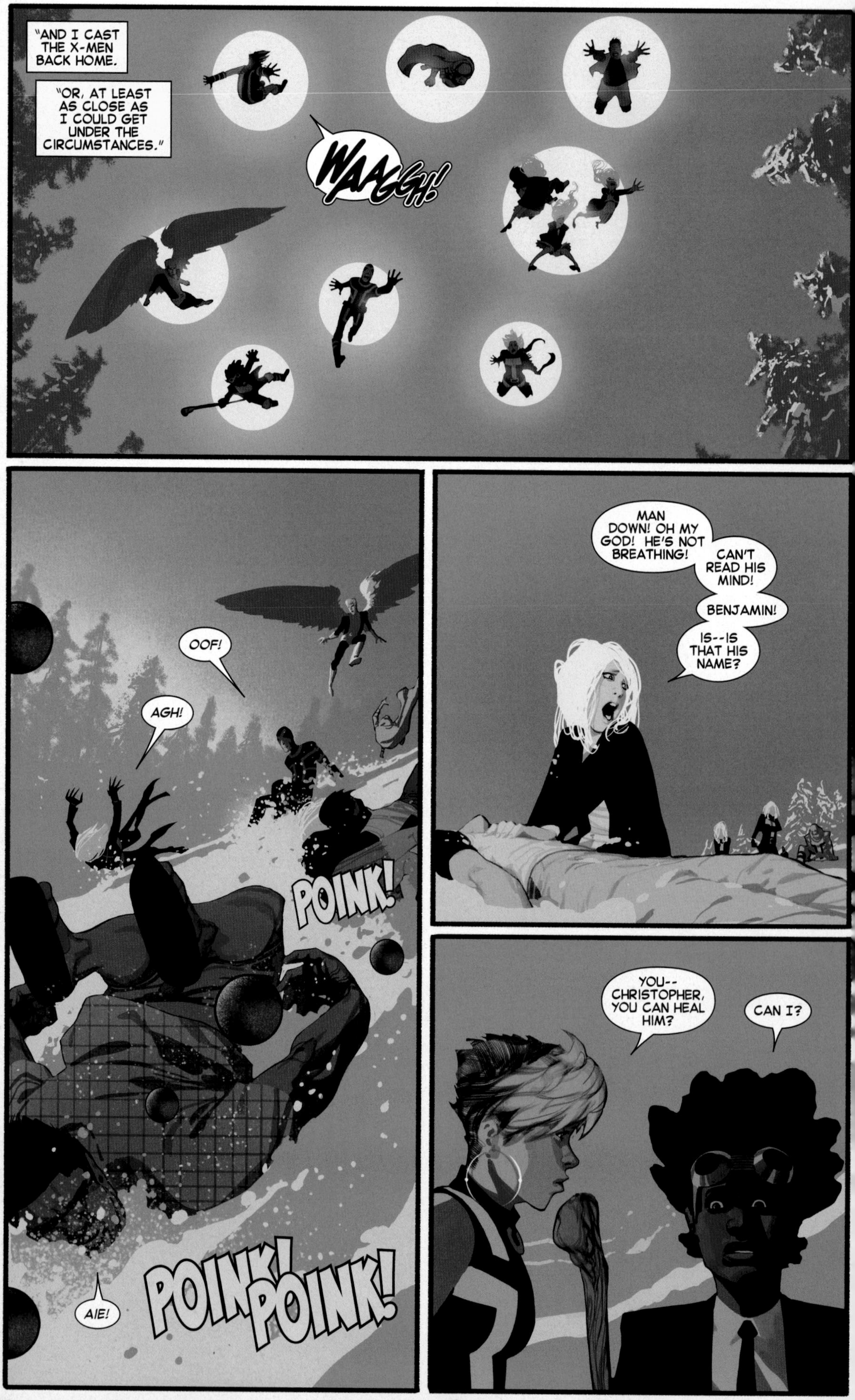
"AND I CAST THE X-MEN BACK HOME.
"OR, AT LEAST AS CLOSE AS I COULD GET UNDER THE CIRCUMSTANCES."
WAAGGH!
OOF!
AGH!
POINK!
AIE!
POINK! POINK!
MAN DOWN! OH MY GOD! HE'S NOT BREATHING!
CAN'T READ HIS MIND!
BENJAMIN!
IS--IS THAT HIS NAME?
YOU-- CHRISTOPHER, YOU CAN HEAL HIM?
CAN I?

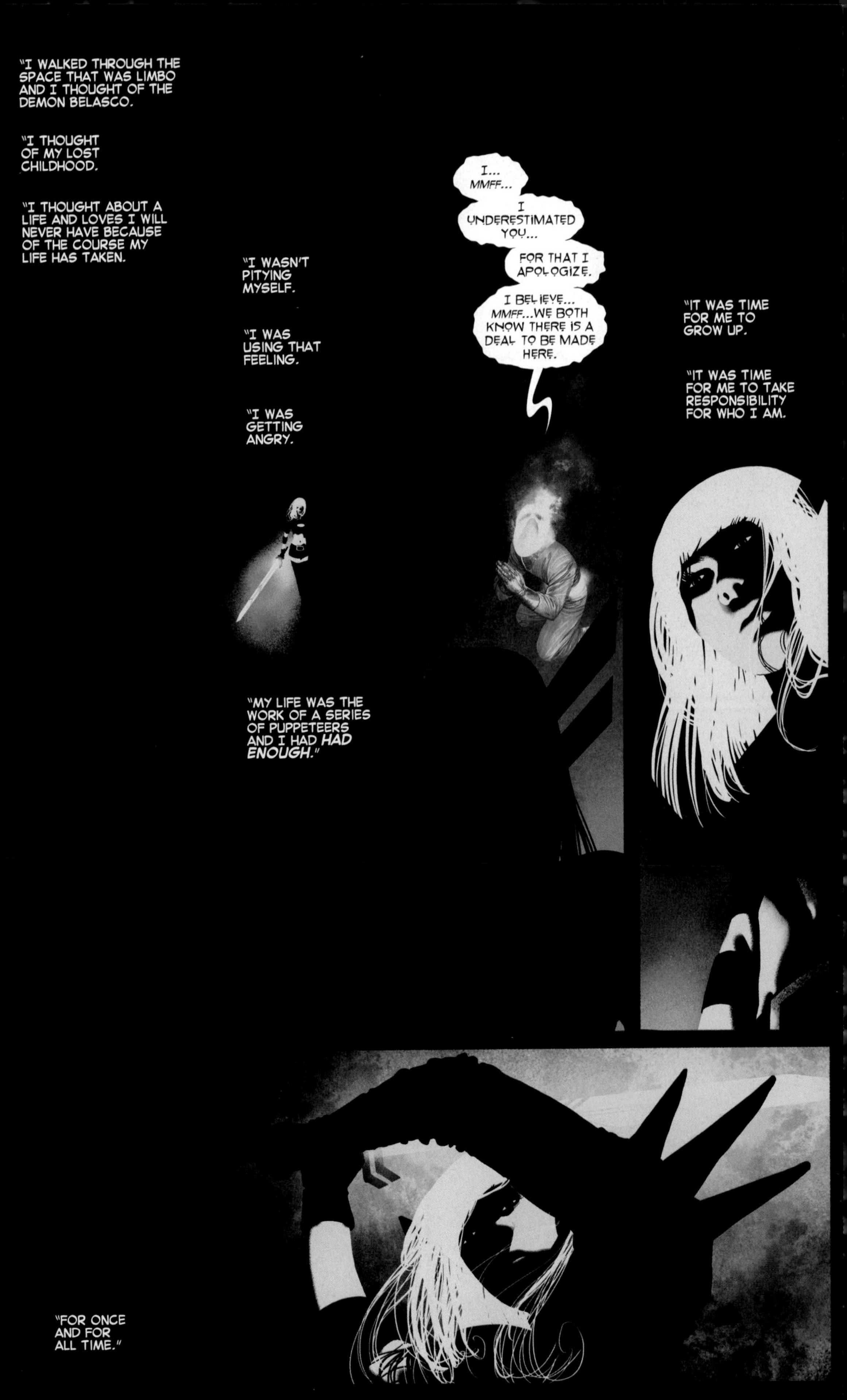
"I WALKED THROUGH THE SPACE THAT WAS LIMBO AND I THOUGHT OF THE DEMON BELASCO.
"I THOUGHT OF MY LOST CHILDHOOD.
"I THOUGHT ABOUT A LIFE AND LOVES I WILL NEVER HAVE BECAUSE OF THE COURSE MY LIFE HAS TAKEN.
"I WASN'T PITYING MYSELF.
"I WAS USING THAT FEELING.
"I WAS GETTING ANGRY.
I... MMFF...
I UNDERESTIMATED YOU...
FOR THAT I APOLOGIZE.
I BELIEVE... MMFF...WE BOTH KNOW THERE IS A DEAL TO BE MADE HERE.
"IT WAS TIME FOR ME TO GROW UP.
"IT WAS TIME FOR ME TO TAKE RESPONSIBILITY FOR WHO I AM.
"MY LIFE WAS THE WORK OF A SERIES OF PUPPETEERS AND I HAD *HAD ENOUGH.*"
"FOR ONCE AND FOR ALL TIME."

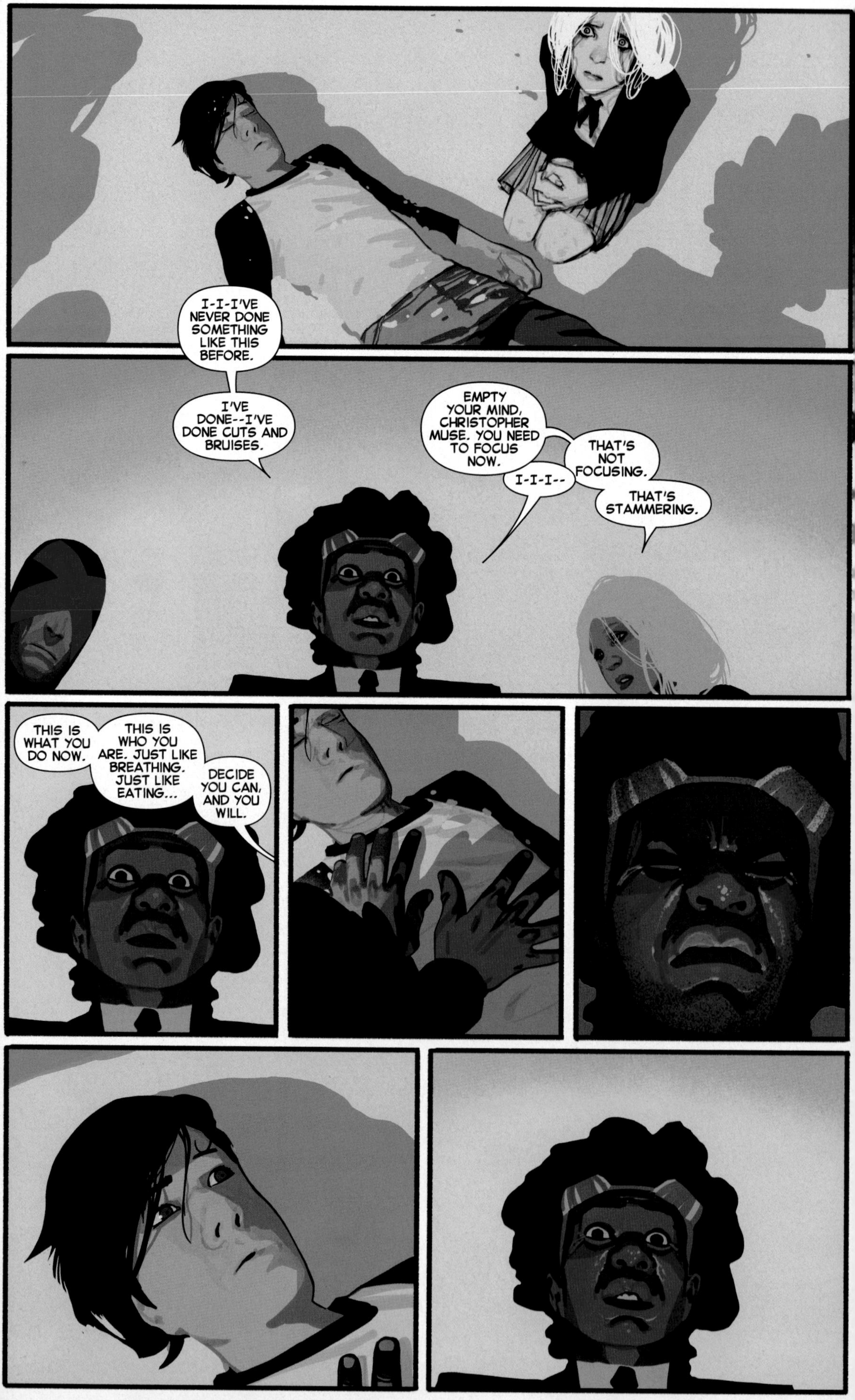
I-I-I'VE NEVER DONE SOMETHING LIKE THIS BEFORE.
I'VE DONE--I'VE DONE CUTS AND BRUISES.
EMPTY YOUR MIND, CHRISTOPHER MUSE. YOU NEED TO FOCUS NOW.
I-I-I--
THAT'S NOT FOCUSING.
THAT'S STAMMERING.
THIS IS WHAT YOU DO NOW.
THIS IS WHO YOU ARE. JUST LIKE BREATHING. JUST LIKE EATING...
DECIDE YOU CAN, AND YOU WILL.

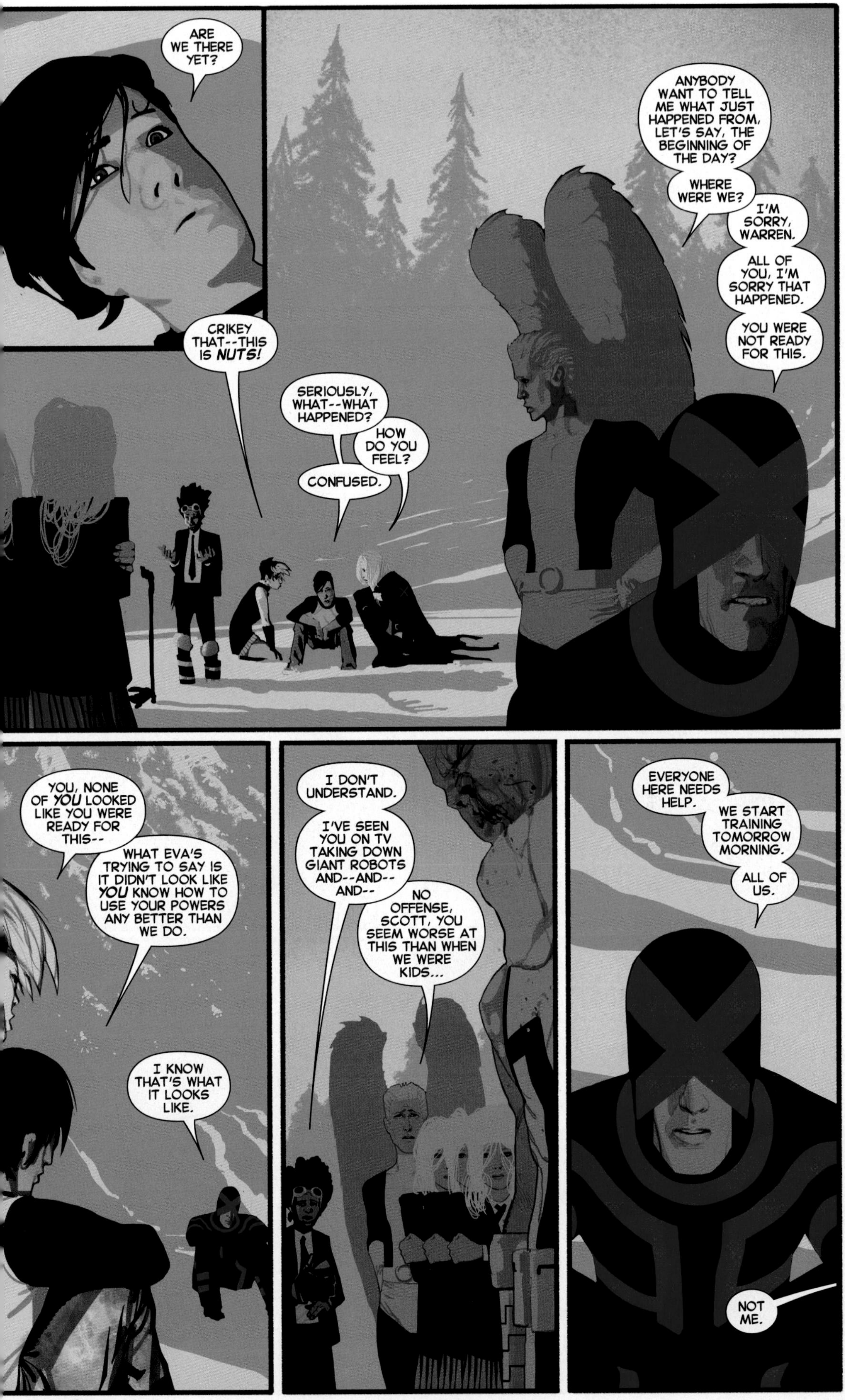
ARE WE THERE YET?
CRIKEY THAT--THIS IS *NUTS!*
SERIOUSLY, WHAT--WHAT HAPPENED?
HOW DO YOU FEEL?
CONFUSED.
ANYBODY WANT TO TELL ME WHAT JUST HAPPENED FROM, LET'S SAY, THE BEGINNING OF THE DAY?
WHERE WERE WE?
I'M SORRY, WARREN.
ALL OF YOU, I'M SORRY THAT HAPPENED.
YOU WERE NOT READY FOR THIS.
YOU, NONE OF *YOU* LOOKED LIKE YOU WERE READY FOR THIS--
WHAT EVA'S TRYING TO SAY IS IT DIDN'T LOOK LIKE *YOU* KNOW HOW TO USE YOUR POWERS ANY BETTER THAN WE DO.
I KNOW THAT'S WHAT IT LOOKS LIKE.
I DON'T UNDERSTAND.
I'VE SEEN YOU ON TV TAKING DOWN GIANT ROBOTS AND--AND--AND--
NO OFFENSE, SCOTT, YOU SEEM WORSE AT THIS THAN WHEN WE WERE KIDS...
EVERYONE HERE NEEDS HELP.
WE START TRAINING TOMORROW MORNING.
ALL OF US.
NOT ME.

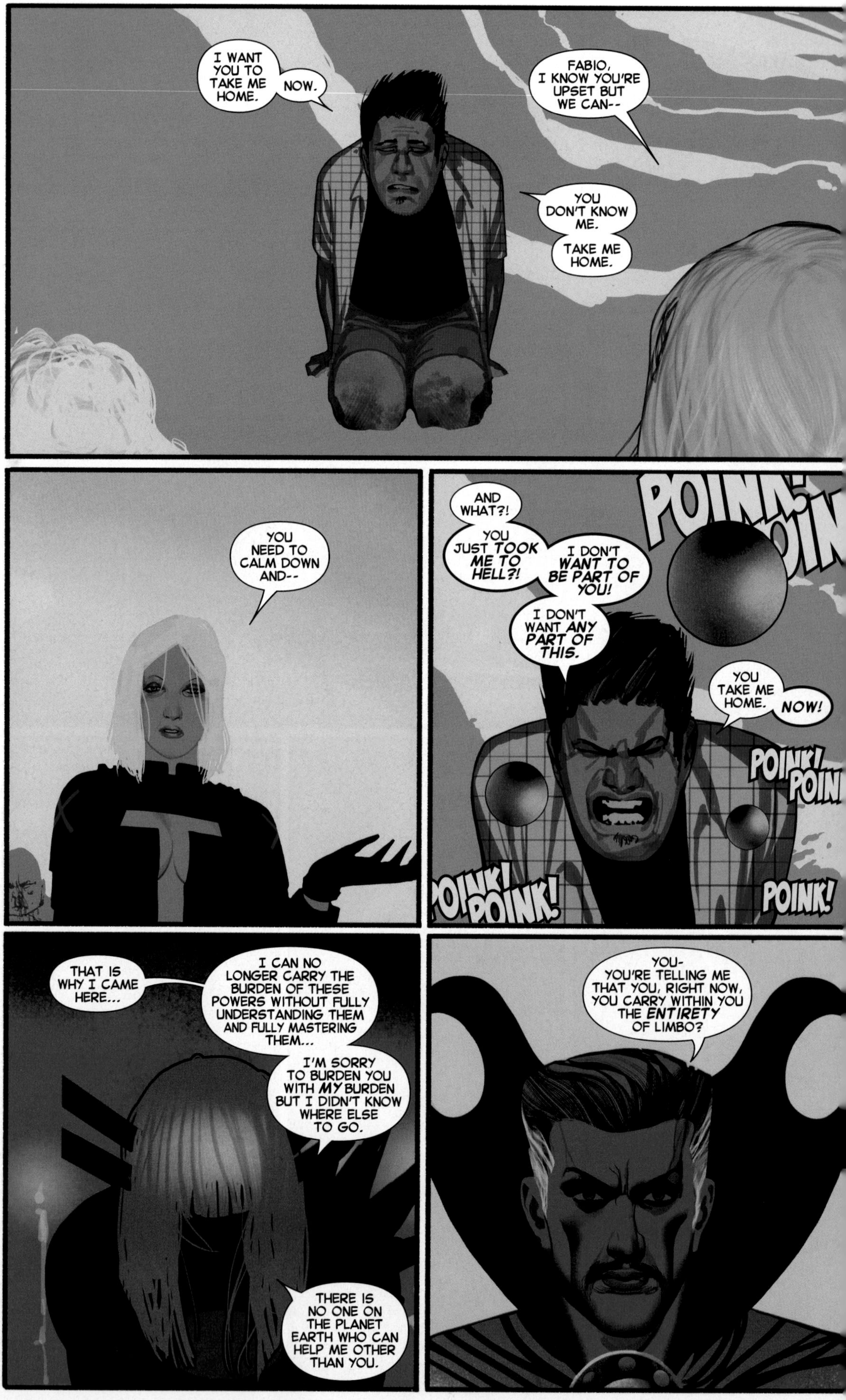

I WANT YOU TO TAKE ME HOME.
NOW.
FABIO, I KNOW YOU'RE UPSET BUT WE CAN--
YOU DON'T KNOW ME.
TAKE ME HOME.
YOU NEED TO CALM DOWN AND--
AND WHAT?!
YOU JUST *TOOK ME TO HELL?!*
I DON'T *WANT TO BE PART OF YOU!*
I DON'T WANT *ANY PART OF THIS.*
POINK! POIN
YOU TAKE ME HOME.
NOW!
POINK! POIN
POINK! POINK!
POINK!
THAT IS WHY I CAME HERE...
I CAN NO LONGER CARRY THE BURDEN OF THESE POWERS WITHOUT FULLY UNDERSTANDING THEM AND FULLY MASTERING THEM...
I'M SORRY TO BURDEN YOU WITH *MY* BURDEN BUT I DIDN'T KNOW WHERE ELSE TO GO.
THERE IS NO ONE ON THE PLANET EARTH WHO CAN HELP ME OTHER THAN YOU.
YOU- YOU'RE TELLING ME THAT YOU, RIGHT NOW, YOU CARRY WITHIN YOU THE *ENTIRETY* OF LIMBO?

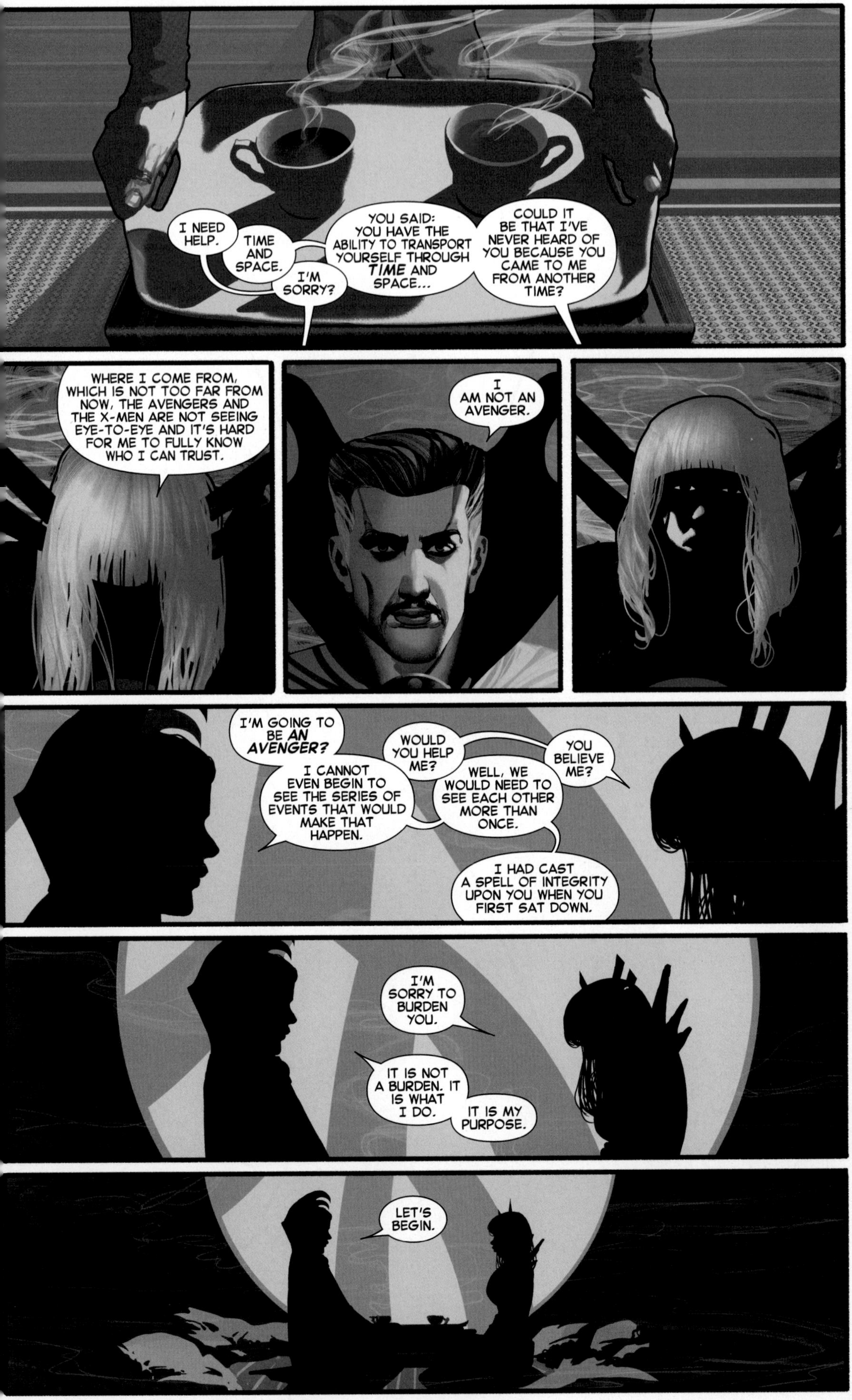
I NEED HELP.
TIME AND SPACE.
I'M SORRY?
YOU SAID: YOU HAVE THE ABILITY TO TRANSPORT YOURSELF THROUGH *TIME* AND SPACE...
COULD IT BE THAT I'VE NEVER HEARD OF YOU BECAUSE YOU CAME TO ME FROM ANOTHER TIME?
WHERE I COME FROM, WHICH IS NOT TOO FAR FROM NOW, THE AVENGERS AND THE X-MEN ARE NOT SEEING EYE-TO-EYE AND IT'S HARD FOR ME TO FULLY KNOW WHO I CAN TRUST.
I AM NOT AN AVENGER.
I'M GOING TO BE *AN AVENGER?*
I CANNOT EVEN BEGIN TO SEE THE SERIES OF EVENTS THAT WOULD MAKE THAT HAPPEN.
WOULD YOU HELP ME?
WELL, WE WOULD NEED TO SEE EACH OTHER MORE THAN ONCE.
YOU BELIEVE ME?
I HAD CAST A SPELL OF INTEGRITY UPON YOU WHEN YOU FIRST SAT DOWN.
I'M SORRY TO BURDEN YOU.
IT IS NOT A BURDEN. IT IS WHAT I DO.
IT IS MY PURPOSE.
LET'S BEGIN.

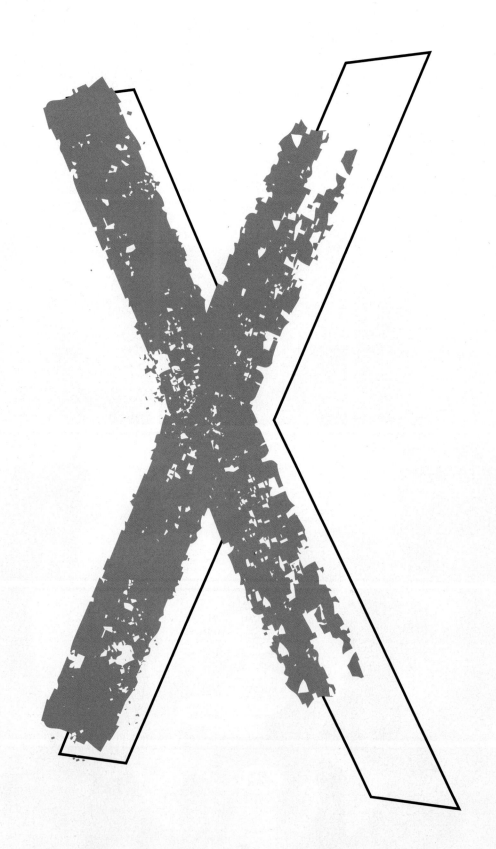

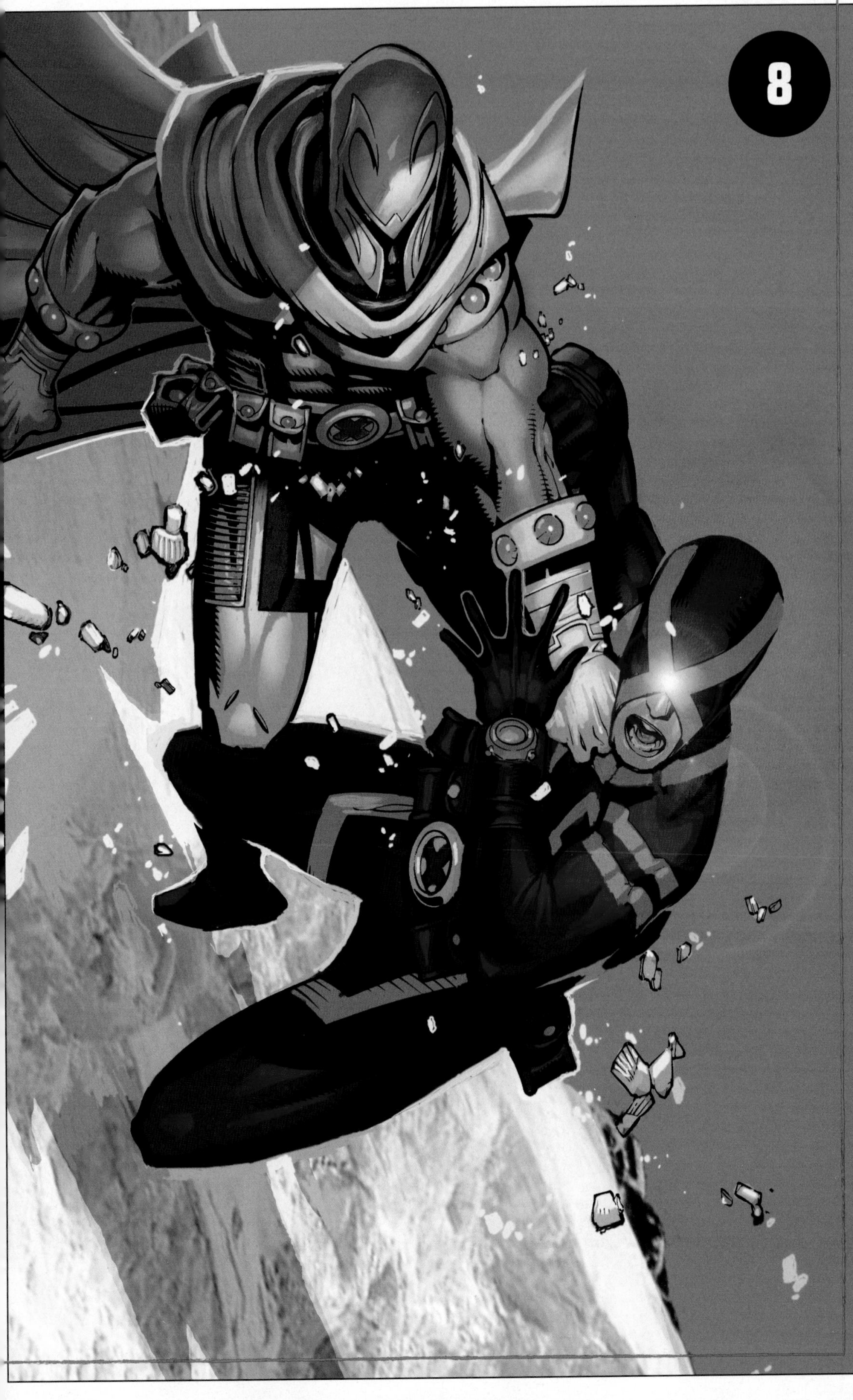
8

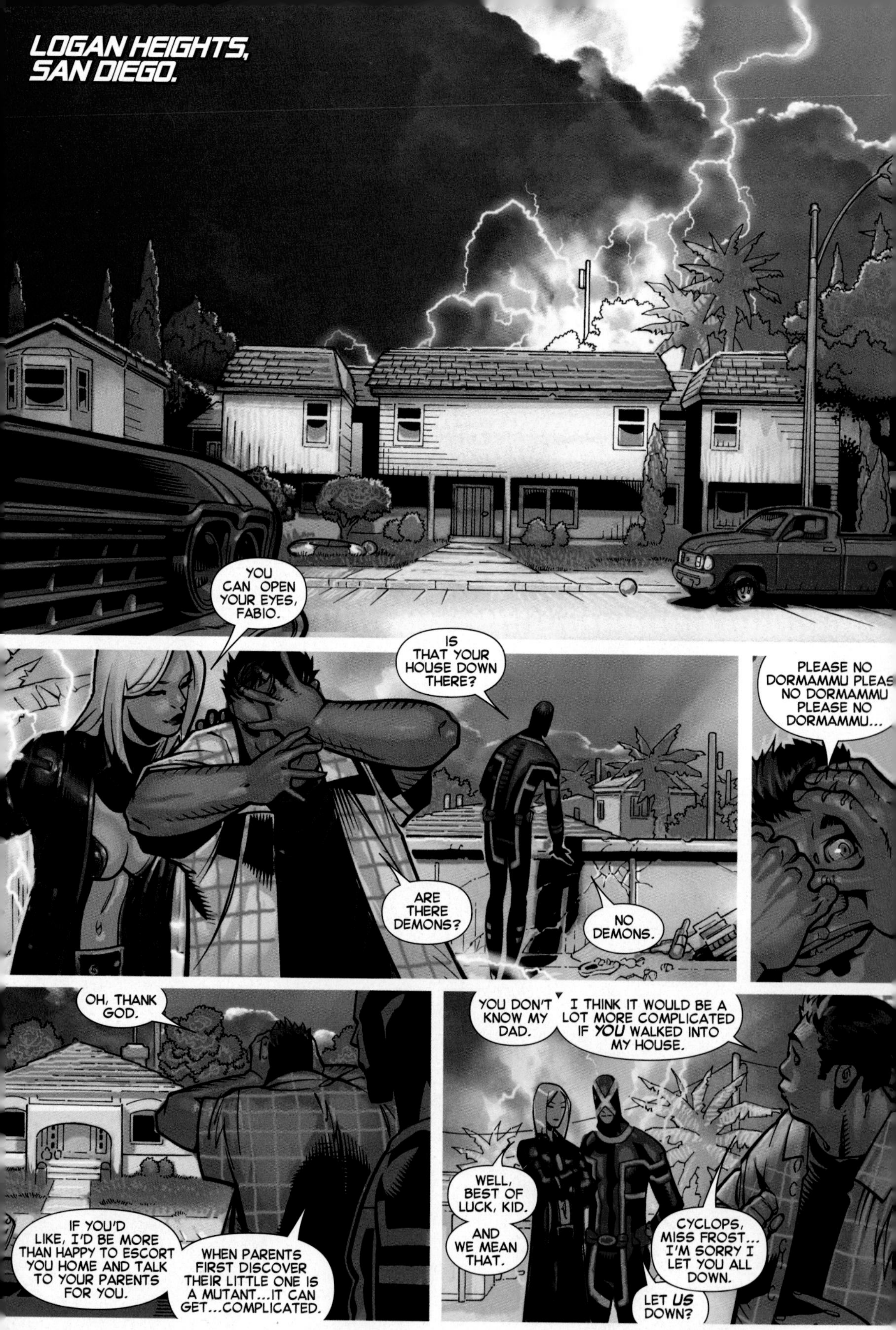
LOGAN HEIGHTS, SAN DIEGO.
YOU CAN OPEN YOUR EYES, FABIO.
IS THAT YOUR HOUSE DOWN THERE?
ARE THERE DEMONS?
NO DEMONS.
PLEASE NO DORMAMMU PLEASE NO DORMAMMU PLEASE NO DORMAMMU...
OH, THANK GOD.
IF YOU'D LIKE, I'D BE MORE THAN HAPPY TO ESCORT YOU HOME AND TALK TO YOUR PARENTS FOR YOU.
WHEN PARENTS FIRST DISCOVER THEIR LITTLE ONE IS A MUTANT...IT CAN GET...COMPLICATED.
YOU DON'T KNOW MY DAD.
I THINK IT WOULD BE A LOT MORE COMPLICATED IF YOU WALKED INTO MY HOUSE.
WELL, BEST OF LUCK, KID.
AND WE MEAN THAT.
CYCLOPS, MISS FROST... I'M SORRY I LET YOU ALL DOWN.
LET US DOWN?

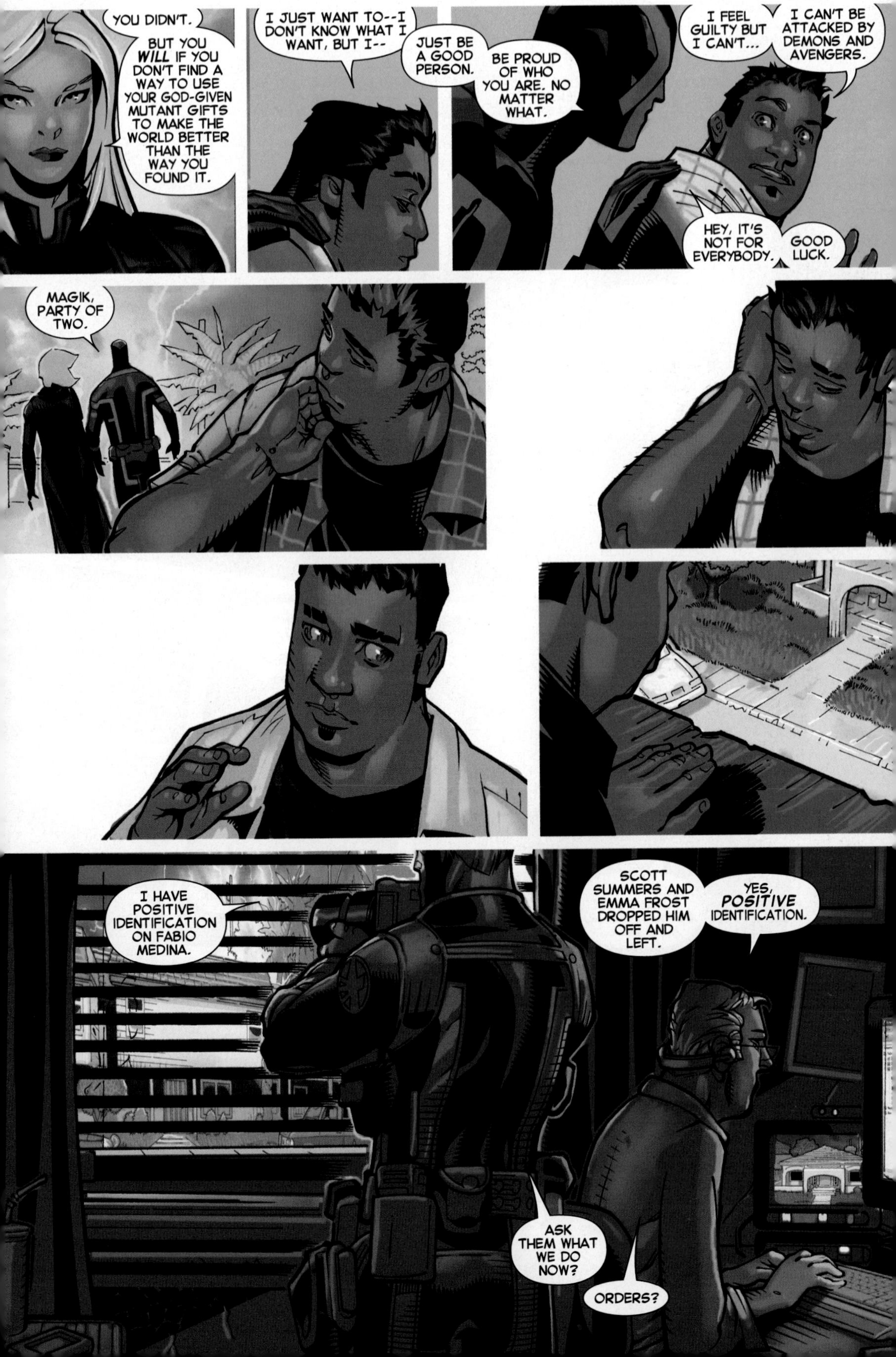

YOU DIDN'T.
BUT YOU *WILL* IF YOU DON'T FIND A WAY TO USE YOUR GOD-GIVEN MUTANT GIFTS TO MAKE THE WORLD BETTER THAN THE WAY YOU FOUND IT.
I JUST WANT TO--I DON'T KNOW WHAT I WANT, BUT I--
JUST BE A GOOD PERSON.
BE PROUD OF WHO YOU ARE. NO MATTER WHAT.
I FEEL GUILTY BUT I CAN'T...
I CAN'T BE ATTACKED BY DEMONS AND AVENGERS.
HEY, IT'S NOT FOR EVERYBODY.
GOOD LUCK.
MAGIK, PARTY OF TWO.
I HAVE POSITIVE IDENTIFICATION ON FABIO MEDINA.
SCOTT SUMMERS AND EMMA FROST DROPPED HIM OFF AND LEFT.
YES, *POSITIVE* IDENTIFICATION.
ASK THEM WHAT WE DO NOW?
ORDERS?

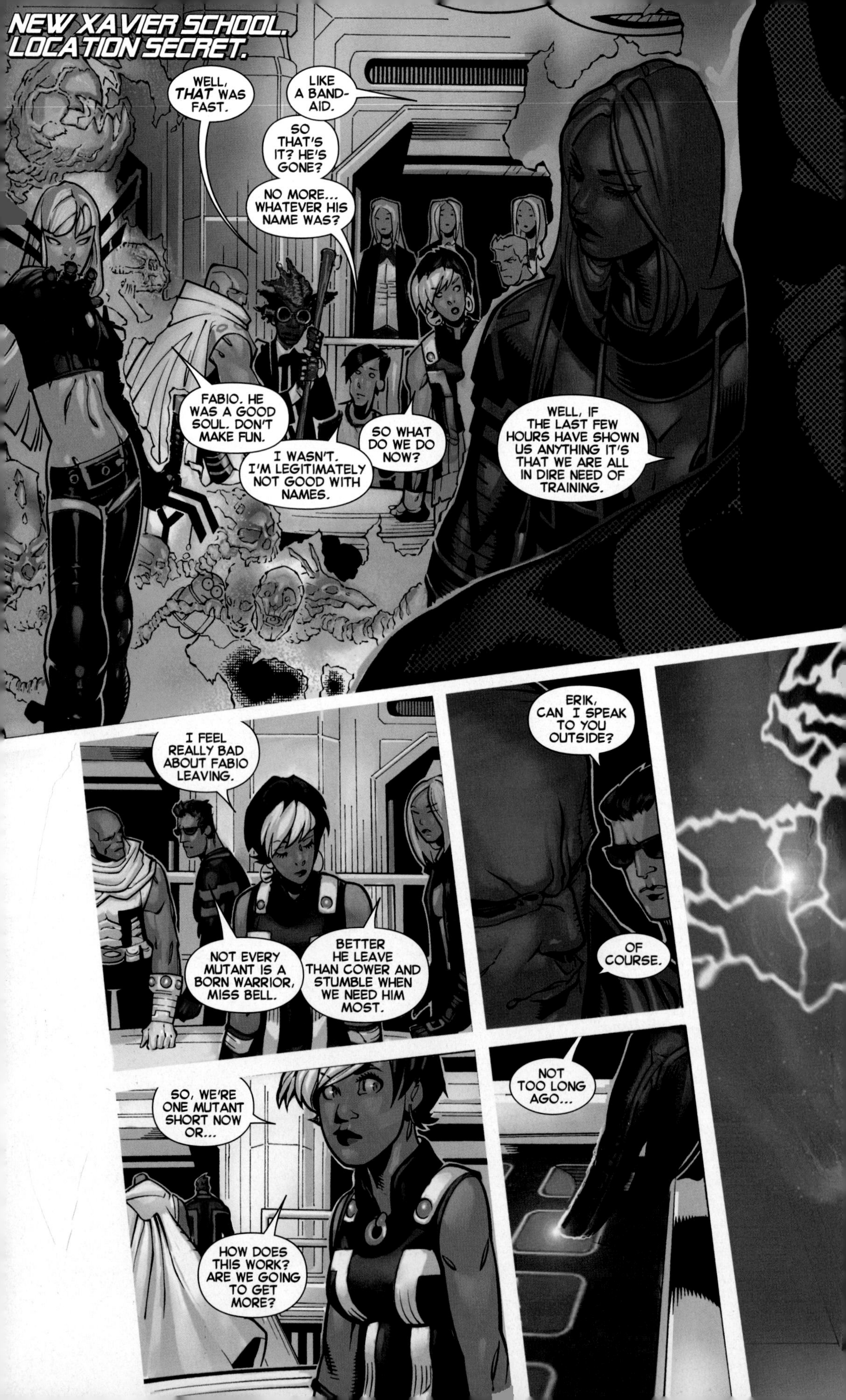
NEW XAVIER SCHOOL. LOCATION SECRET.
WELL, THAT WAS FAST.
LIKE A BAND-AID.
SO THAT'S IT? HE'S GONE?
NO MORE... WHATEVER HIS NAME WAS?
FABIO. HE WAS A GOOD SOUL. DON'T MAKE FUN.
I WASN'T. I'M LEGITIMATELY NOT GOOD WITH NAMES.
SO WHAT DO WE DO NOW?
WELL, IF THE LAST FEW HOURS HAVE SHOWN US ANYTHING IT'S THAT WE ARE ALL IN DIRE NEED OF TRAINING.
I FEEL REALLY BAD ABOUT FABIO LEAVING.
NOT EVERY MUTANT IS A BORN WARRIOR, MISS BELL.
BETTER HE LEAVE THAN COWER AND STUMBLE WHEN WE NEED HIM MOST.
ERIK, CAN I SPEAK TO YOU OUTSIDE?
OF COURSE.
SO, WE'RE ONE MUTANT SHORT NOW OR...
HOW DOES THIS WORK? ARE WE GOING TO GET MORE?
NOT TOO LONG AGO...

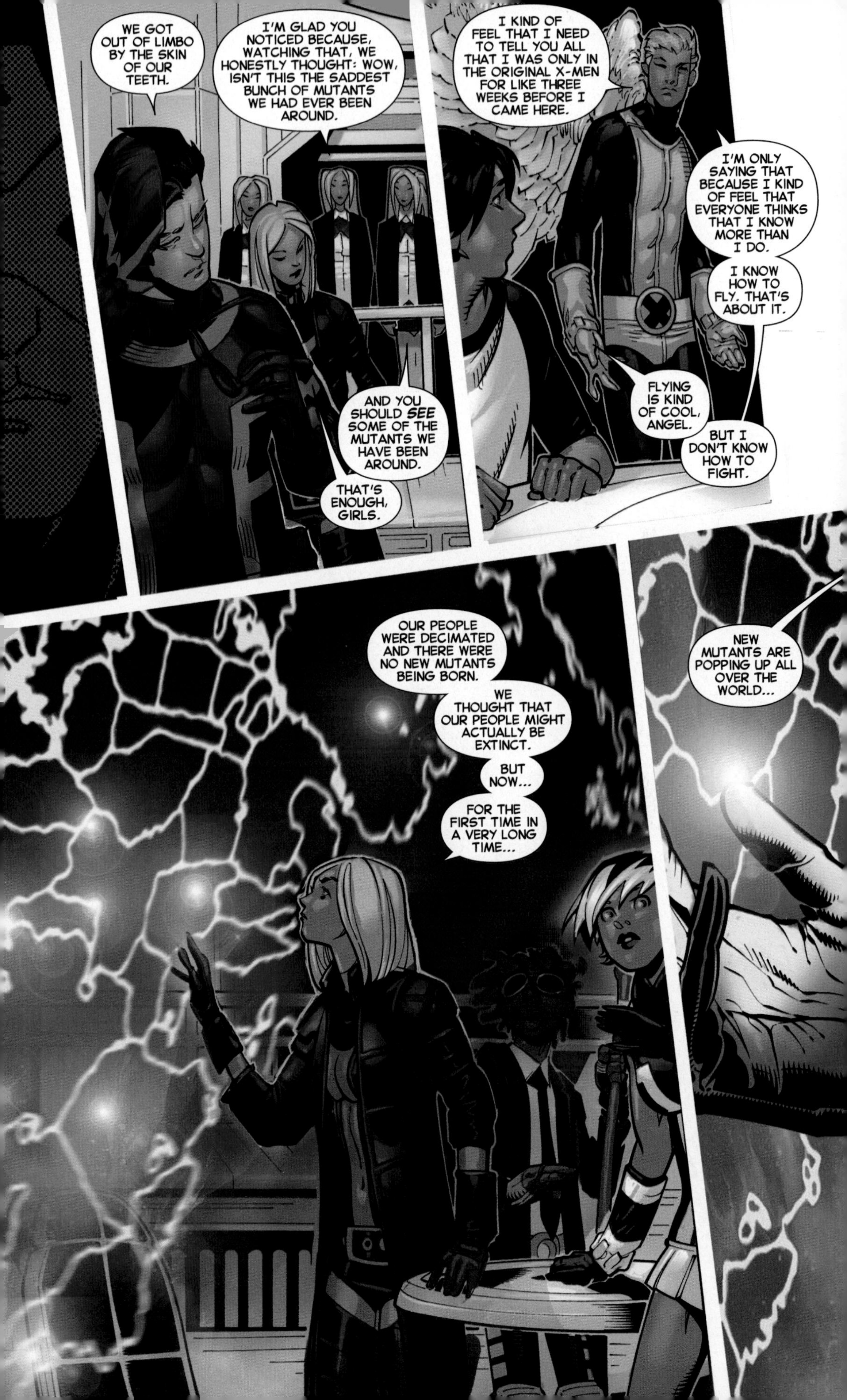
WE GOT OUT OF LIMBO BY THE SKIN OF OUR TEETH.
I'M GLAD YOU NOTICED BECAUSE, WATCHING THAT, WE HONESTLY THOUGHT: WOW, ISN'T THIS THE SADDEST BUNCH OF MUTANTS WE HAD EVER BEEN AROUND.
AND YOU SHOULD SEE SOME OF THE MUTANTS WE HAVE BEEN AROUND.
THAT'S ENOUGH, GIRLS.
I KIND OF FEEL THAT I NEED TO TELL YOU ALL THAT I WAS ONLY IN THE ORIGINAL X-MEN FOR LIKE THREE WEEKS BEFORE I CAME HERE.
I'M ONLY SAYING THAT BECAUSE I KIND OF FEEL THAT EVERYONE THINKS THAT I KNOW MORE THAN I DO.
I KNOW HOW TO FLY. THAT'S ABOUT IT.
FLYING IS KIND OF COOL, ANGEL.
BUT I DON'T KNOW HOW TO FIGHT.
OUR PEOPLE WERE DECIMATED AND THERE WERE NO NEW MUTANTS BEING BORN.
WE THOUGHT THAT OUR PEOPLE MIGHT ACTUALLY BE EXTINCT.
BUT NOW...
FOR THE FIRST TIME IN A VERY LONG TIME...
NEW MUTANTS ARE POPPING UP ALL OVER THE WORLD...

X

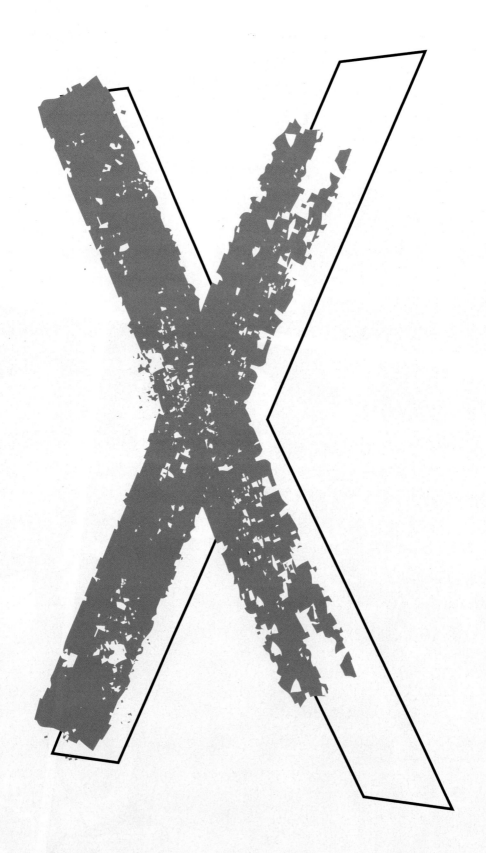

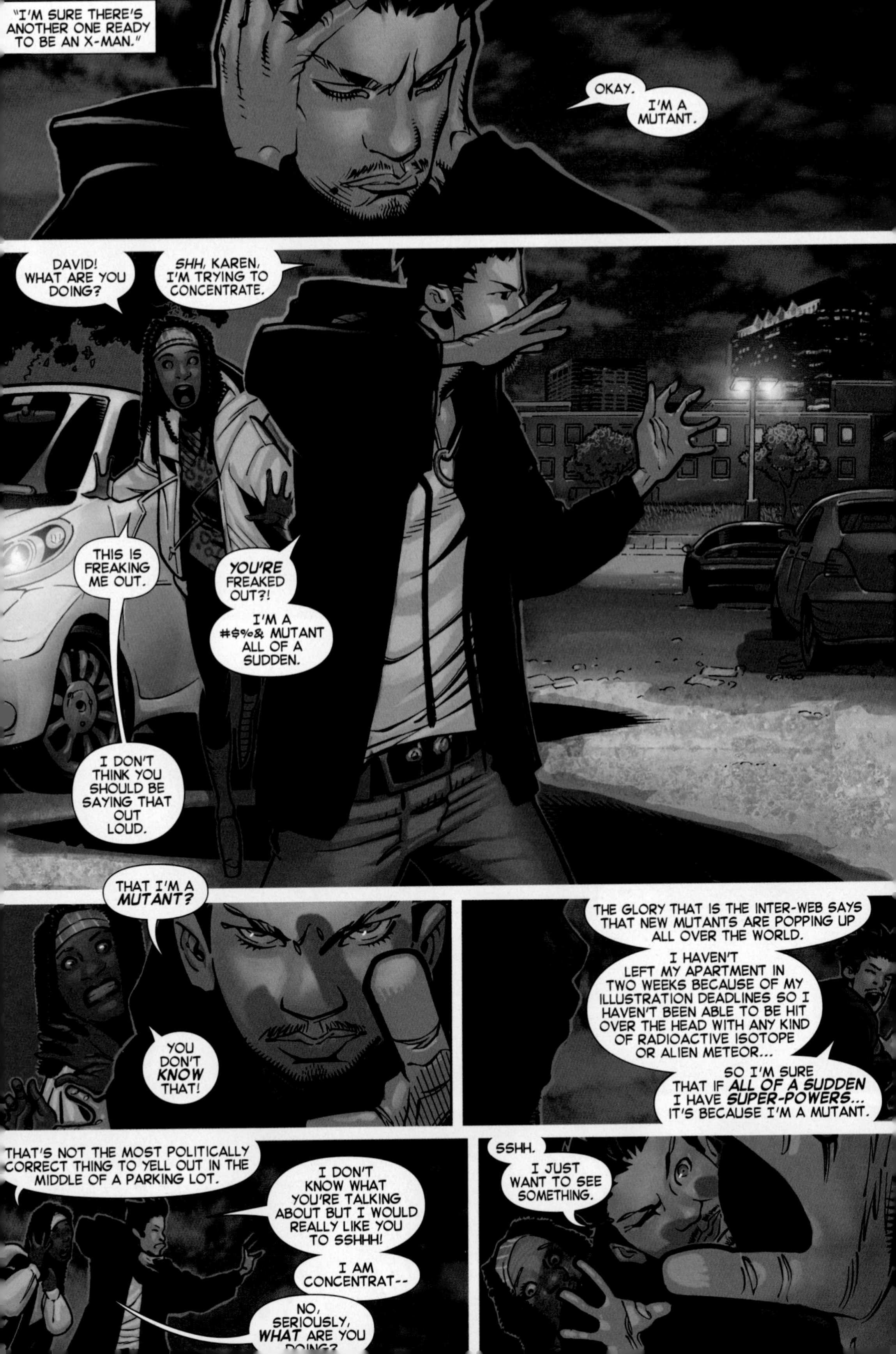
"I'M SURE THERE'S ANOTHER ONE READY TO BE AN X-MAN."
OKAY.
I'M A MUTANT.
DAVID! WHAT ARE YOU DOING?
SHH, KAREN, I'M TRYING TO CONCENTRATE.
THIS IS FREAKING ME OUT.
YOU'RE FREAKED OUT?!
I'M A #$%& MUTANT ALL OF A SUDDEN.
I DON'T THINK YOU SHOULD BE SAYING THAT OUT LOUD.
THAT I'M A MUTANT?
YOU DON'T KNOW THAT!
THE GLORY THAT IS THE INTER-WEB SAYS THAT NEW MUTANTS ARE POPPING UP ALL OVER THE WORLD.
I HAVEN'T LEFT MY APARTMENT IN TWO WEEKS BECAUSE OF MY ILLUSTRATION DEADLINES SO I HAVEN'T BEEN ABLE TO BE HIT OVER THE HEAD WITH ANY KIND OF RADIOACTIVE ISOTOPE OR ALIEN METEOR...
SO I'M SURE THAT IF ALL OF A SUDDEN I HAVE SUPER-POWERS... IT'S BECAUSE I'M A MUTANT.
THAT'S NOT THE MOST POLITICALLY CORRECT THING TO YELL OUT IN THE MIDDLE OF A PARKING LOT.
I DON'T KNOW WHAT YOU'RE TALKING ABOUT BUT I WOULD REALLY LIKE YOU TO SSHHH!
I AM CONCENTRAT--
NO, SERIOUSLY, WHAT ARE YOU
SSHH.
I JUST WANT TO SEE SOMETHING.

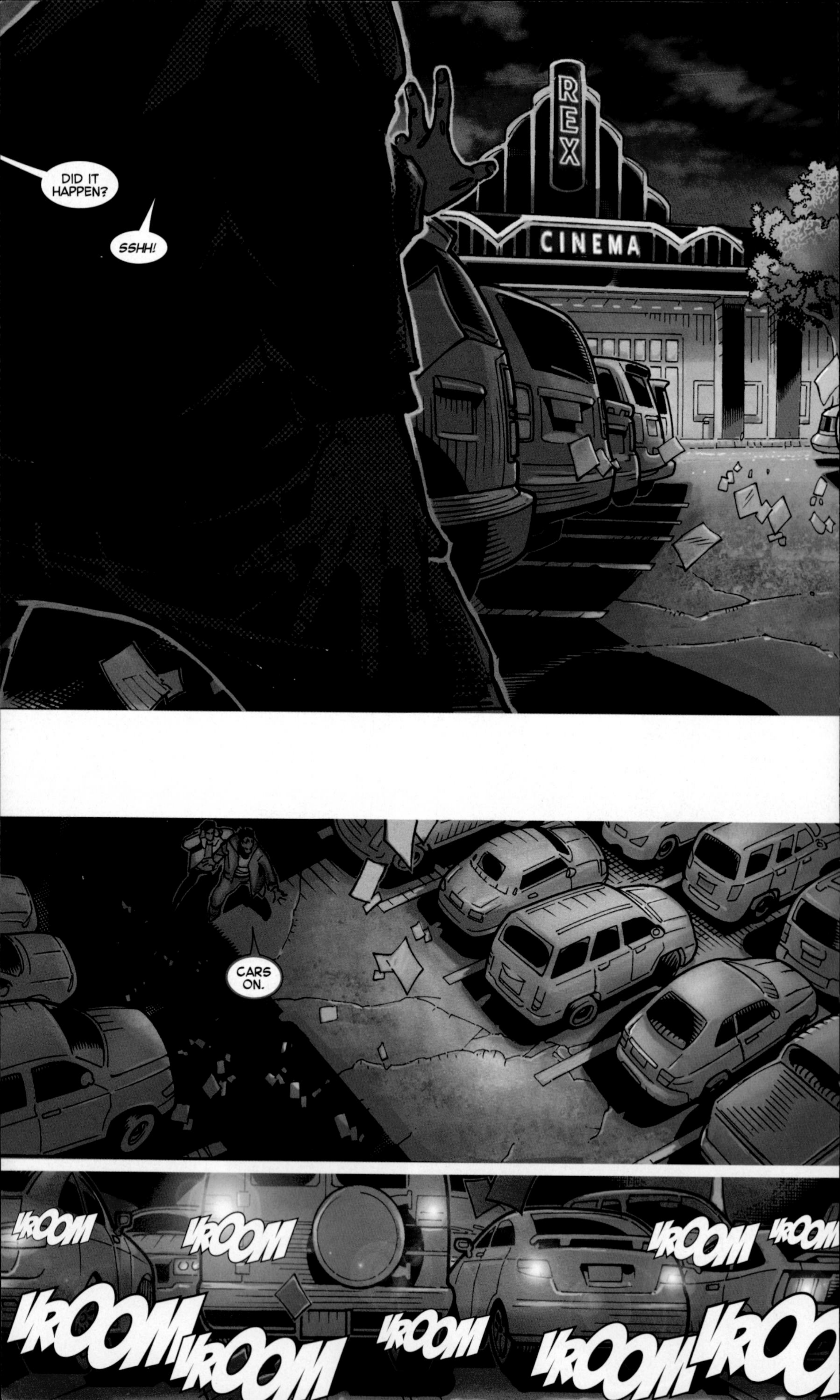
DID IT HAPPEN?
SSHH!
REX
CINEMA
CARS ON.
VROOM
VROOM
VROOM
VROOM
VROOM
VROOM
VROOM
VROOM

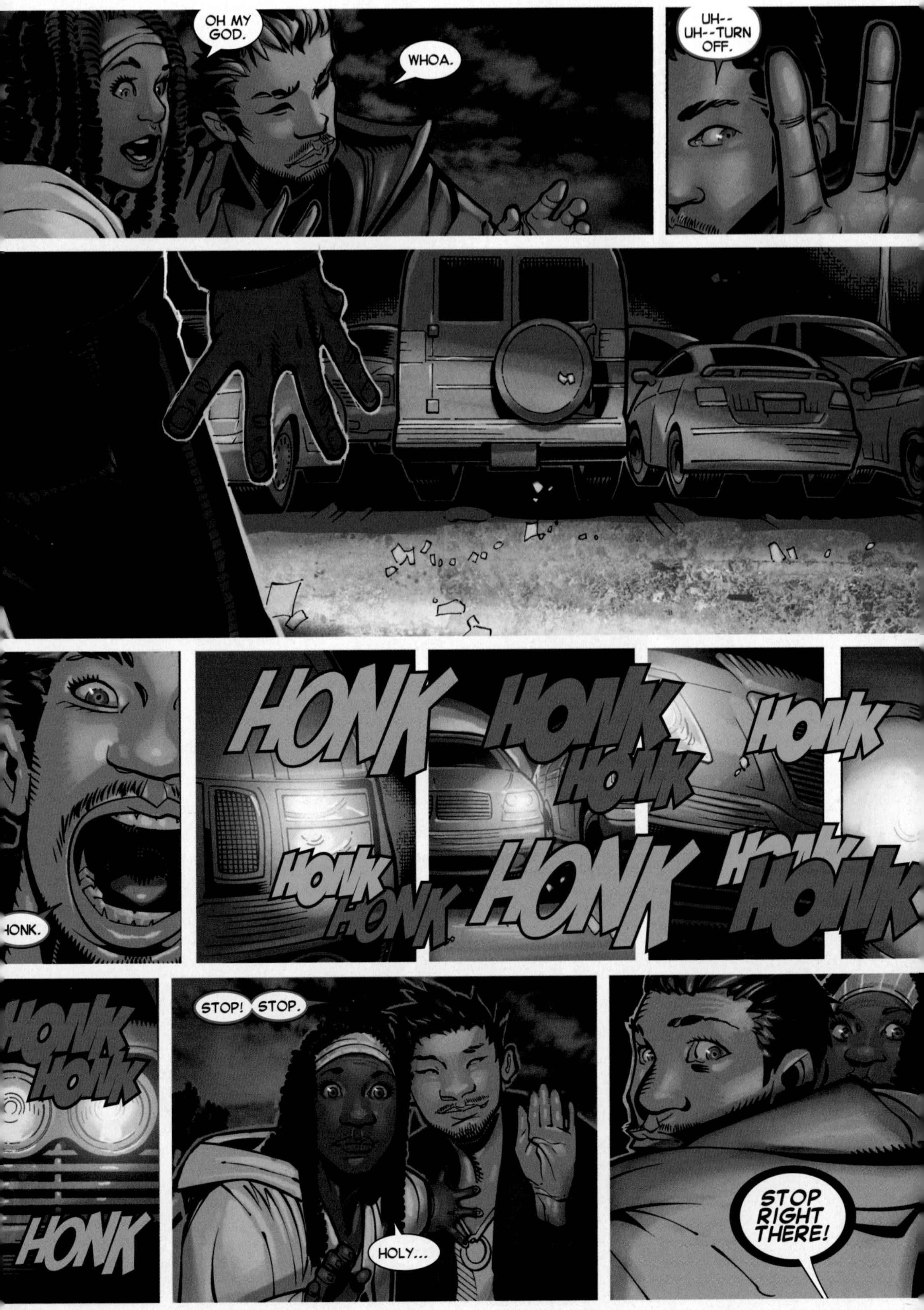
OH MY GOD.
WHOA.
UH-- UH--TURN OFF.
HONK HONK HONK HONK HONK HONK HONK HONK HONK
HONK.
HONK HONK HONK
STOP! STOP.
HOLY...
STOP RIGHT THERE!

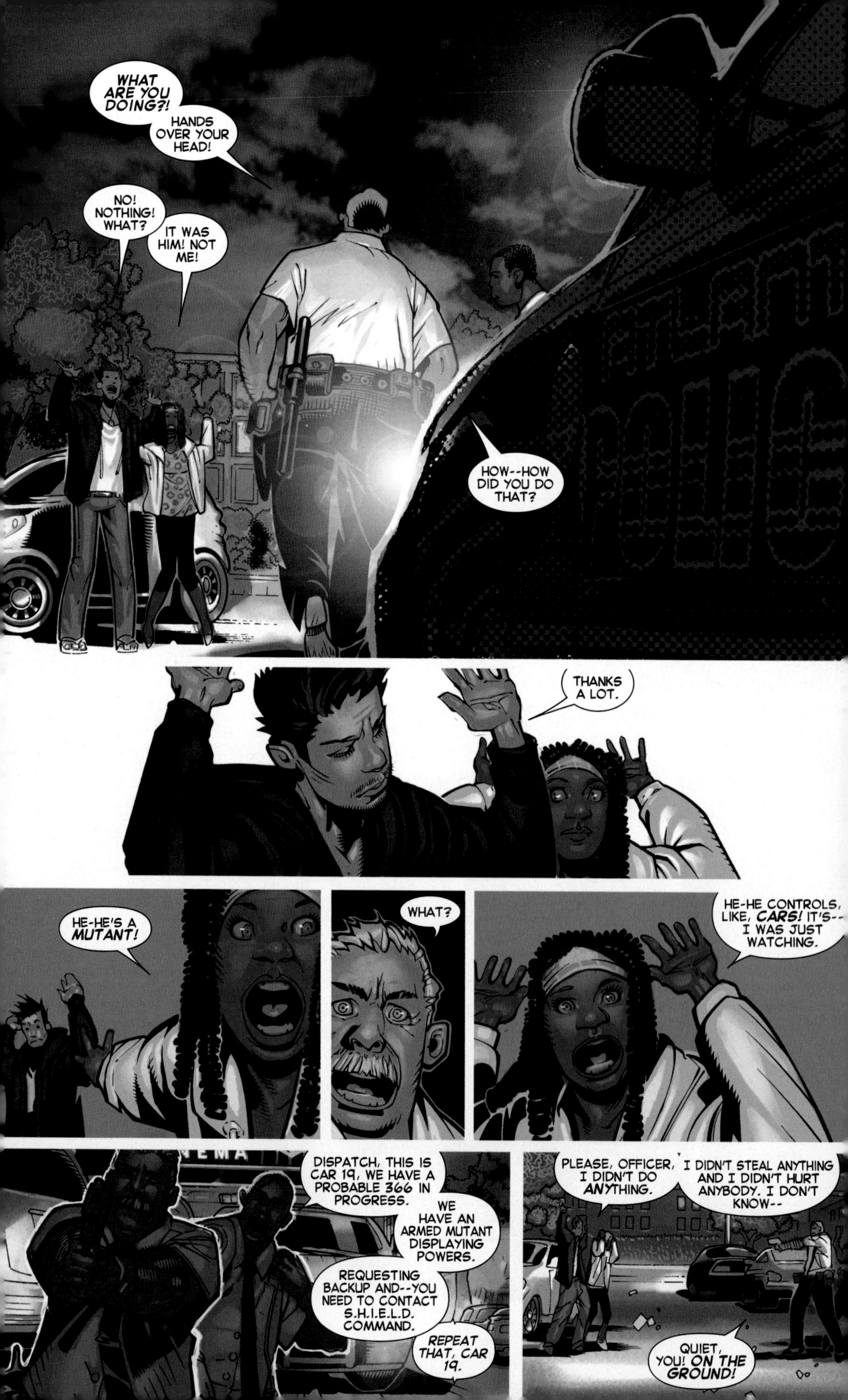

WHAT ARE YOU DOING?!
HANDS OVER YOUR HEAD!
NO! NOTHING! WHAT?
IT WAS HIM! NOT ME!
HOW--HOW DID YOU DO THAT?
THANKS A LOT.
HE-HE'S A MUTANT!
WHAT?
HE-HE CONTROLS, LIKE, CARS! IT'S-- I WAS JUST WATCHING.
DISPATCH, THIS IS CAR 19, WE HAVE A PROBABLE 366 IN PROGRESS.
WE HAVE AN ARMED MUTANT DISPLAYING POWERS.
REQUESTING BACKUP AND--YOU NEED TO CONTACT S.H.I.E.L.D. COMMAND.
REPEAT THAT, CAR 19.
PLEASE, OFFICER, I DIDN'T DO ANYTHING.
I DIDN'T STEAL ANYTHING AND I DIDN'T HURT ANYBODY. I DON'T KNOW--
QUIET, YOU! ON THE GROUND!

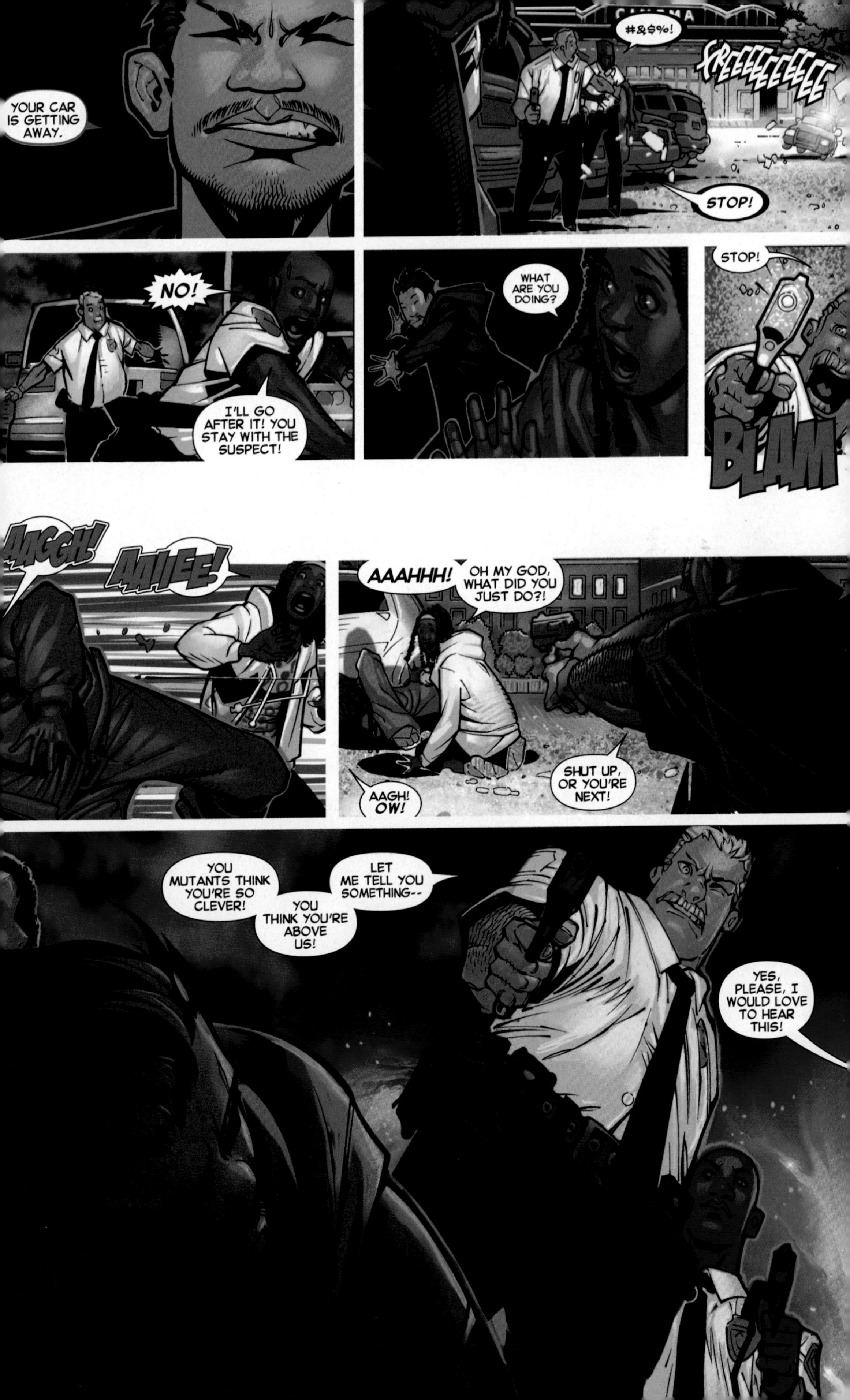
YOUR CAR IS GETTING AWAY.
#&$%!
STOP!
NO!
I'LL GO AFTER IT! YOU STAY WITH THE SUSPECT!
WHAT ARE YOU DOING?
STOP!
BLAM
AAGGH!
AAIIEE!
AAAHHH!
OH MY GOD, WHAT DID YOU JUST DO?!
AAGH! OW!
SHUT UP, OR YOU'RE NEXT!
YOU MUTANTS THINK YOU'RE SO CLEVER!
YOU THINK YOU'RE ABOVE US!
LET ME TELL YOU SOMETHING--
YES, PLEASE, I WOULD LOVE TO HEAR THIS!

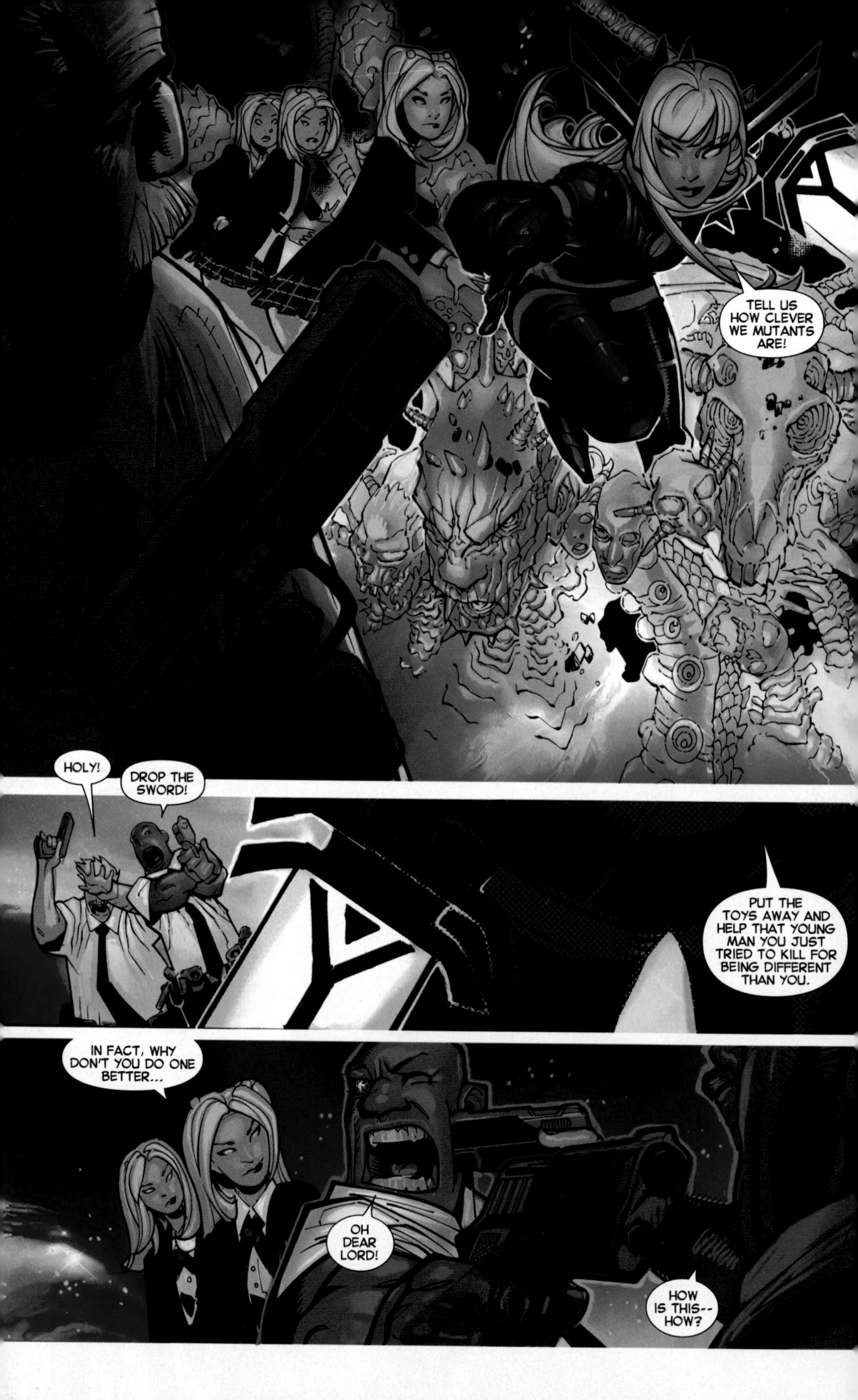
TELL US HOW CLEVER WE MUTANTS ARE!
HOLY!
DROP THE SWORD!
PUT THE TOYS AWAY AND HELP THAT YOUNG MAN YOU JUST TRIED TO KILL FOR BEING DIFFERENT THAN YOU.
IN FACT, WHY DON'T YOU DO ONE BETTER...
OH DEAR LORD!
HOW IS THIS-- HOW?

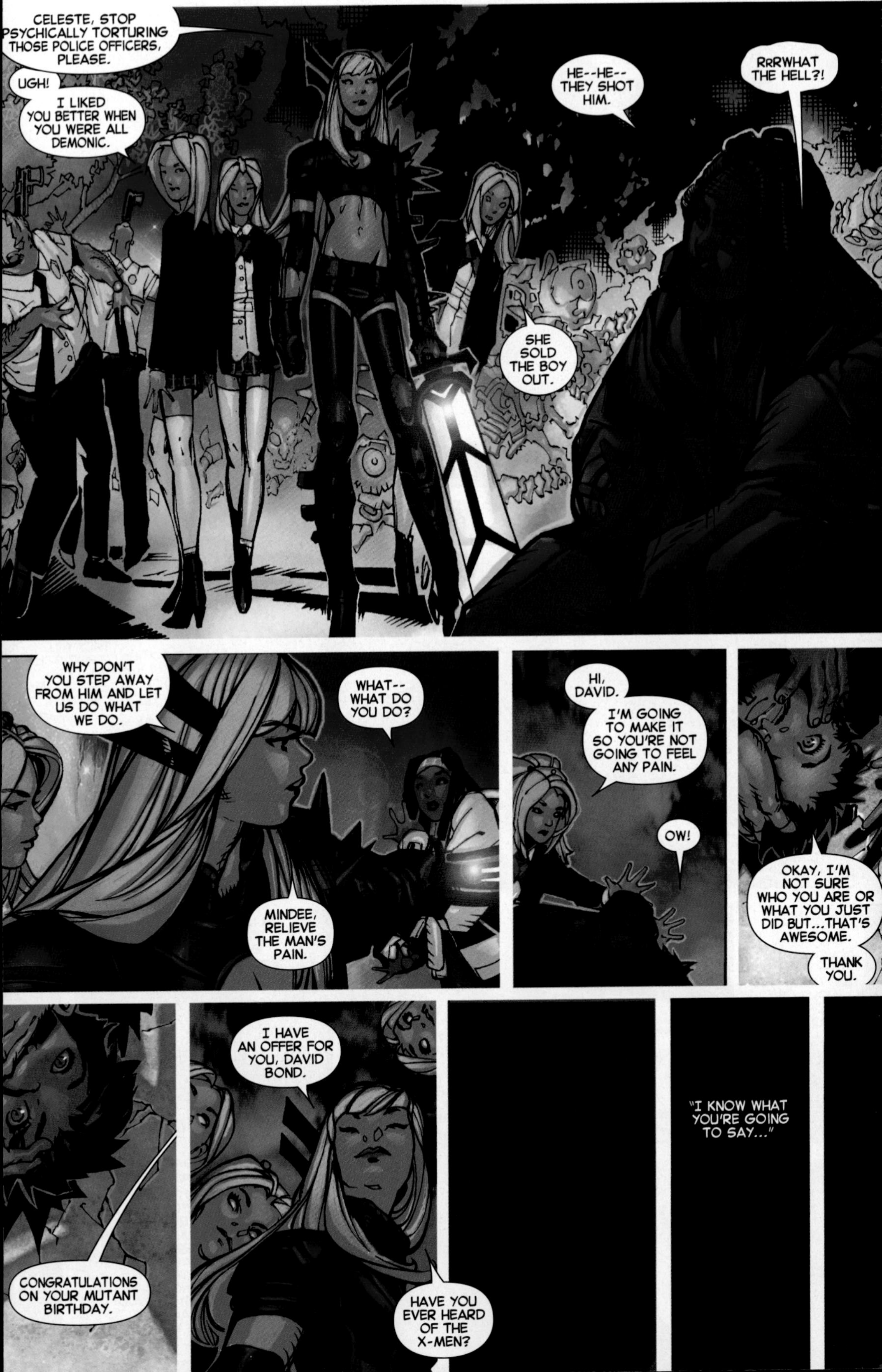
CELESTE, STOP PSYCHICALLY TORTURING THOSE POLICE OFFICERS, PLEASE.
UGH!
I LIKED YOU BETTER WHEN YOU WERE ALL DEMONIC.
HE--HE--THEY SHOT HIM.
RRRWHAT THE HELL?!
SHE SOLD THE BOY OUT.
WHY DON'T YOU STEP AWAY FROM HIM AND LET US DO WHAT WE DO.
WHAT--WHAT DO YOU DO?
MINDEE, RELIEVE THE MAN'S PAIN.
HI, DAVID.
I'M GOING TO MAKE IT SO YOU'RE NOT GOING TO FEEL ANY PAIN.
OW!
OKAY, I'M NOT SURE WHO YOU ARE OR WHAT YOU JUST DID BUT...THAT'S AWESOME.
THANK YOU.
CONGRATULATIONS ON YOUR MUTANT BIRTHDAY.
I HAVE AN OFFER FOR YOU, DAVID BOND.
HAVE YOU EVER HEARD OF THE X-MEN?
"I KNOW WHAT YOU'RE GOING TO SAY..."

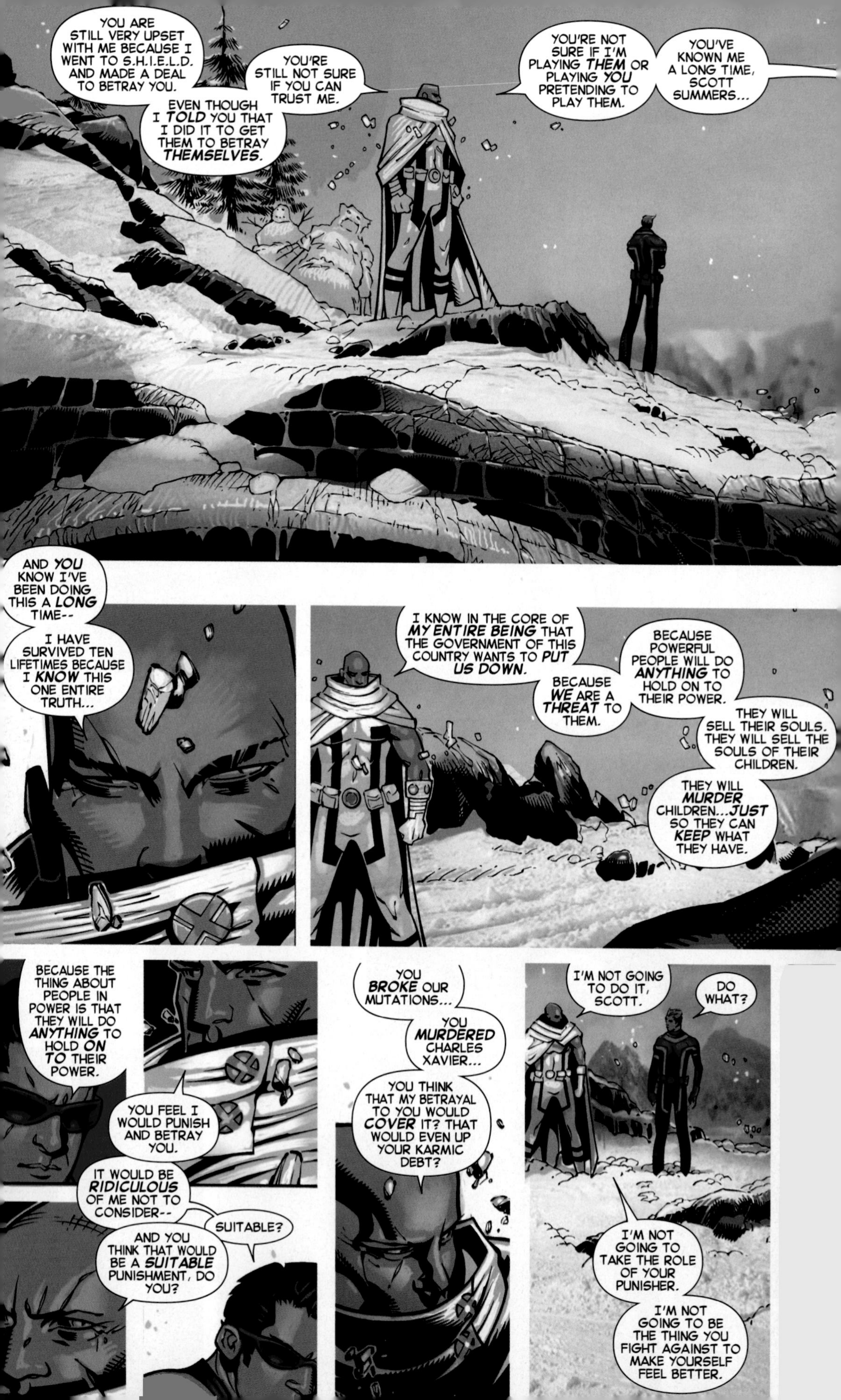

YOU ARE STILL VERY UPSET WITH ME BECAUSE I WENT TO S.H.I.E.L.D. AND MADE A DEAL TO BETRAY YOU.
EVEN THOUGH I *TOLD* YOU THAT I DID IT TO GET THEM TO BETRAY *THEMSELVES.*
YOU'RE STILL NOT SURE IF YOU CAN TRUST ME.
YOU'RE NOT SURE IF I'M PLAYING *THEM* OR PLAYING *YOU* PRETENDING TO PLAY THEM.
YOU'VE KNOWN ME A LONG TIME, SCOTT SUMMERS...
AND *YOU* KNOW I'VE BEEN DOING THIS A *LONG* TIME--
I HAVE SURVIVED TEN LIFETIMES BECAUSE I *KNOW* THIS ONE ENTIRE TRUTH...
I KNOW IN THE CORE OF *MY ENTIRE BEING* THAT THE GOVERNMENT OF THIS COUNTRY WANTS TO *PUT US DOWN.*
BECAUSE *WE* ARE A *THREAT* TO THEM.
BECAUSE POWERFUL PEOPLE WILL DO *ANYTHING* TO HOLD ON TO THEIR POWER.
THEY WILL SELL THEIR SOULS. THEY WILL SELL THE SOULS OF THEIR CHILDREN.
THEY WILL *MURDER* CHILDREN...*JUST* SO THEY CAN *KEEP* WHAT THEY HAVE.
BECAUSE THE THING ABOUT PEOPLE IN POWER IS THAT THEY WILL DO *ANYTHING* TO HOLD *ON TO* THEIR POWER.
YOU FEEL I WOULD PUNISH AND BETRAY YOU.
IT WOULD BE *RIDICULOUS* OF ME NOT TO CONSIDER--
SUITABLE?
AND YOU THINK THAT WOULD BE A *SUITABLE* PUNISHMENT, DO YOU?
YOU *BROKE* OUR MUTATIONS...
YOU *MURDERED* CHARLES XAVIER...
YOU THINK THAT MY BETRAYAL TO YOU WOULD *COVER* IT? THAT WOULD EVEN UP YOUR KARMIC DEBT?
I'M NOT GOING TO DO IT, SCOTT.
DO WHAT?
I'M NOT GOING TO TAKE THE ROLE OF YOUR PUNISHER.
I'M NOT GOING TO BE THE THING YOU FIGHT AGAINST TO MAKE YOURSELF FEEL BETTER.

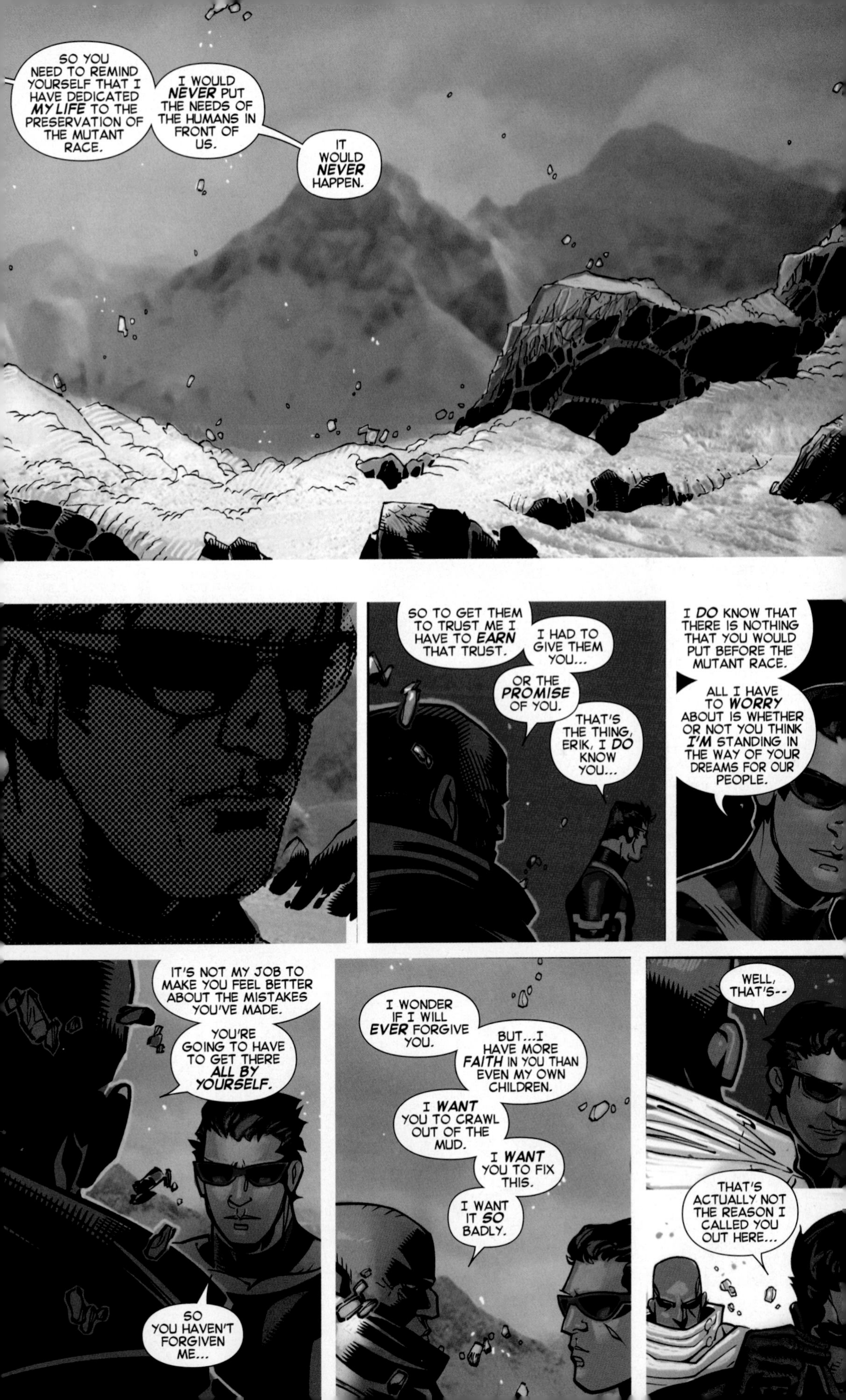
SO YOU NEED TO REMIND YOURSELF THAT I HAVE DEDICATED MY LIFE TO THE PRESERVATION OF THE MUTANT RACE.
I WOULD NEVER PUT THE NEEDS OF THE HUMANS IN FRONT OF US.
IT WOULD NEVER HAPPEN.
SO TO GET THEM TO TRUST ME I HAVE TO EARN THAT TRUST.
I HAD TO GIVE THEM YOU...
OR THE PROMISE OF YOU.
THAT'S THE THING, ERIK, I DO KNOW YOU...
I DO KNOW THAT THERE IS NOTHING THAT YOU WOULD PUT BEFORE THE MUTANT RACE.
ALL I HAVE TO WORRY ABOUT IS WHETHER OR NOT YOU THINK I'M STANDING IN THE WAY OF YOUR DREAMS FOR OUR PEOPLE.
IT'S NOT MY JOB TO MAKE YOU FEEL BETTER ABOUT THE MISTAKES YOU'VE MADE.
YOU'RE GOING TO HAVE TO GET THERE ALL BY YOURSELF.
SO YOU HAVEN'T FORGIVEN ME...
I WONDER IF I WILL EVER FORGIVE YOU.
BUT...I HAVE MORE FAITH IN YOU THAN EVEN MY OWN CHILDREN.
I WANT YOU TO CRAWL OUT OF THE MUD.
I WANT YOU TO FIX THIS.
I WANT IT SO BADLY.
WELL, THAT'S--
THAT'S ACTUALLY NOT THE REASON I CALLED YOU OUT HERE...

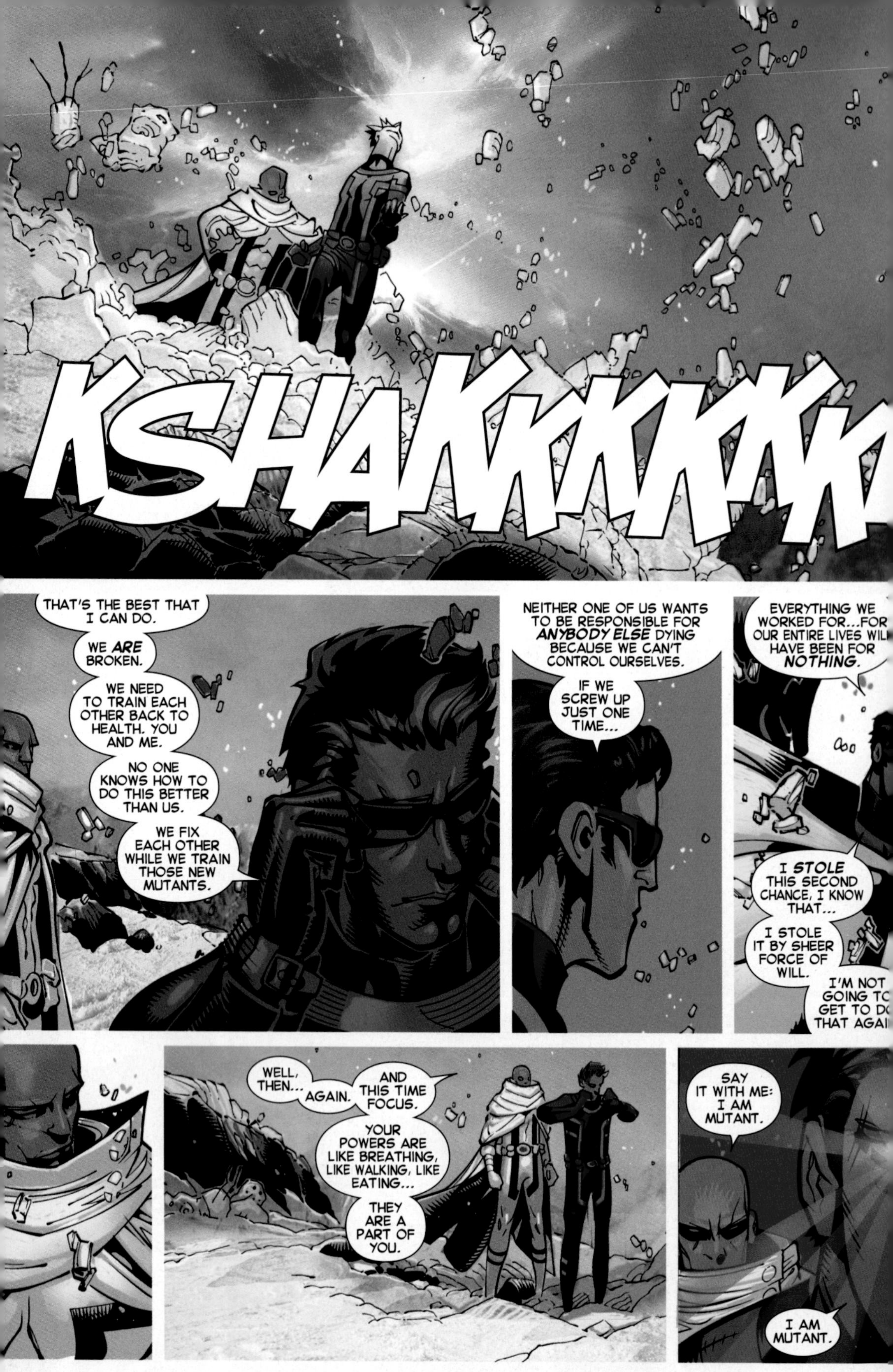
KSHAKKKKKK
THAT'S THE BEST THAT I CAN DO.
WE *ARE* BROKEN.
WE NEED TO TRAIN EACH OTHER BACK TO HEALTH. YOU AND ME.
NO ONE KNOWS HOW TO DO THIS BETTER THAN US.
WE FIX EACH OTHER WHILE WE TRAIN THOSE NEW MUTANTS.
NEITHER ONE OF US WANTS TO BE RESPONSIBLE FOR *ANYBODY ELSE* DYING BECAUSE WE CAN'T CONTROL OURSELVES.
IF WE SCREW UP JUST ONE TIME...
EVERYTHING WE WORKED FOR...FOR OUR ENTIRE LIVES WIL HAVE BEEN FOR *NOTHING.*
I *STOLE* THIS SECOND CHANCE, I KNOW THAT...
I STOLE IT BY SHEER FORCE OF WILL.
I'M NOT GOING TO GET TO DO THAT AGAI
WELL, THEN...
AGAIN.
AND THIS TIME FOCUS.
YOUR POWERS ARE LIKE BREATHING, LIKE WALKING, LIKE EATING...
THEY ARE A PART OF YOU.
SAY IT WITH ME: I AM MUTANT.
I AM MUTANT.

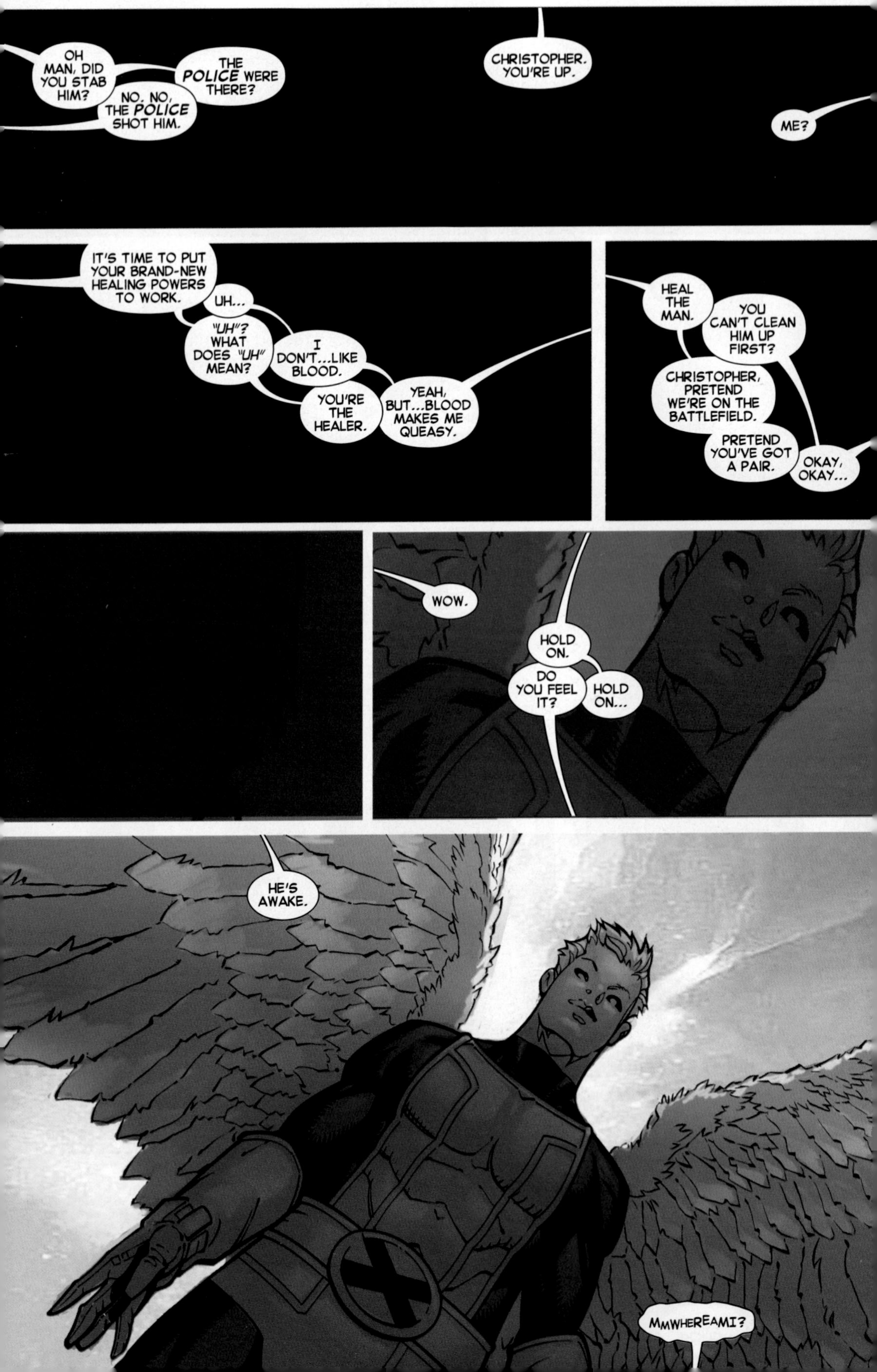
OH MAN, DID YOU STAB HIM?
THE POLICE WERE THERE?
NO. NO, THE POLICE SHOT HIM.
CHRISTOPHER. YOU'RE UP.
ME?
IT'S TIME TO PUT YOUR BRAND-NEW HEALING POWERS TO WORK.
UH...
"UH"? WHAT DOES "UH" MEAN?
I DON'T...LIKE BLOOD.
YOU'RE THE HEALER.
YEAH, BUT...BLOOD MAKES ME QUEASY.
HEAL THE MAN.
YOU CAN'T CLEAN HIM UP FIRST?
CHRISTOPHER, PRETEND WE'RE ON THE BATTLEFIELD.
PRETEND YOU'VE GOT A PAIR.
OKAY, OKAY...
WOW.
HOLD ON.
DO YOU FEEL IT?
HOLD ON...
HE'S AWAKE.
MMWHEREAMI?

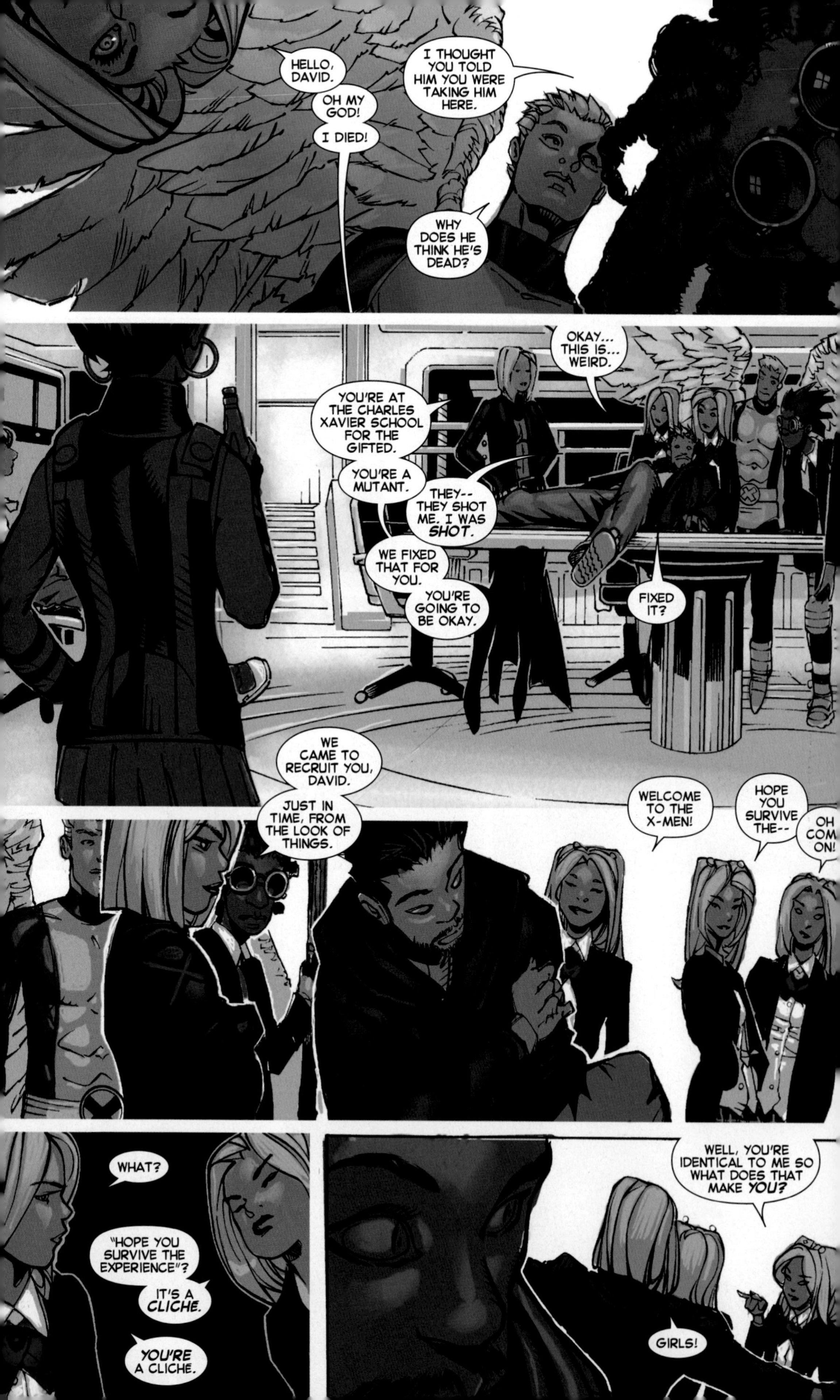
HELLO, DAVID.
OH MY GOD!
I DIED!
I THOUGHT YOU TOLD HIM YOU WERE TAKING HIM HERE.
WHY DOES HE THINK HE'S DEAD?
OKAY... THIS IS... WEIRD.
YOU'RE AT THE CHARLES XAVIER SCHOOL FOR THE GIFTED.
YOU'RE A MUTANT.
THEY-- THEY SHOT ME. I WAS SHOT.
WE FIXED THAT FOR YOU.
YOU'RE GOING TO BE OKAY.
FIXED IT?
WE CAME TO RECRUIT YOU, DAVID.
JUST IN TIME, FROM THE LOOK OF THINGS.
WELCOME TO THE X-MEN!
HOPE YOU SURVIVE THE--
OH COM ON!
WHAT?
"HOPE YOU SURVIVE THE EXPERIENCE"?
IT'S A CLICHE.
YOU'RE A CLICHE.
WELL, YOU'RE IDENTICAL TO ME SO WHAT DOES THAT MAKE YOU?
GIRLS!

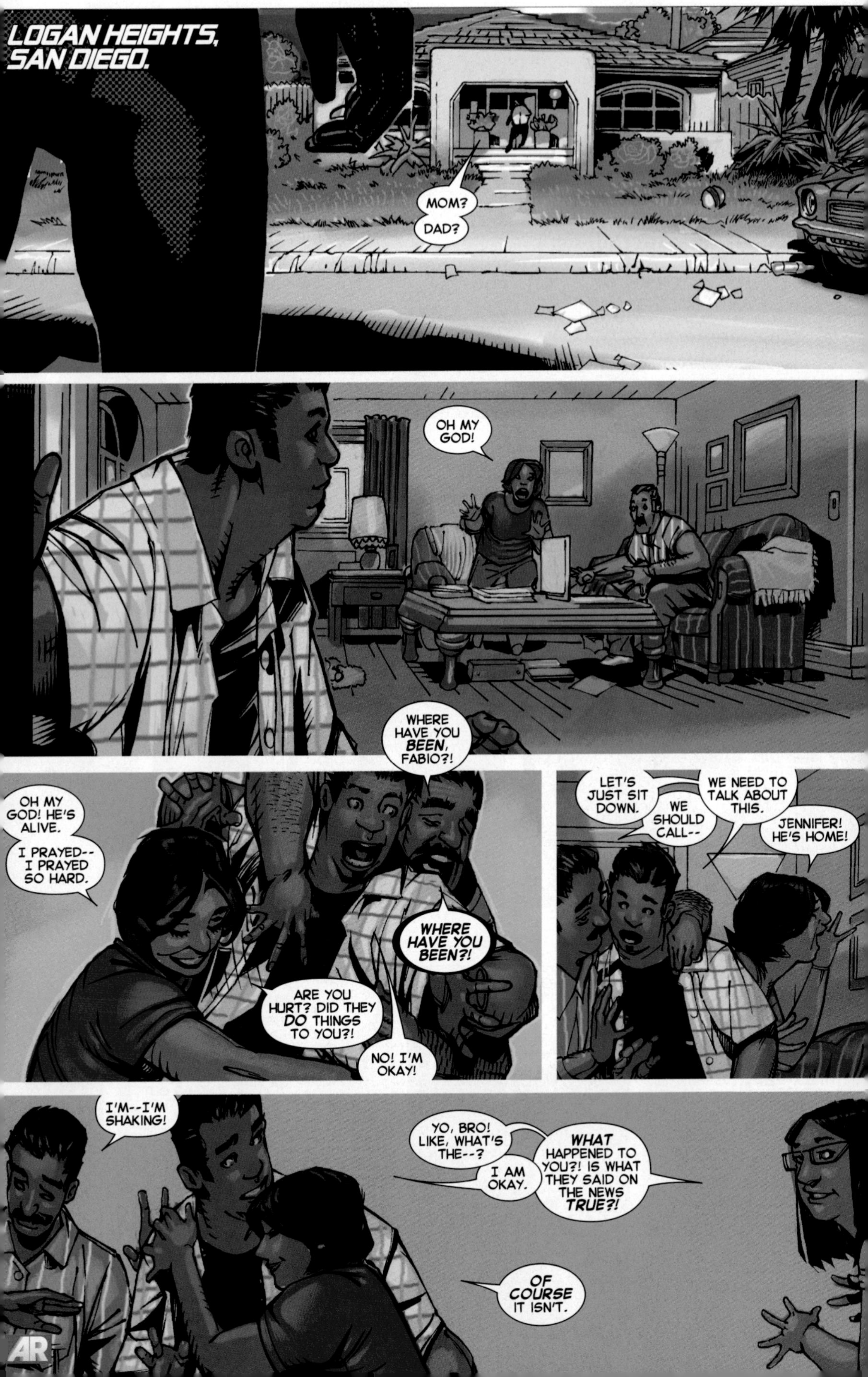
LOGAN HEIGHTS, SAN DIEGO.
MOM?
DAD?
OH MY GOD!
WHERE HAVE YOU BEEN, FABIO?!
OH MY GOD! HE'S ALIVE.
I PRAYED-- I PRAYED SO HARD.
WHERE HAVE YOU BEEN?!
ARE YOU HURT? DID THEY DO THINGS TO YOU?!
NO! I'M OKAY!
LET'S JUST SIT DOWN.
WE SHOULD CALL--
WE NEED TO TALK ABOUT THIS.
JENNIFER! HE'S HOME!
I'M--I'M SHAKING!
YO, BRO! LIKE, WHAT'S THE--?
I AM OKAY.
WHAT HAPPENED TO YOU?! IS WHAT THEY SAID ON THE NEWS TRUE?!
OF COURSE IT ISN'T.

ACTUALLY, I DON'T KNOW WHAT THEY SAID ON THE NEWS... BUT HERE'S THE DEAL.

I AM JUST GOING TO SAY IT... I AM A MUTANT.

NO.

THEY-- THEY JUST *TOLD* YOU THAT SO THEY COULD--

MOM.

I AM.

I WAS ATTACKED AND THE X-MEN *SAVED* ME.

THE X-MEN?

SCOTT SUMMERS. CYCLOPS.

YOU *MET* HIM?

THAT'S WHERE I'VE BEEN.

WE'RE GOING TO THE HOSPITAL.

DAD!

THEY *DID* SOMETHING TO YOU.

DAD.

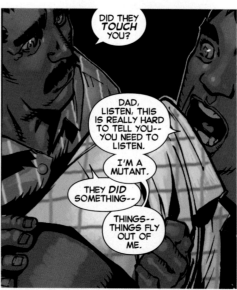

DID THEY *TOUCH* YOU?

DAD, LISTEN, THIS IS REALLY HARD TO TELL YOU-- YOU NEED TO LISTEN.

I'M A MUTANT.

THEY *DID* SOMETHING--

THINGS-- THINGS FLY OUT OF ME.

WHAT THEY SAID-- THE POLICE-- WHAT THEY SAID *WAS TRUE?*

HOLD ON...LIKE WHAT? SHOW US.

I DON'T WANT TO DO IT RIGHT NOW BECAUSE I DON'T WANT TO HURT YOU.

HURT US?

LISTEN, THE X-MEN *HELPED* ME!

THE POLICE CAME HERE. THEY SAID YOU WERE A FUGITIVE.

I *TOLD YOU* HE WAS A GOOD BOY.

I'M NOT.

WHY DIDN'T YOU *CALL* US?

THEY DIDN'T HAVE A PHONE.

THE X-MEN DON'T HAVE A *PHONE?*

THEY DON'T WANT ANYONE FINDING OUT WHERE THEY ARE.

BECAUSE THEY'RE *TERRORISTS,* DOG.

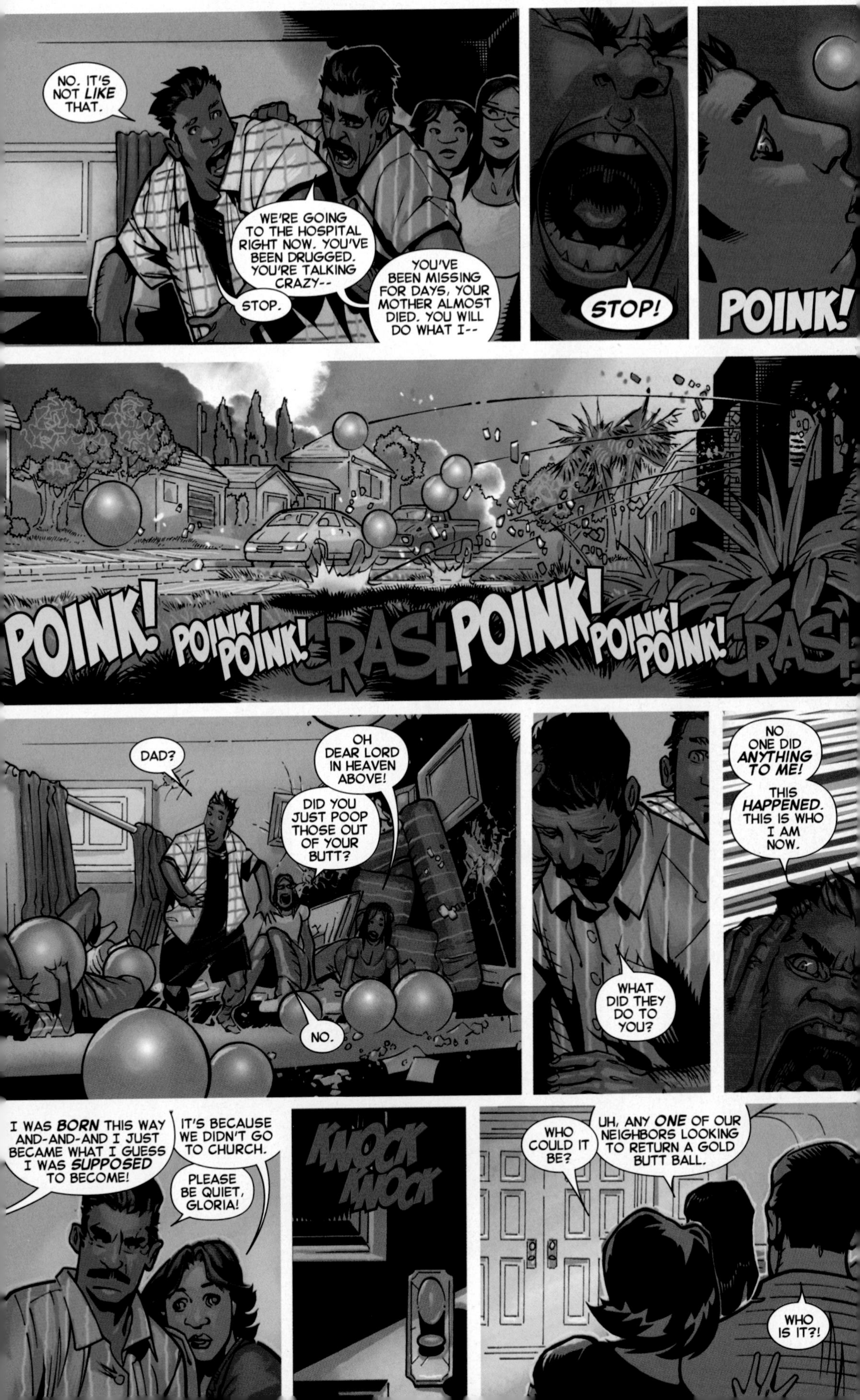
NO. IT'S NOT *LIKE* THAT.
WE'RE GOING TO THE HOSPITAL RIGHT NOW. YOU'VE BEEN DRUGGED. YOU'RE TALKING CRAZY--
YOU'VE BEEN MISSING FOR DAYS, YOUR MOTHER ALMOST DIED. YOU WILL DO WHAT I--
STOP.
STOP!
POINK!
POINK!
POINK!
POINK!
CRASH
POINK!
POINK!
POINK!
CRASH
DAD?
OH DEAR LORD IN HEAVEN ABOVE!
DID YOU JUST POOP THOSE OUT OF YOUR BUTT?
NO.
WHAT DID THEY DO TO YOU?
NO ONE DID *ANYTHING TO ME!*
THIS *HAPPENED.* THIS IS WHO I AM NOW.
I WAS *BORN* THIS WAY AND-AND-AND I JUST BECAME WHAT I GUESS I WAS *SUPPOSED* TO BECOME!
IT'S BECAUSE WE DIDN'T GO TO CHURCH.
PLEASE BE QUIET, GLORIA!
KNOCK KNOCK
WHO COULD IT BE?
UH, ANY *ONE* OF OUR NEIGHBORS LOOKING TO RETURN A GOLD BUTT BALL.
WHO IS IT?!

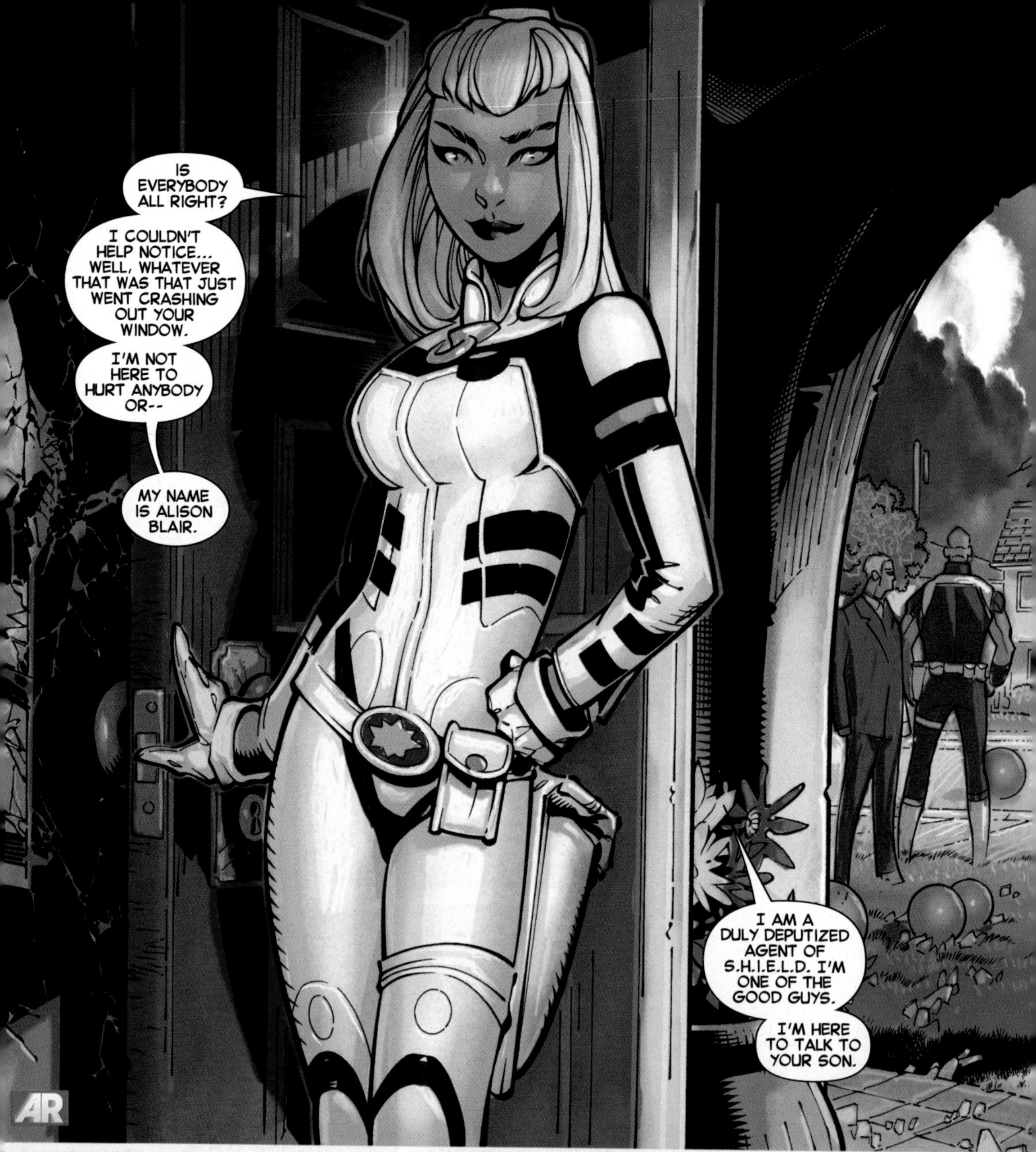
IS EVERYBODY ALL RIGHT?
I COULDN'T HELP NOTICE... WELL, WHATEVER THAT WAS THAT JUST WENT CRASHING OUT YOUR WINDOW.
I'M NOT HERE TO HURT ANYBODY OR--
MY NAME IS ALISON BLAIR.
I AM A DULY DEPUTIZED AGENT OF S.H.I.E.L.D. I'M ONE OF THE GOOD GUYS.
I'M HERE TO TALK TO YOUR SON.

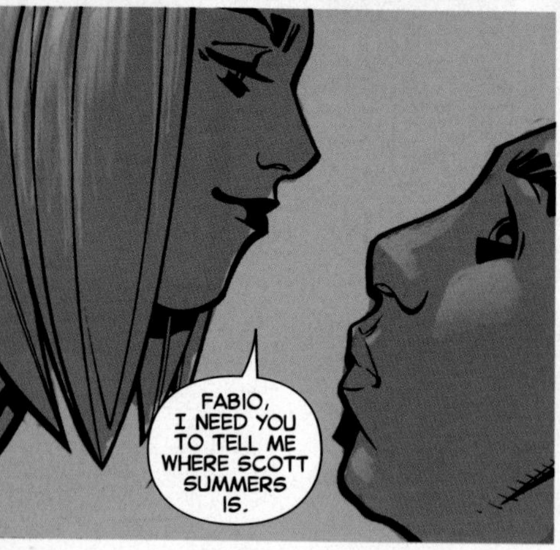
FABIO, I NEED YOU TO TELL ME WHERE SCOTT SUMMERS IS.

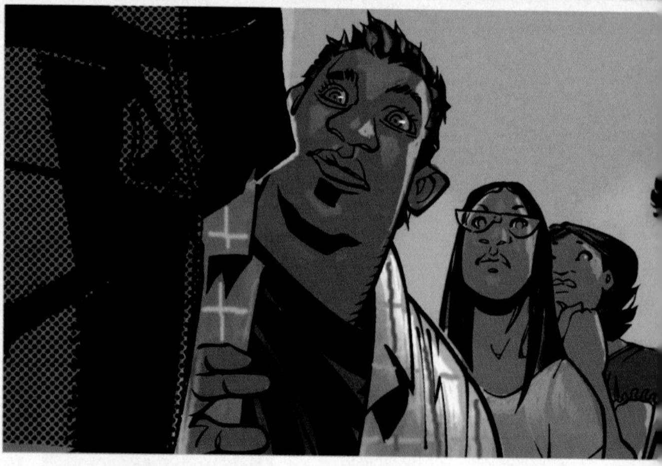

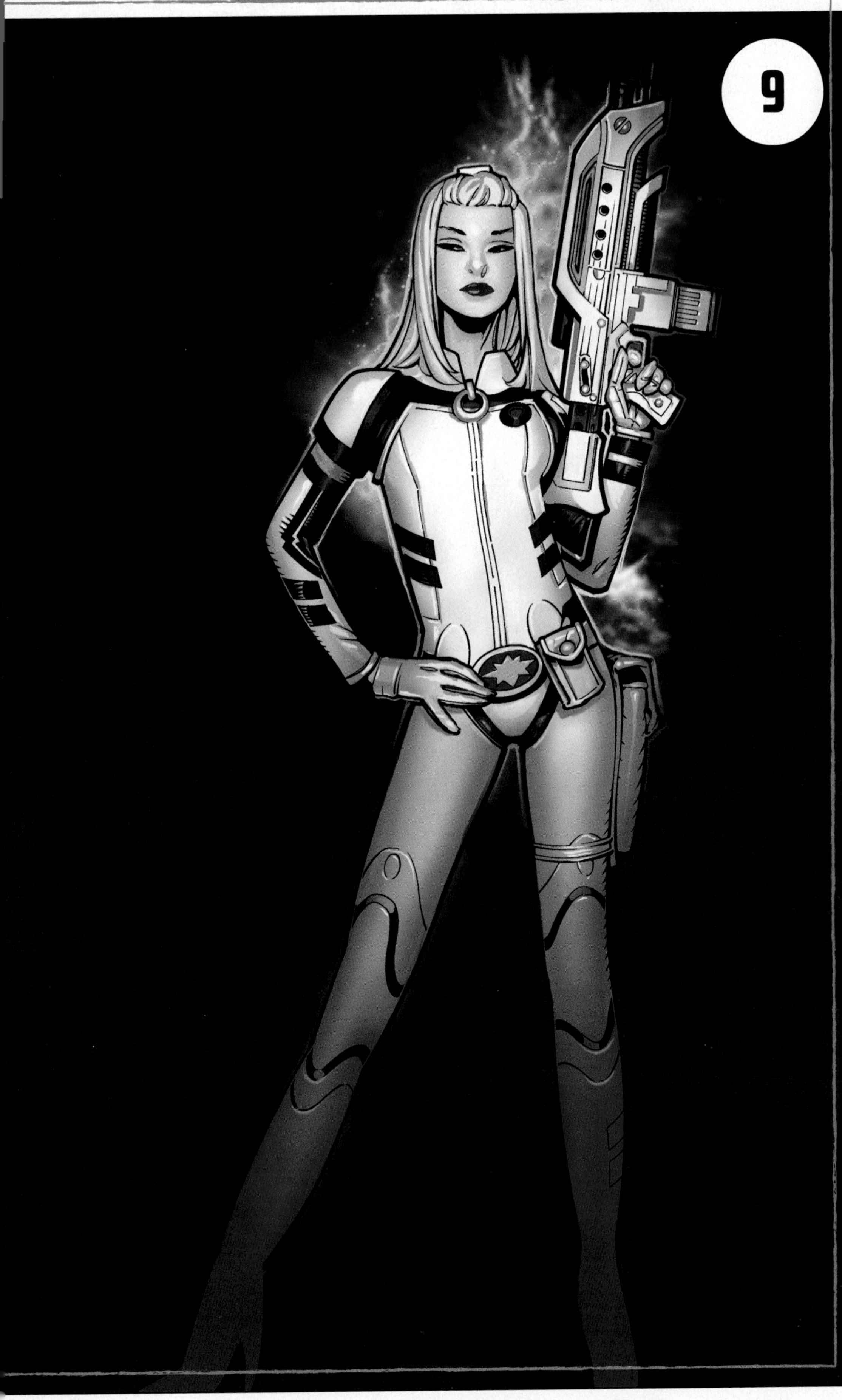
9

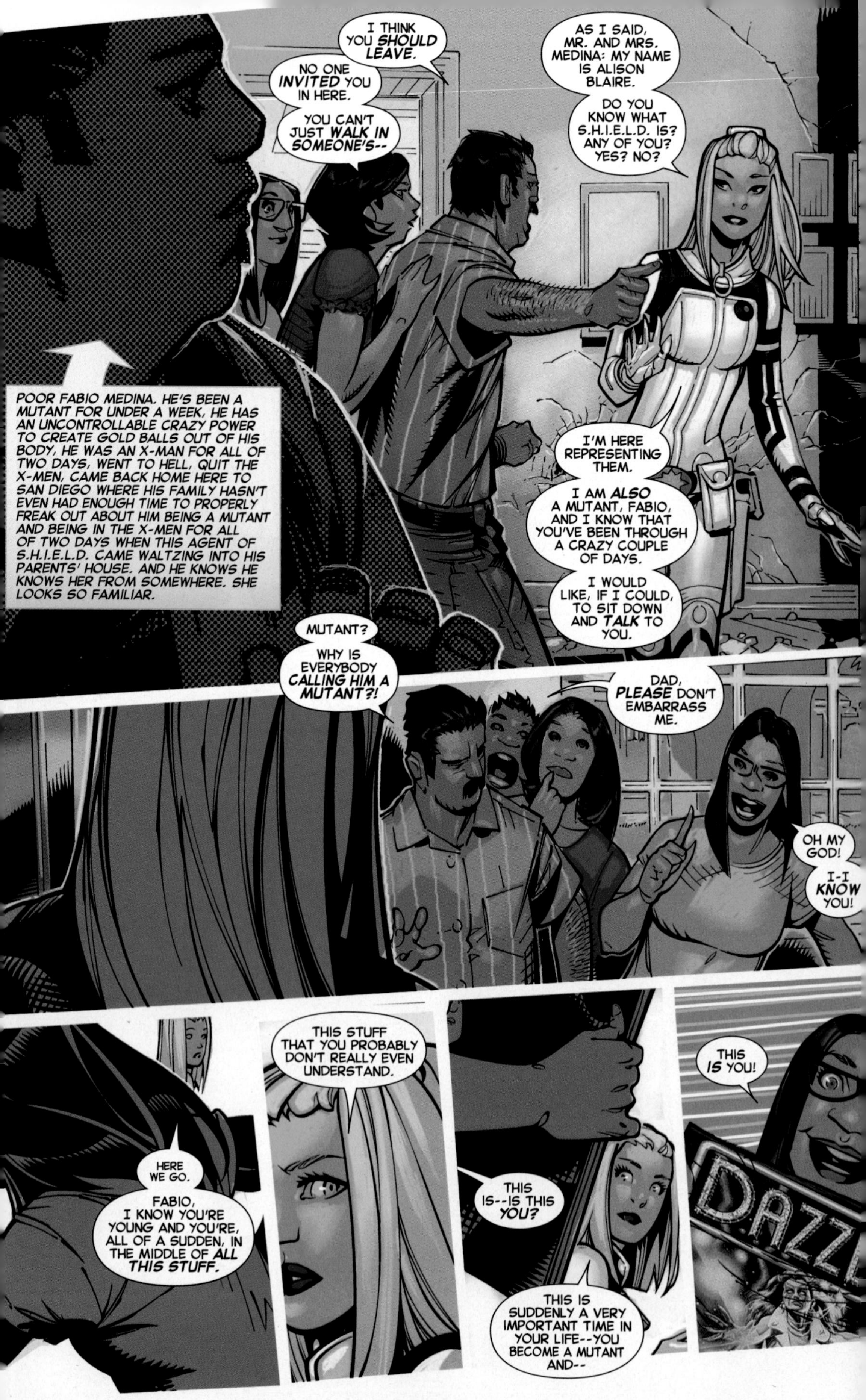
NO ONE INVITED YOU IN HERE.
I THINK YOU SHOULD LEAVE.
YOU CAN'T JUST WALK IN SOMEONE'S--
AS I SAID, MR. AND MRS. MEDINA: MY NAME IS ALISON BLAIRE.
DO YOU KNOW WHAT S.H.I.E.L.D. IS? ANY OF YOU? YES? NO?
POOR FABIO MEDINA. HE'S BEEN A MUTANT FOR UNDER A WEEK, HE HAS AN UNCONTROLLABLE CRAZY POWER TO CREATE GOLD BALLS OUT OF HIS BODY, HE WAS AN X-MAN FOR ALL OF TWO DAYS, WENT TO HELL, QUIT THE X-MEN, CAME BACK HOME HERE TO SAN DIEGO WHERE HIS FAMILY HASN'T EVEN HAD ENOUGH TIME TO PROPERLY FREAK OUT ABOUT HIM BEING A MUTANT AND BEING IN THE X-MEN FOR ALL OF TWO DAYS WHEN THIS AGENT OF S.H.I.E.L.D. CAME WALTZING INTO HIS PARENTS' HOUSE. AND HE KNOWS HE KNOWS HER FROM SOMEWHERE. SHE LOOKS SO FAMILIAR.
I'M HERE REPRESENTING THEM.
I AM ALSO A MUTANT, FABIO, AND I KNOW THAT YOU'VE BEEN THROUGH A CRAZY COUPLE OF DAYS.
I WOULD LIKE, IF I COULD, TO SIT DOWN AND TALK TO YOU.
MUTANT?
WHY IS EVERYBODY CALLING HIM A MUTANT?!
DAD, PLEASE DON'T EMBARRASS ME.
OH MY GOD!
I-I KNOW YOU!
HERE WE GO.
FABIO, I KNOW YOU'RE YOUNG AND YOU'RE, ALL OF A SUDDEN, IN THE MIDDLE OF ALL THIS STUFF.
THIS STUFF THAT YOU PROBABLY DON'T REALLY EVEN UNDERSTAND.
THIS IS--IS THIS YOU?
THIS IS SUDDENLY A VERY IMPORTANT TIME IN YOUR LIFE--YOU BECOME A MUTANT AND--
THIS IS YOU!
DAZZL

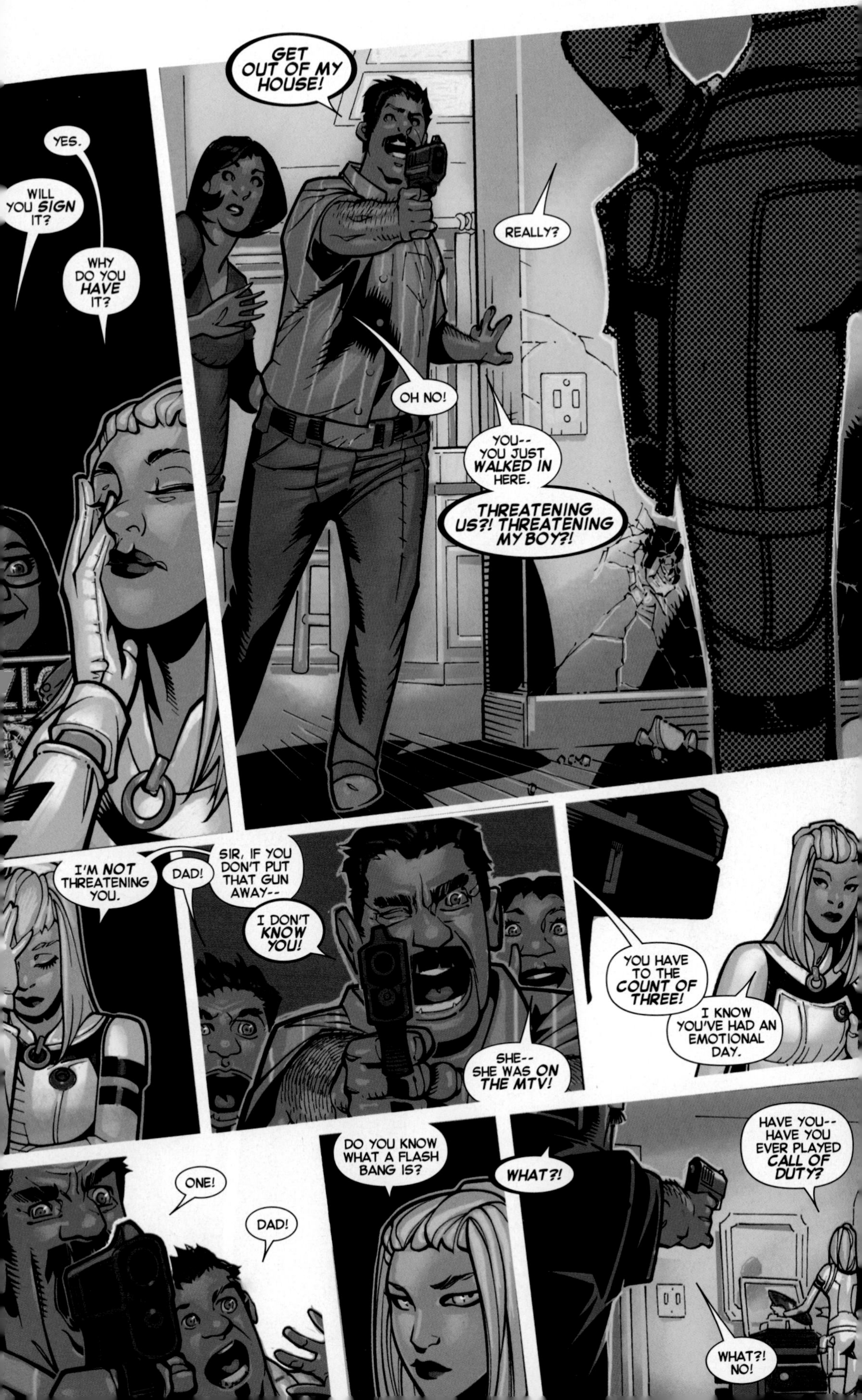

YES.
WILL YOU SIGN IT?
WHY DO YOU HAVE IT?
GET OUT OF MY HOUSE!
OH NO!
REALLY?
YOU-- YOU JUST WALKED IN HERE.
THREATENING US?! THREATENING MY BOY?!
I'M NOT THREATENING YOU.
DAD!
SIR, IF YOU DON'T PUT THAT GUN AWAY--
I DON'T KNOW YOU!
SHE-- SHE WAS ON THE MTV!
YOU HAVE TO THE COUNT OF THREE!
I KNOW YOU'VE HAD AN EMOTIONAL DAY.
ONE!
DAD!
DO YOU KNOW WHAT A FLASH BANG IS?
WHAT?!
HAVE YOU-- HAVE YOU EVER PLAYED CALL OF DUTY?
WHAT?! NO!

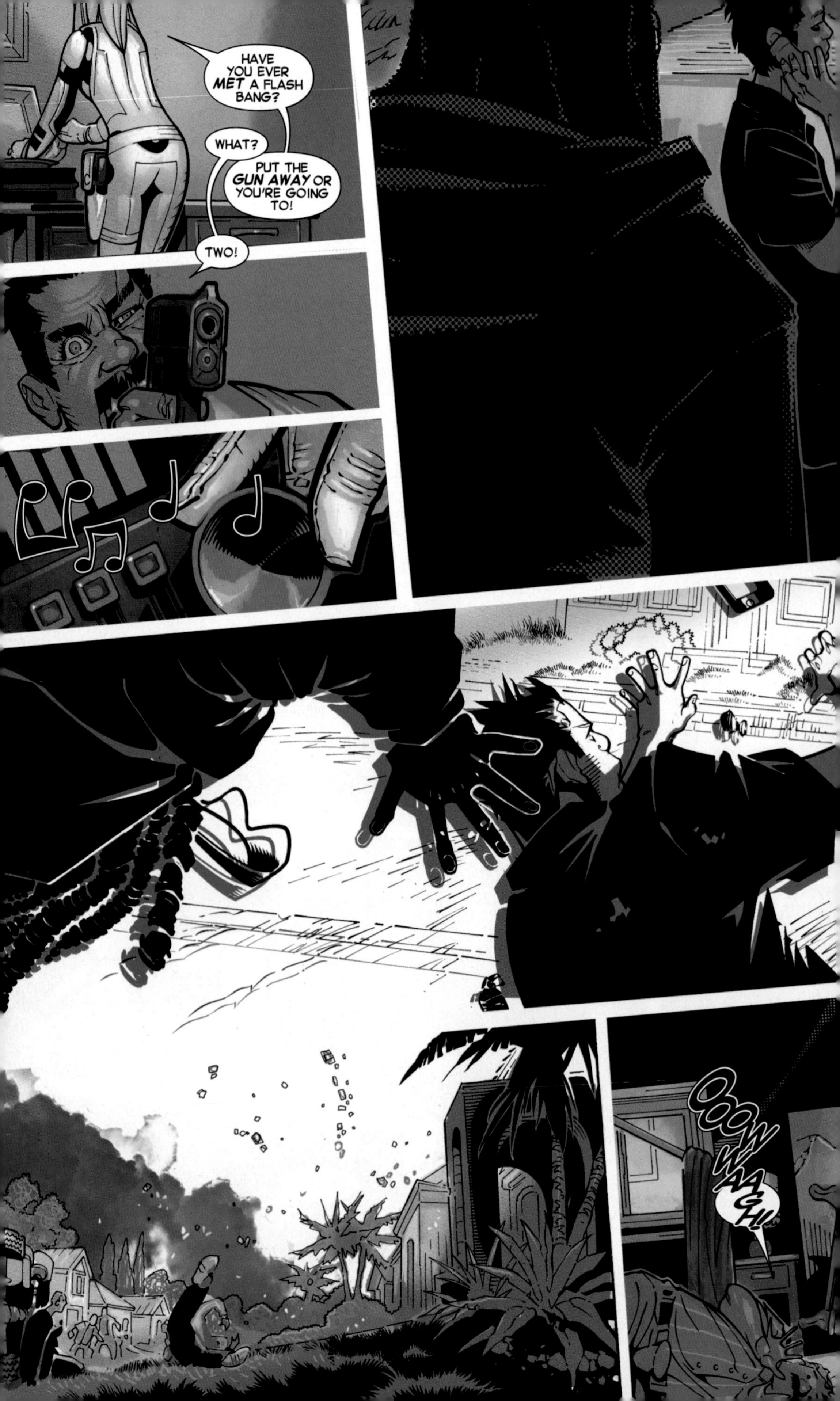
HAVE YOU EVER MET A FLASH BANG?
WHAT?
PUT THE GUN AWAY OR YOU'RE GOING TO!
TWO!
OOOWWAAGH!!

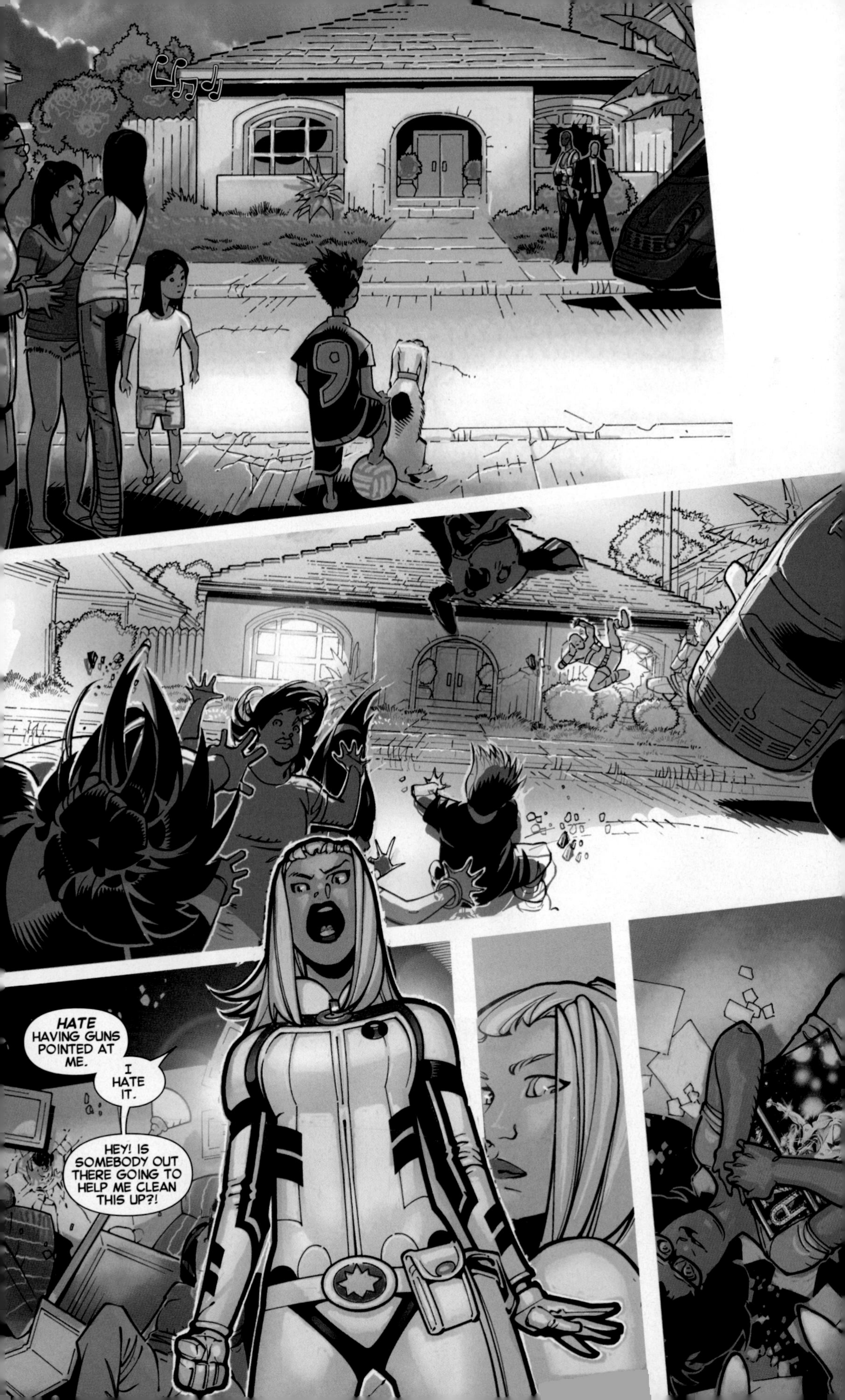
HATE HAVING GUNS POINTED AT ME.
I HATE IT.
HEY! IS SOMEBODY OUT THERE GOING TO HELP ME CLEAN THIS UP?!

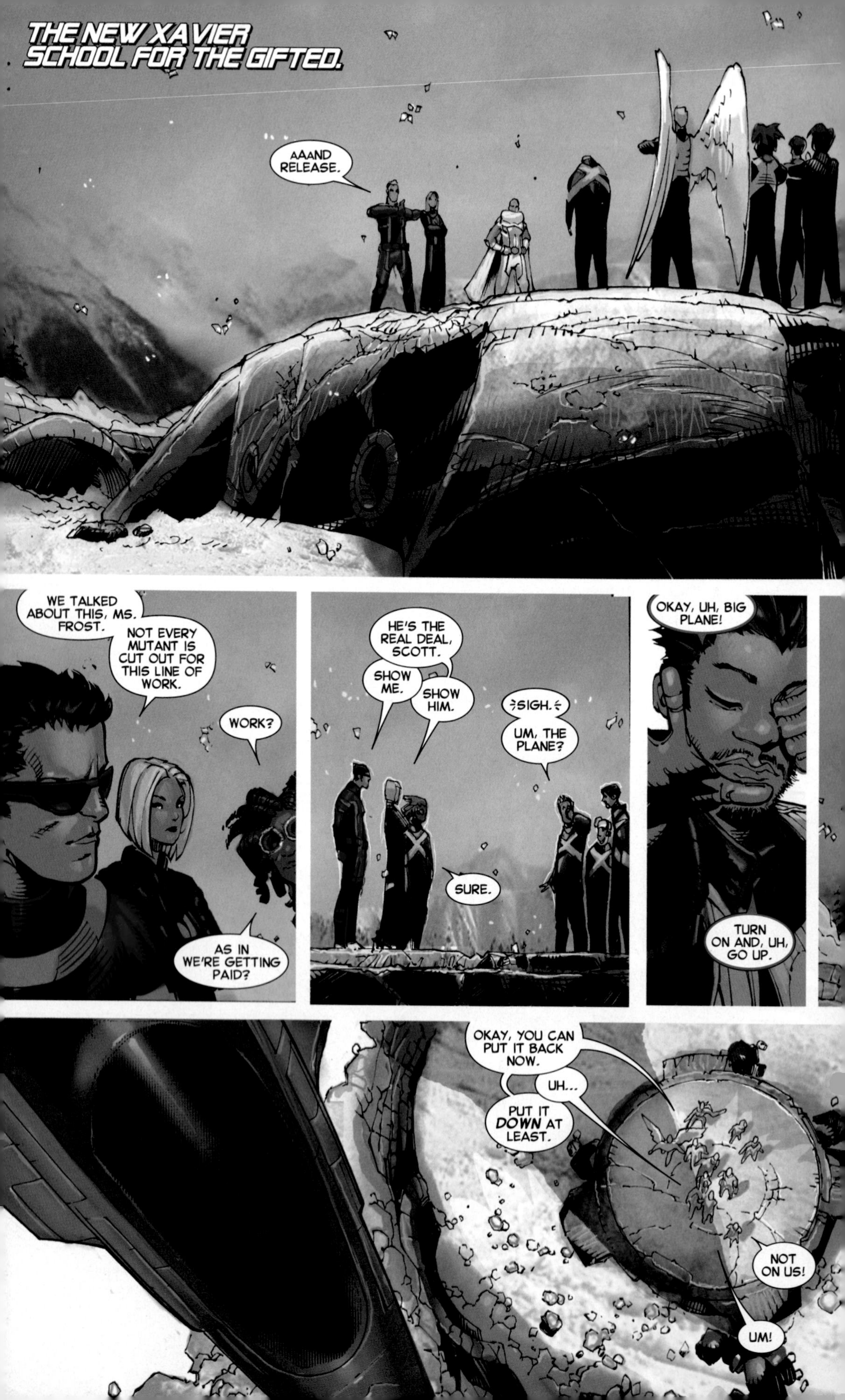
THE NEW XAVIER SCHOOL FOR THE GIFTED.
AAAND RELEASE.
WE TALKED ABOUT THIS, MS. FROST.
NOT EVERY MUTANT IS CUT OUT FOR THIS LINE OF WORK.
WORK?
AS IN WE'RE GETTING PAID?
HE'S THE REAL DEAL, SCOTT.
SHOW ME.
SHOW HIM.
SURE.
SIGH.
UM, THE PLANE?
OKAY, UH, BIG PLANE!
TURN ON AND, UH, GO UP.
OKAY, YOU CAN PUT IT BACK NOW.
UH...
PUT IT DOWN AT LEAST.
NOT ON US!
UM!

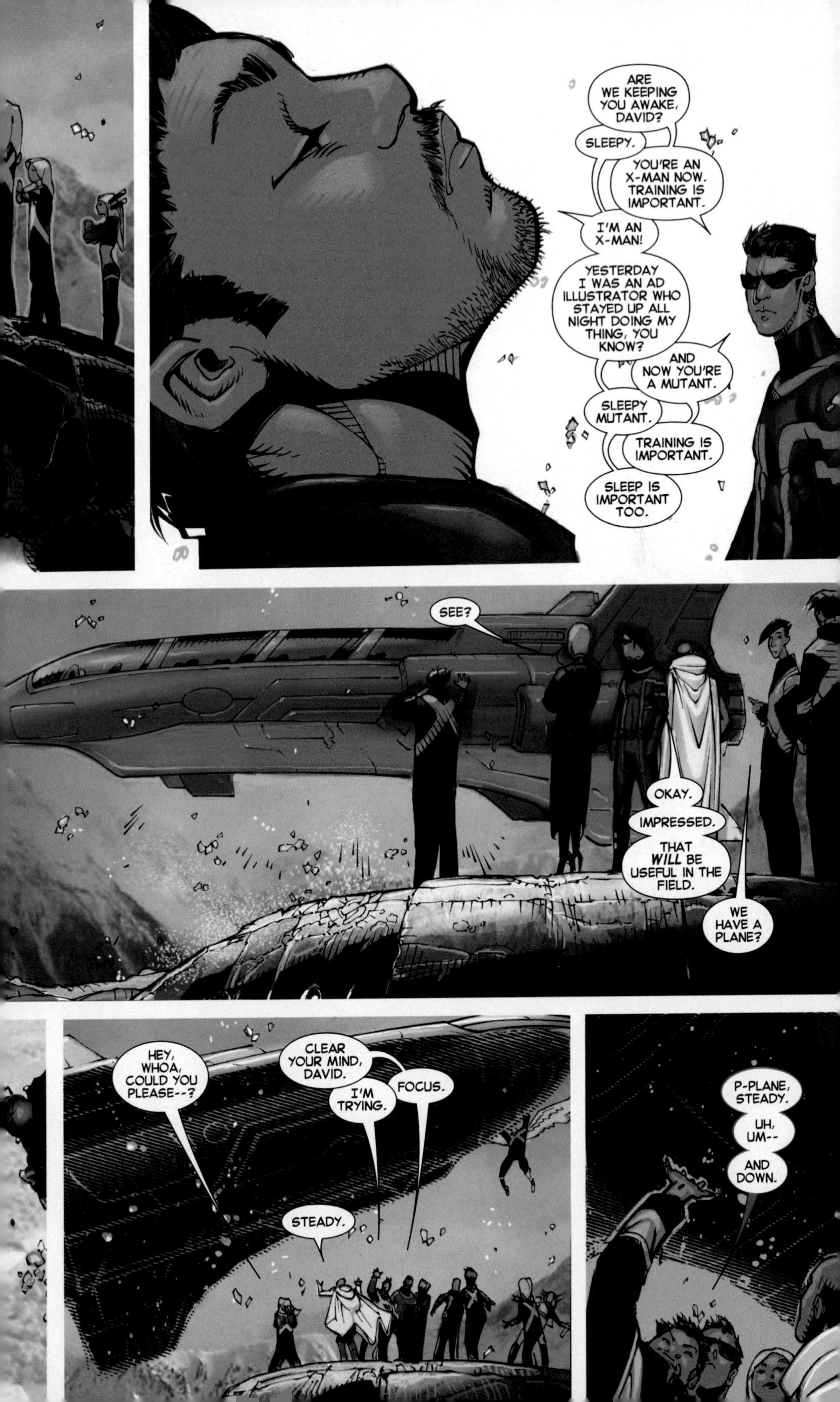
ARE WE KEEPING YOU AWAKE, DAVID?
SLEEPY.
YOU'RE AN X-MAN NOW. TRAINING IS IMPORTANT.
I'M AN X-MAN!
YESTERDAY I WAS AN AD ILLUSTRATOR WHO STAYED UP ALL NIGHT DOING MY THING, YOU KNOW?
AND NOW YOU'RE A MUTANT.
SLEEPY MUTANT.
TRAINING IS IMPORTANT.
SLEEP IS IMPORTANT TOO.
SEE?
OKAY.
IMPRESSED.
THAT *WILL* BE USEFUL IN THE FIELD.
WE HAVE A PLANE?
HEY, WHOA, COULD YOU PLEASE--?
CLEAR YOUR MIND, DAVID.
I'M TRYING.
FOCUS.
STEADY.
P-PLANE, STEADY.
UH, UM--
AND DOWN.

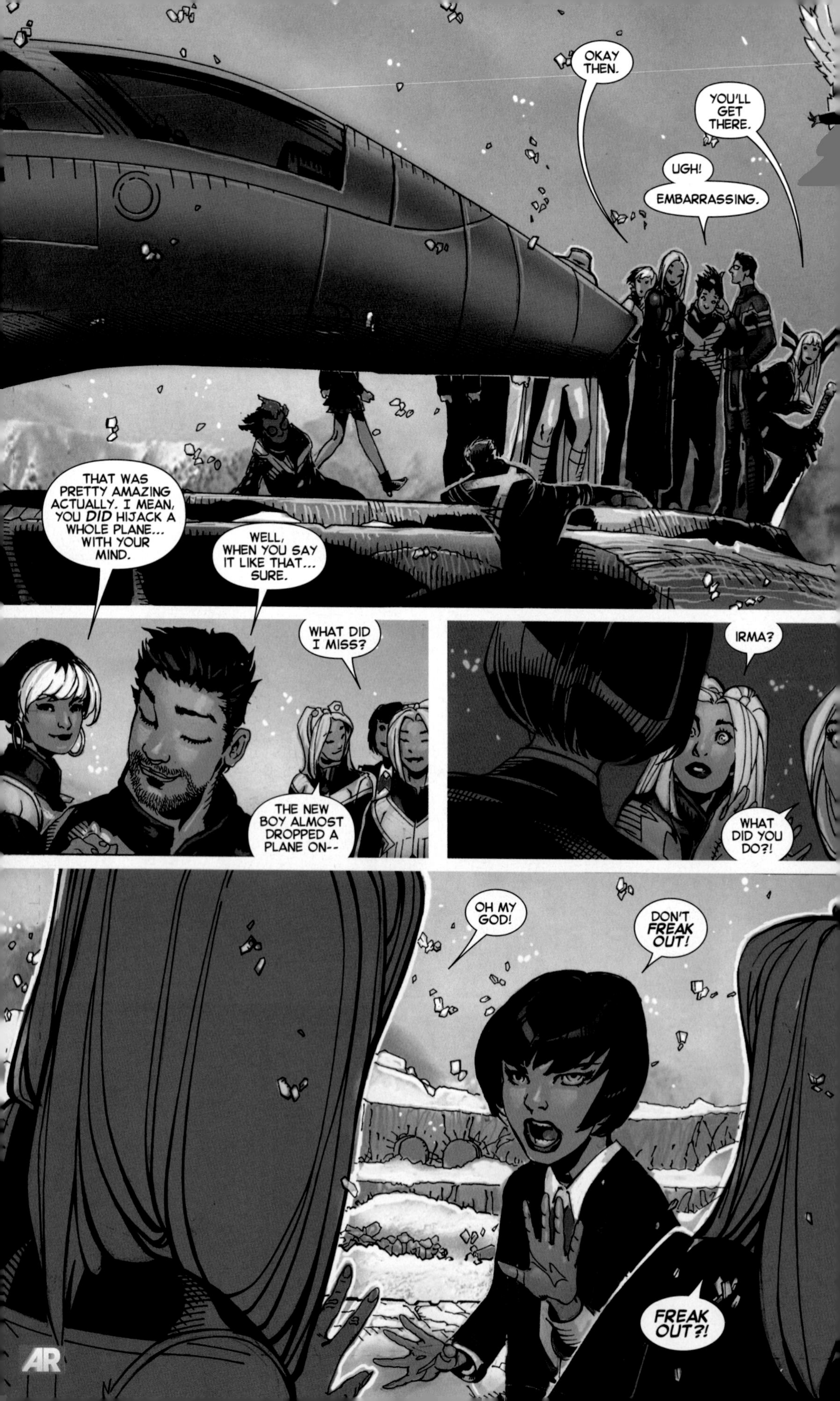
OKAY THEN.
YOU'LL GET THERE.
UGH!
EMBARRASSING.
THAT WAS PRETTY AMAZING ACTUALLY. I MEAN, YOU DID HIJACK A WHOLE PLANE... WITH YOUR MIND.
WELL, WHEN YOU SAY IT LIKE THAT... SURE.
WHAT DID I MISS?
THE NEW BOY ALMOST DROPPED A PLANE ON--
IRMA?
WHAT DID YOU DO?!
OH MY GOD!
DON'T FREAK OUT!
FREAK OUT?!

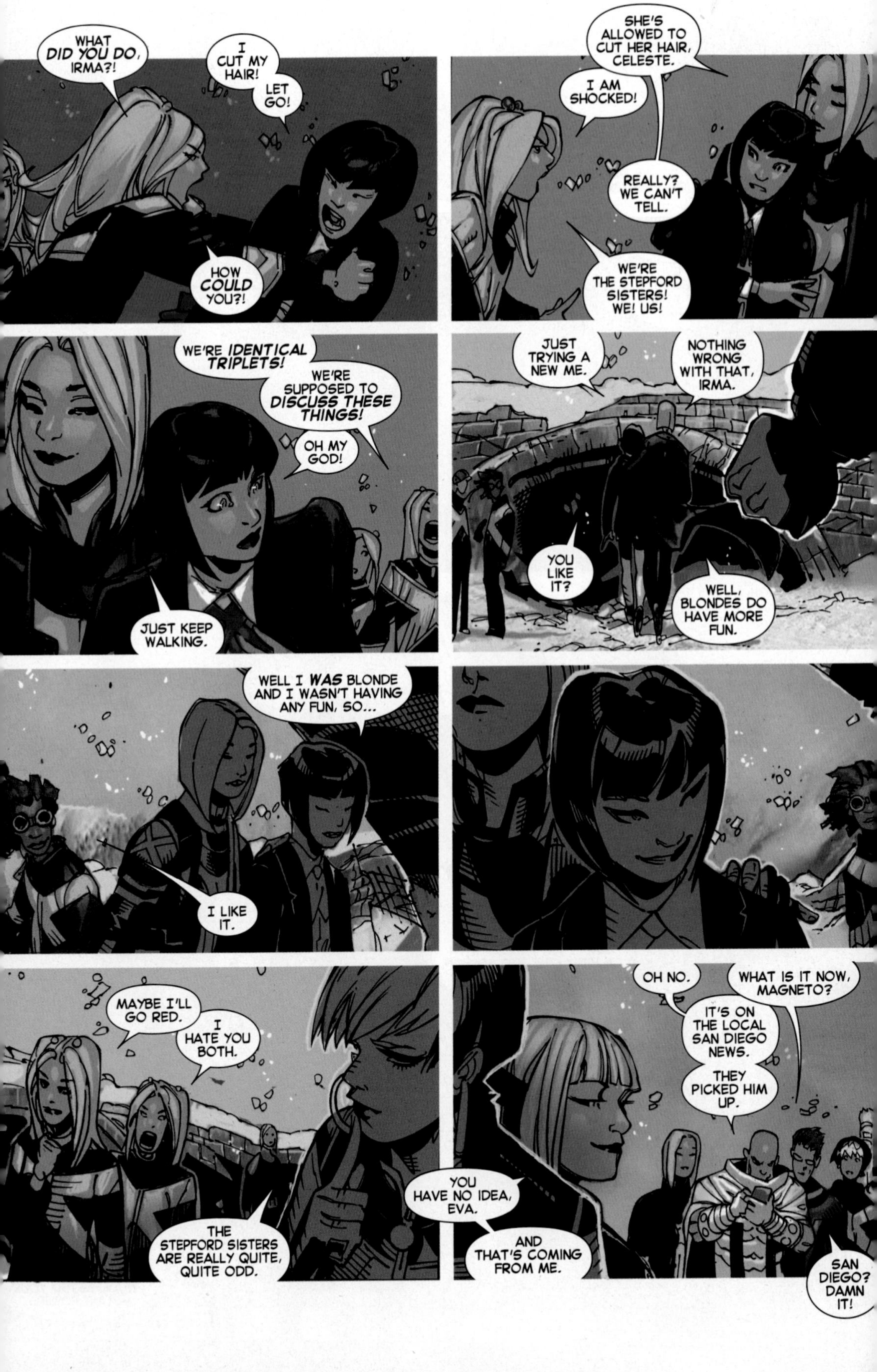
WHAT DID YOU DO, IRMA?!
I CUT MY HAIR!
LET GO!
HOW COULD YOU?!
SHE'S ALLOWED TO CUT HER HAIR, CELESTE.
I AM SHOCKED!
REALLY? WE CAN'T TELL.
WE'RE THE STEPFORD SISTERS! WE! US!
WE'RE IDENTICAL TRIPLETS!
WE'RE SUPPOSED TO DISCUSS THESE THINGS!
OH MY GOD!
JUST KEEP WALKING.
JUST TRYING A NEW ME.
NOTHING WRONG WITH THAT, IRMA.
YOU LIKE IT?
WELL, BLONDES DO HAVE MORE FUN.
WELL I WAS BLONDE AND I WASN'T HAVING ANY FUN, SO...
I LIKE IT.
MAYBE I'LL GO RED.
I HATE YOU BOTH.
THE STEPFORD SISTERS ARE REALLY QUITE, QUITE ODD.
YOU HAVE NO IDEA, EVA.
AND THAT'S COMING FROM ME.
OH NO.
WHAT IS IT NOW, MAGNETO?
IT'S ON THE LOCAL SAN DIEGO NEWS.
THEY PICKED HIM UP.
SAN DIEGO? DAMN IT!

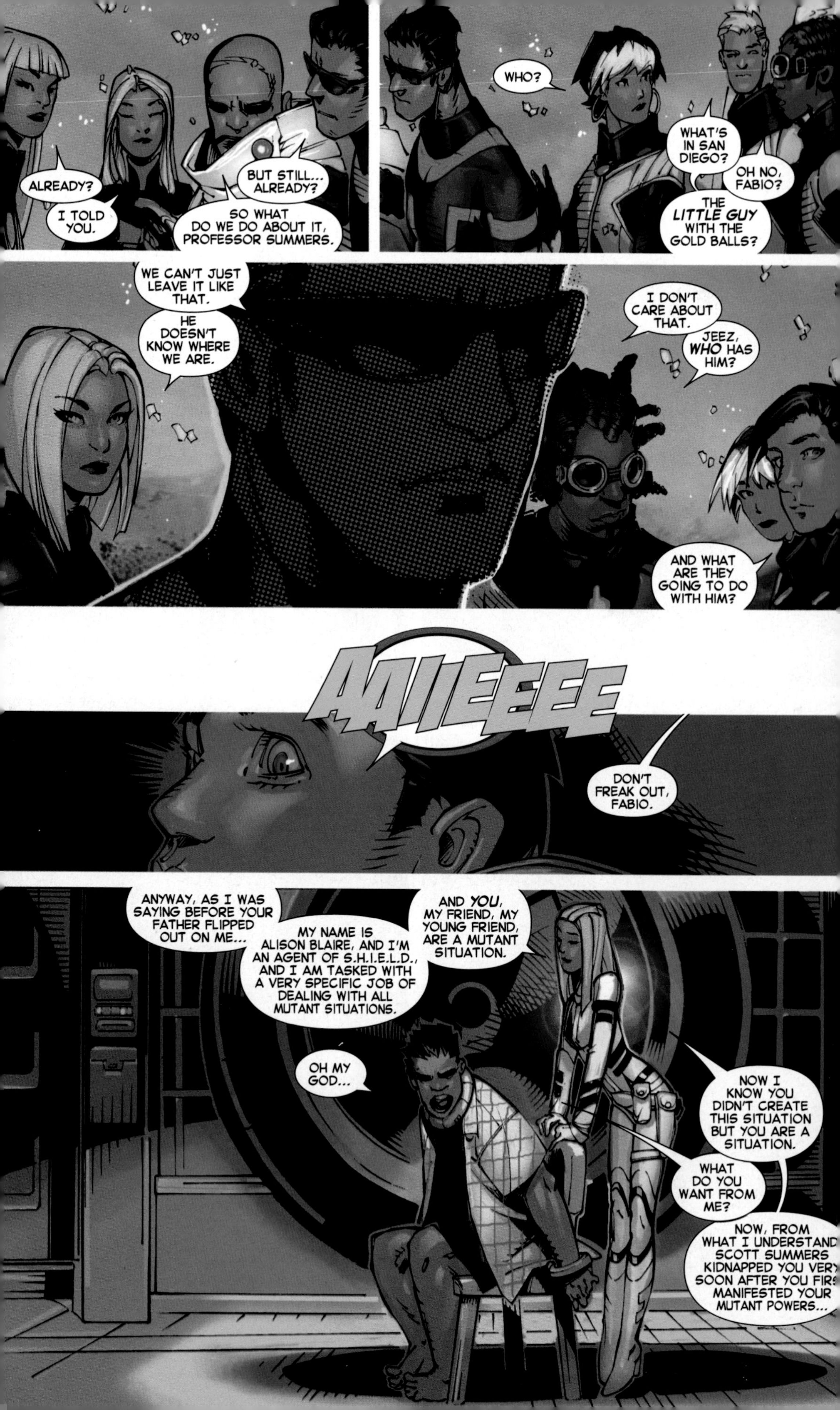

ALREADY?
I TOLD YOU.
BUT STILL... ALREADY?
SO WHAT DO WE DO ABOUT IT, PROFESSOR SUMMERS.
WHO?
WHAT'S IN SAN DIEGO?
OH NO, FABIO?
THE LITTLE GUY WITH THE GOLD BALLS?
WE CAN'T JUST LEAVE IT LIKE THAT.
HE DOESN'T KNOW WHERE WE ARE.
I DON'T CARE ABOUT THAT.
JEEZ, WHO HAS HIM?
AND WHAT ARE THEY GOING TO DO WITH HIM?
AAIIEEEE
DON'T FREAK OUT, FABIO.
ANYWAY, AS I WAS SAYING BEFORE YOUR FATHER FLIPPED OUT ON ME...
MY NAME IS ALISON BLAIRE, AND I'M AN AGENT OF S.H.I.E.L.D., AND I AM TASKED WITH A VERY SPECIFIC JOB OF DEALING WITH ALL MUTANT SITUATIONS.
AND YOU, MY FRIEND, MY YOUNG FRIEND, ARE A MUTANT SITUATION.
OH MY GOD...
NOW I KNOW YOU DIDN'T CREATE THIS SITUATION BUT YOU ARE A SITUATION.
WHAT DO YOU WANT FROM ME?
NOW, FROM WHAT I UNDERSTAND SCOTT SUMMERS KIDNAPPED YOU VERY SOON AFTER YOU FIRS MANIFESTED YOUR MUTANT POWERS...

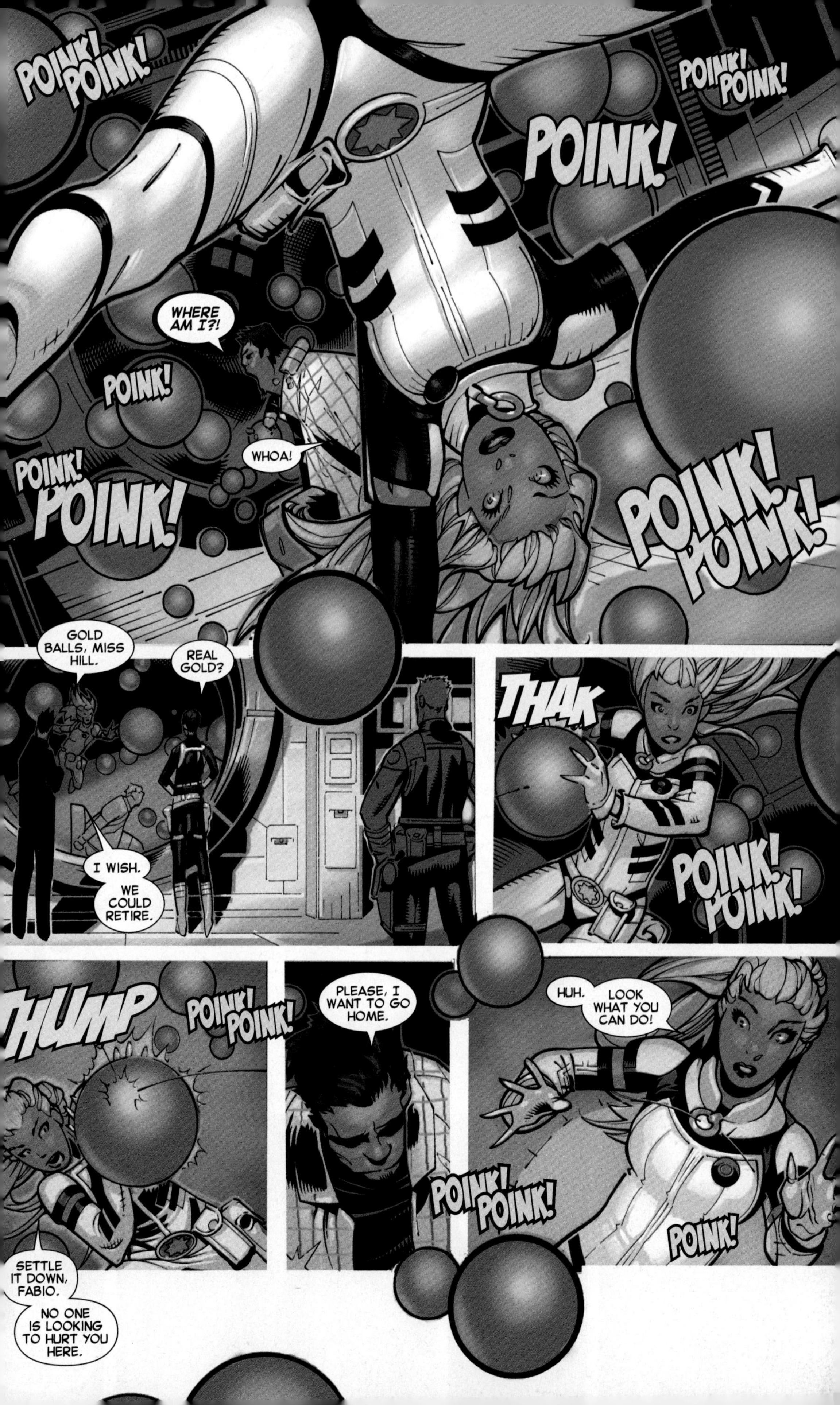
POINK! POINK!
POINK! POINK!
POINK!
WHERE AM I?!
POINK!
POINK! POINK!
WHOA!
POINK! POINK!
GOLD BALLS, MISS HILL.
REAL GOLD?
I WISH.
WE COULD RETIRE.
THAK
POINK! POINK!
THUMP
POINK! POINK!
SETTLE IT DOWN, FABIO.
NO ONE IS LOOKING TO HURT YOU HERE.
PLEASE, I WANT TO GO HOME.
POINK! POINK!
HUH.
LOOK WHAT YOU CAN DO!
POINK!

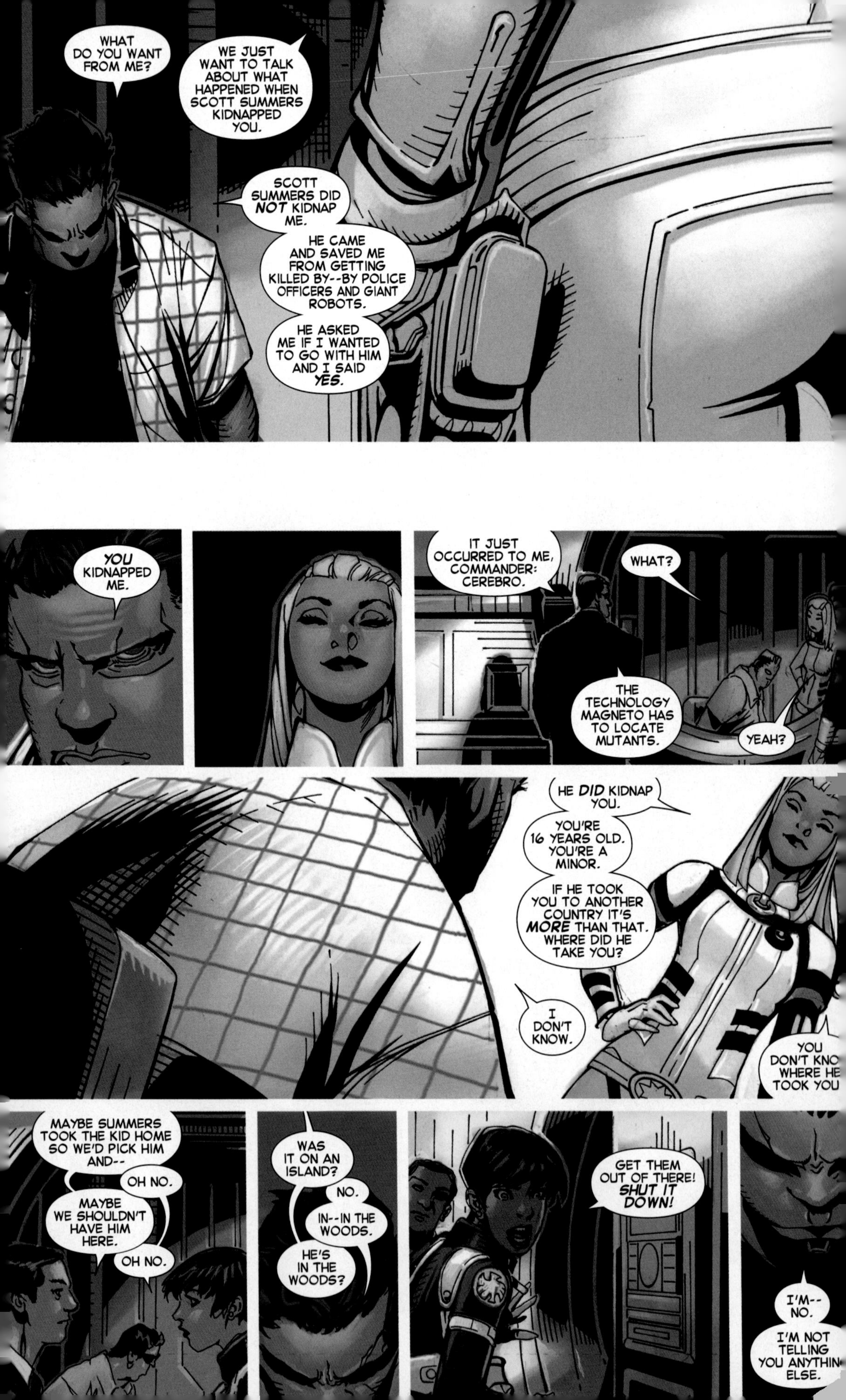
WHAT DO YOU WANT FROM ME?
WE JUST WANT TO TALK ABOUT WHAT HAPPENED WHEN SCOTT SUMMERS KIDNAPPED YOU.
SCOTT SUMMERS DID NOT KIDNAP ME.
HE CAME AND SAVED ME FROM GETTING KILLED BY--BY POLICE OFFICERS AND GIANT ROBOTS.
HE ASKED ME IF I WANTED TO GO WITH HIM AND I SAID YES.
YOU KIDNAPPED ME.
IT JUST OCCURRED TO ME, COMMANDER: CEREBRO.
WHAT?
THE TECHNOLOGY MAGNETO HAS TO LOCATE MUTANTS.
YEAH?
HE DID KIDNAP YOU.
YOU'RE 16 YEARS OLD. YOU'RE A MINOR.
IF HE TOOK YOU TO ANOTHER COUNTRY IT'S MORE THAN THAT. WHERE DID HE TAKE YOU?
I DON'T KNOW.
YOU DON'T KNO WHERE HE TOOK YOU
MAYBE SUMMERS TOOK THE KID HOME SO WE'D PICK HIM AND--
OH NO.
MAYBE WE SHOULDN'T HAVE HIM HERE.
OH NO.
WAS IT ON AN ISLAND?
NO.
IN--IN THE WOODS.
HE'S IN THE WOODS?
GET THEM OUT OF THERE! SHUT IT DOWN!
I'M-- NO.
I'M NOT TELLING YOU ANYTHIN ELSE.

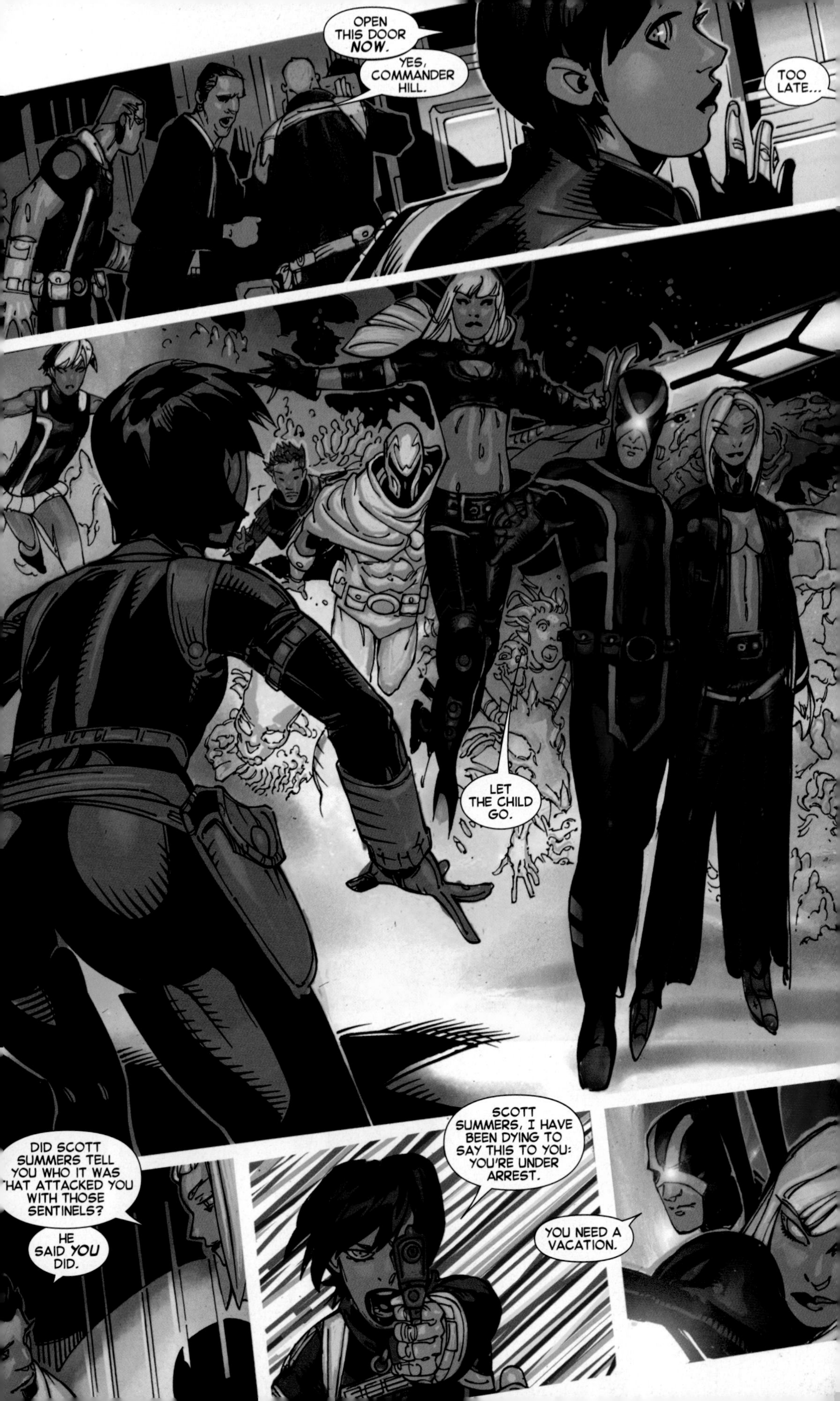
OPEN THIS DOOR NOW.
YES, COMMANDER HILL.
TOO LATE...
LET THE CHILD GO.
DID SCOTT SUMMERS TELL YOU WHO IT WAS THAT ATTACKED YOU WITH THOSE SENTINELS?
HE SAID YOU DID.
SCOTT SUMMERS, I HAVE BEEN DYING TO SAY THIS TO YOU: YOU'RE UNDER ARREST.
YOU NEED A VACATION.

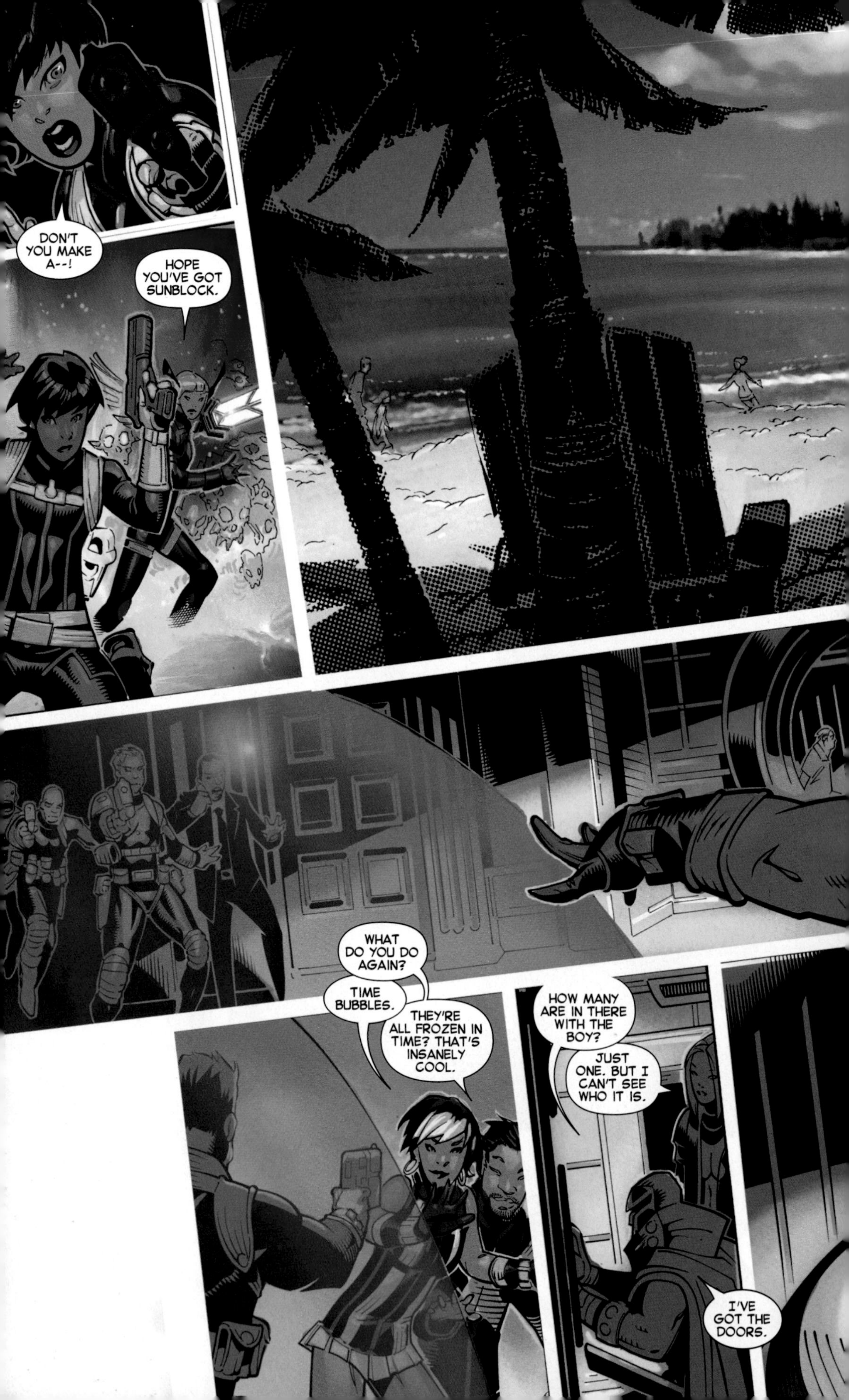
DON'T YOU MAKE A--!
HOPE YOU'VE GOT SUNBLOCK.
WHAT DO YOU DO AGAIN?
TIME BUBBLES.
THEY'RE ALL FROZEN IN TIME? THAT'S INSANELY COOL.
HOW MANY ARE IN THERE WITH THE BOY?
JUST ONE. BUT I CAN'T SEE WHO IT IS.
I'VE GOT THE DOORS.

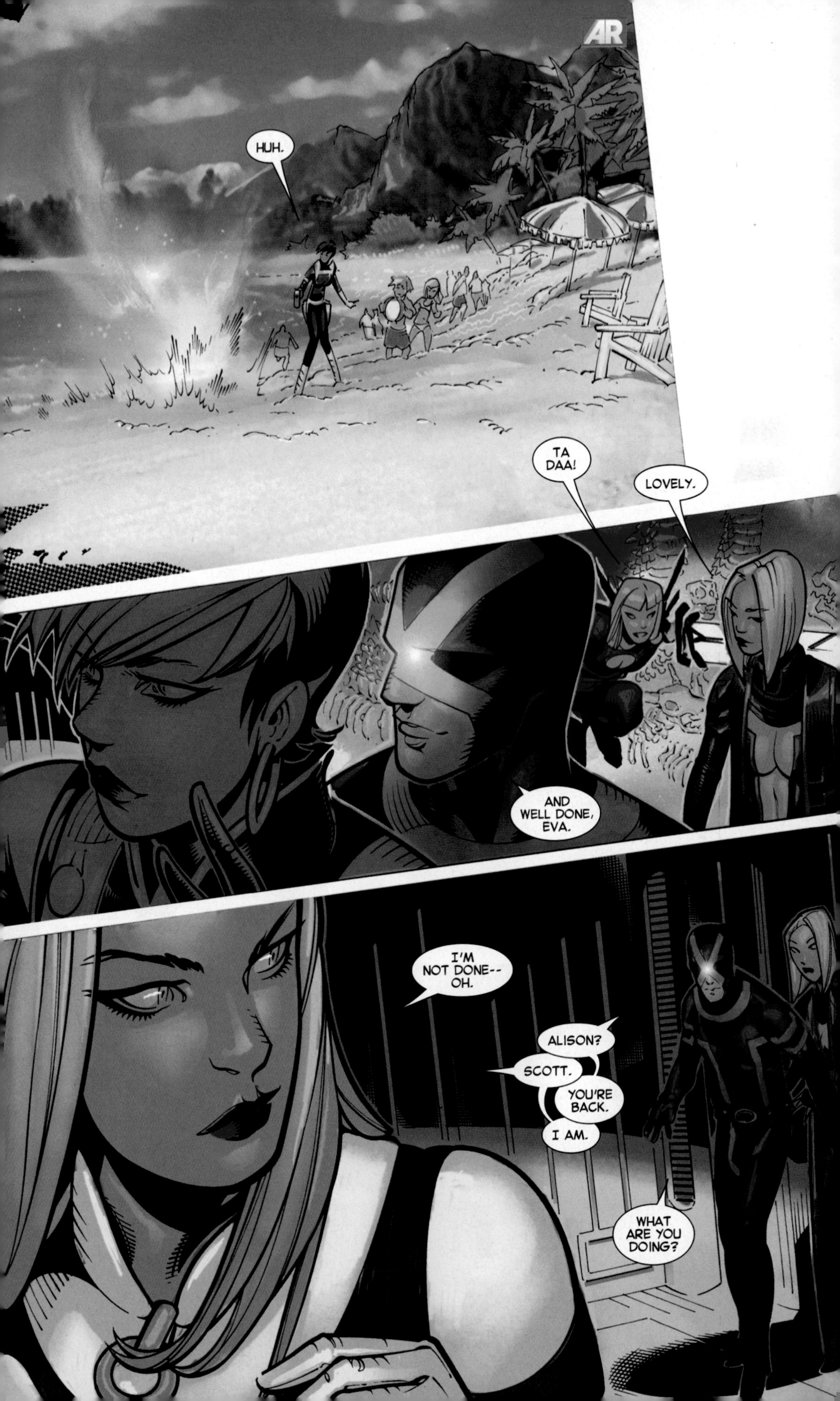
HUH.
TA DAA!
LOVELY.
AND WELL DONE, EVA.
I'M NOT DONE-- OH.
ALISON?
SCOTT.
YOU'RE BACK.
I AM.
WHAT ARE YOU DOING?

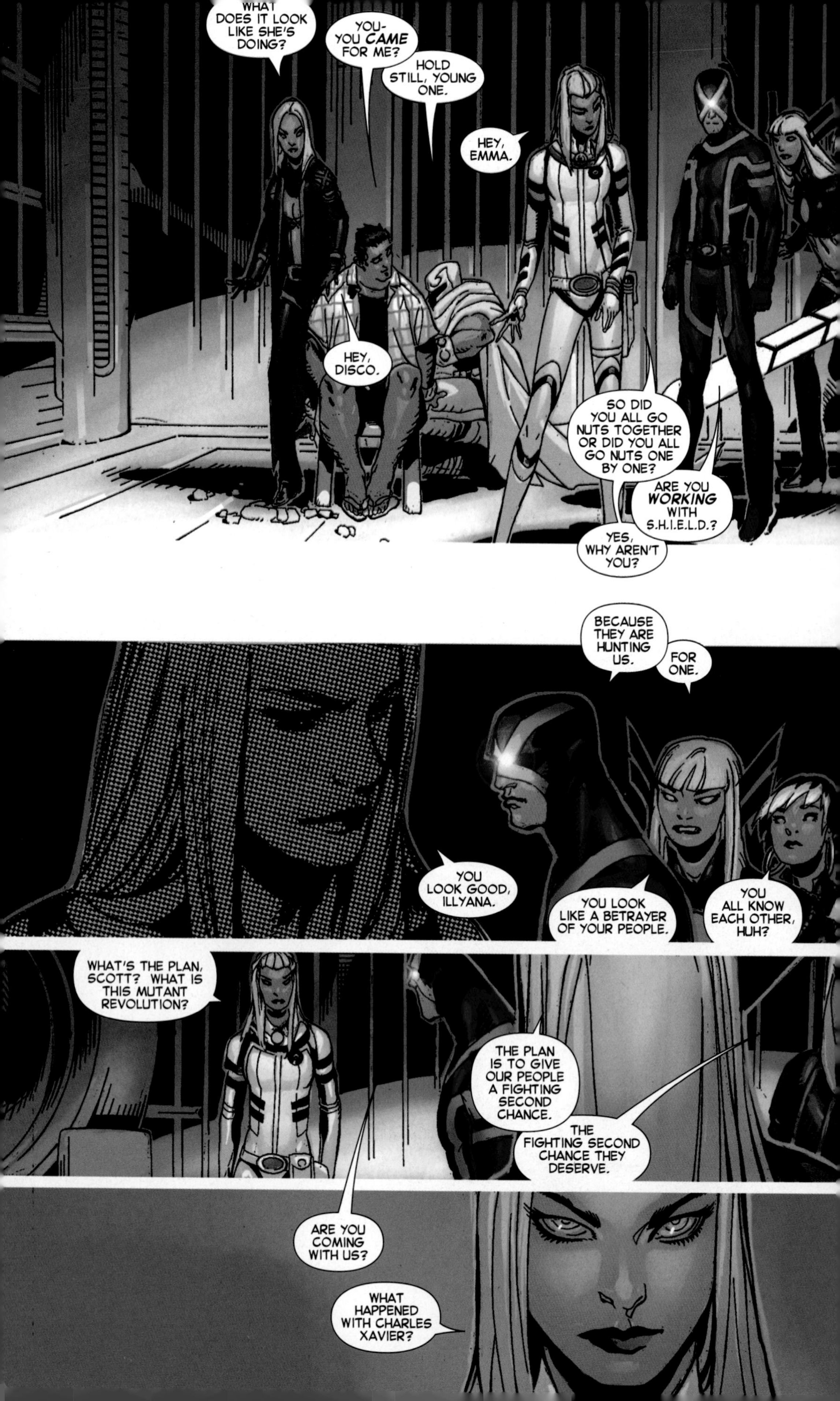

WHAT DOES IT LOOK LIKE SHE'S DOING?
YOU- YOU **CAME** FOR ME?
HOLD STILL, YOUNG ONE.
HEY, EMMA.
HEY, DISCO.
SO DID YOU ALL GO NUTS TOGETHER OR DID YOU ALL GO NUTS ONE BY ONE?
ARE YOU **WORKING** WITH S.H.I.E.L.D.?
YES, WHY AREN'T YOU?
BECAUSE THEY ARE HUNTING US.
FOR ONE.
YOU LOOK GOOD, ILLYANA.
YOU LOOK LIKE A BETRAYER OF YOUR PEOPLE.
YOU ALL KNOW EACH OTHER, HUH?
WHAT'S THE PLAN, SCOTT? WHAT IS THIS MUTANT REVOLUTION?
THE PLAN IS TO GIVE OUR PEOPLE A FIGHTING SECOND CHANCE.
THE FIGHTING SECOND CHANCE THEY DESERVE.
ARE YOU COMING WITH US?
WHAT HAPPENED WITH CHARLES XAVIER?

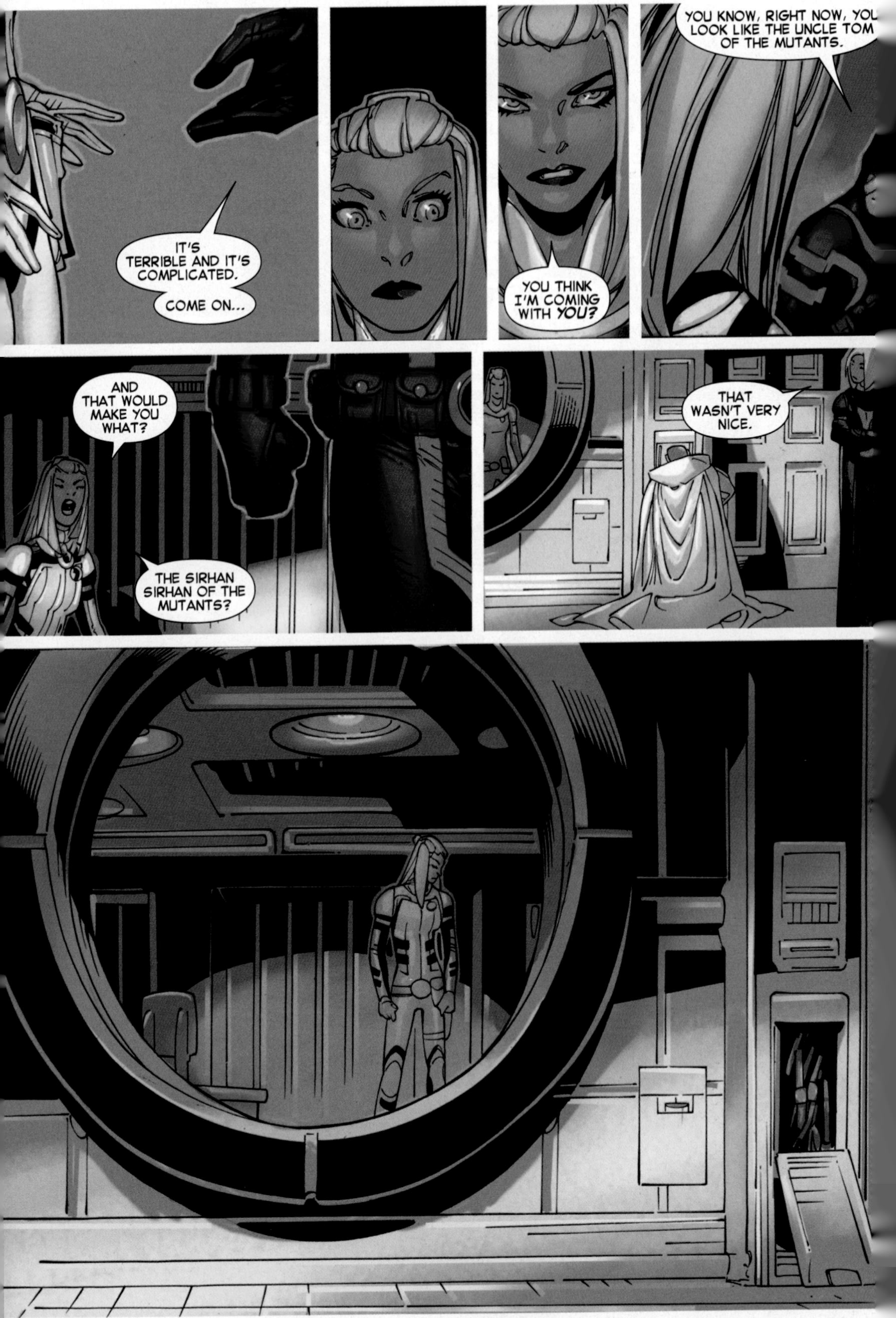
IT'S TERRIBLE AND IT'S COMPLICATED.
COME ON...
YOU THINK I'M COMING WITH *YOU?*
YOU KNOW, RIGHT NOW, YOU LOOK LIKE THE UNCLE TOM OF THE MUTANTS.
AND THAT WOULD MAKE YOU WHAT?
THE SIRHAN SIRHAN OF THE MUTANTS?
THAT WASN'T VERY NICE.

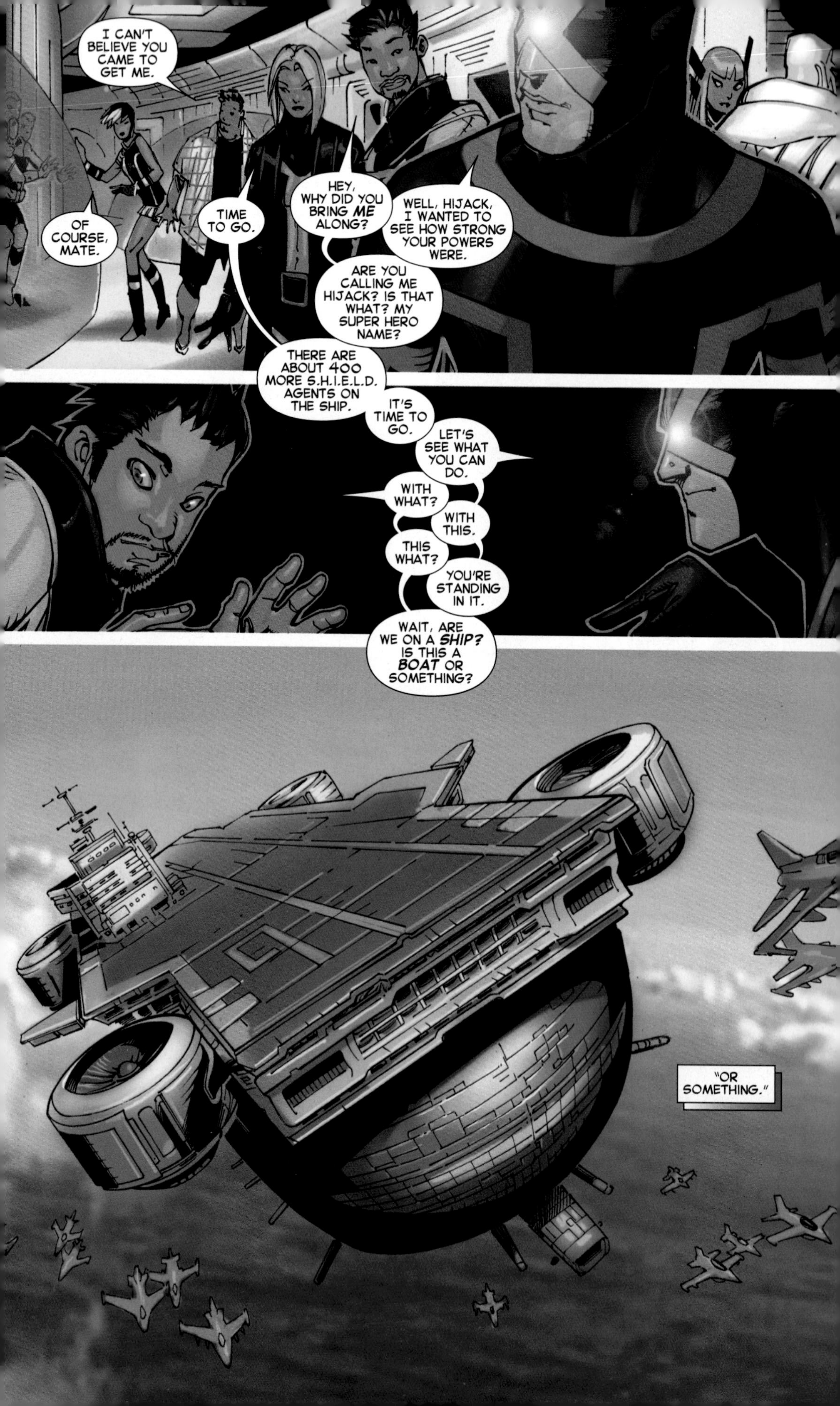
I CAN'T BELIEVE YOU CAME TO GET ME.
OF COURSE, MATE.
TIME TO GO.
HEY, WHY DID YOU BRING ME ALONG?
WELL, HIJACK, I WANTED TO SEE HOW STRONG YOUR POWERS WERE.
ARE YOU CALLING ME HIJACK? IS THAT WHAT? MY SUPER HERO NAME?
THERE ARE ABOUT 400 MORE S.H.I.E.L.D. AGENTS ON THE SHIP.
IT'S TIME TO GO.
LET'S SEE WHAT YOU CAN DO.
WITH WHAT?
WITH THIS.
THIS WHAT?
YOU'RE STANDING IN IT.
WAIT, ARE WE ON A SHIP? IS THIS A BOAT OR SOMETHING?
"OR SOMETHING."

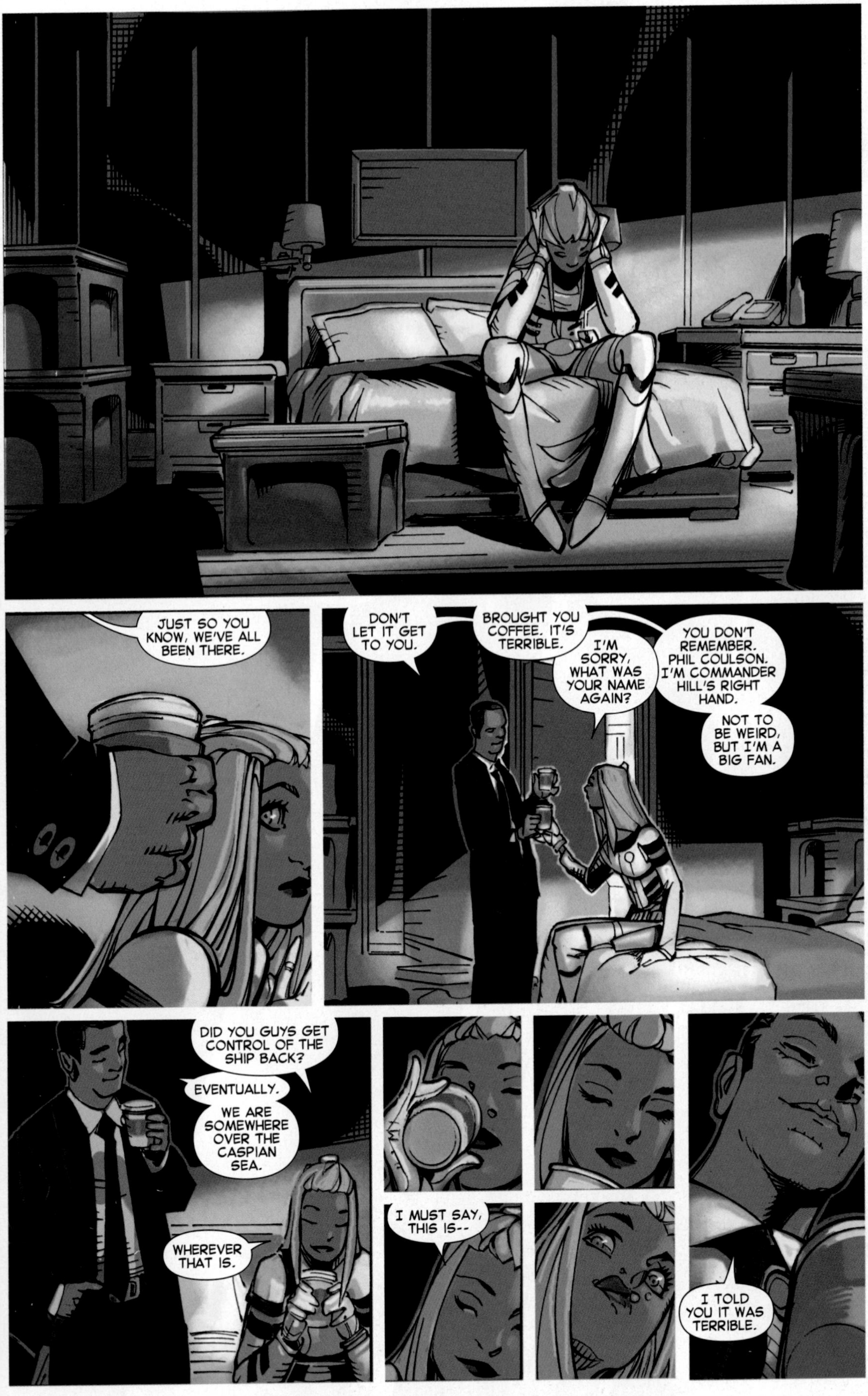
JUST SO YOU KNOW, WE'VE ALL BEEN THERE.
DON'T LET IT GET TO YOU.
BROUGHT YOU COFFEE. IT'S TERRIBLE.
I'M SORRY, WHAT WAS YOUR NAME AGAIN?
YOU DON'T REMEMBER. PHIL COULSON. I'M COMMANDER HILL'S RIGHT HAND.
NOT TO BE WEIRD, BUT I'M A BIG FAN.
DID YOU GUYS GET CONTROL OF THE SHIP BACK?
EVENTUALLY.
WE ARE SOMEWHERE OVER THE CASPIAN SEA.
WHEREVER THAT IS.
I MUST SAY, THIS IS--
I TOLD YOU IT WAS TERRIBLE.

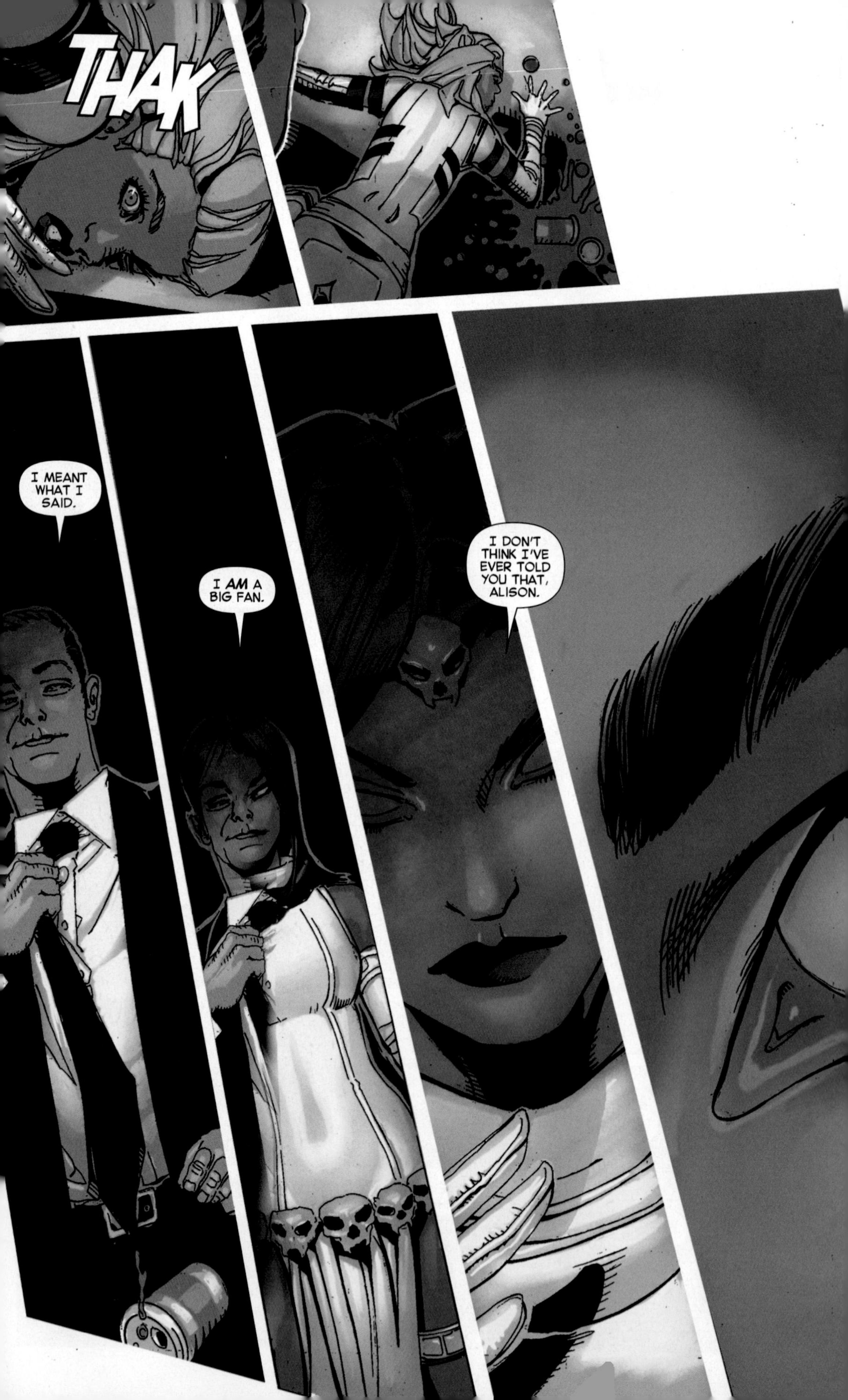
THAK
I MEANT WHAT I SAID.
I AM A BIG FAN.
I DON'T THINK I'VE EVER TOLD YOU THAT, ALISON.

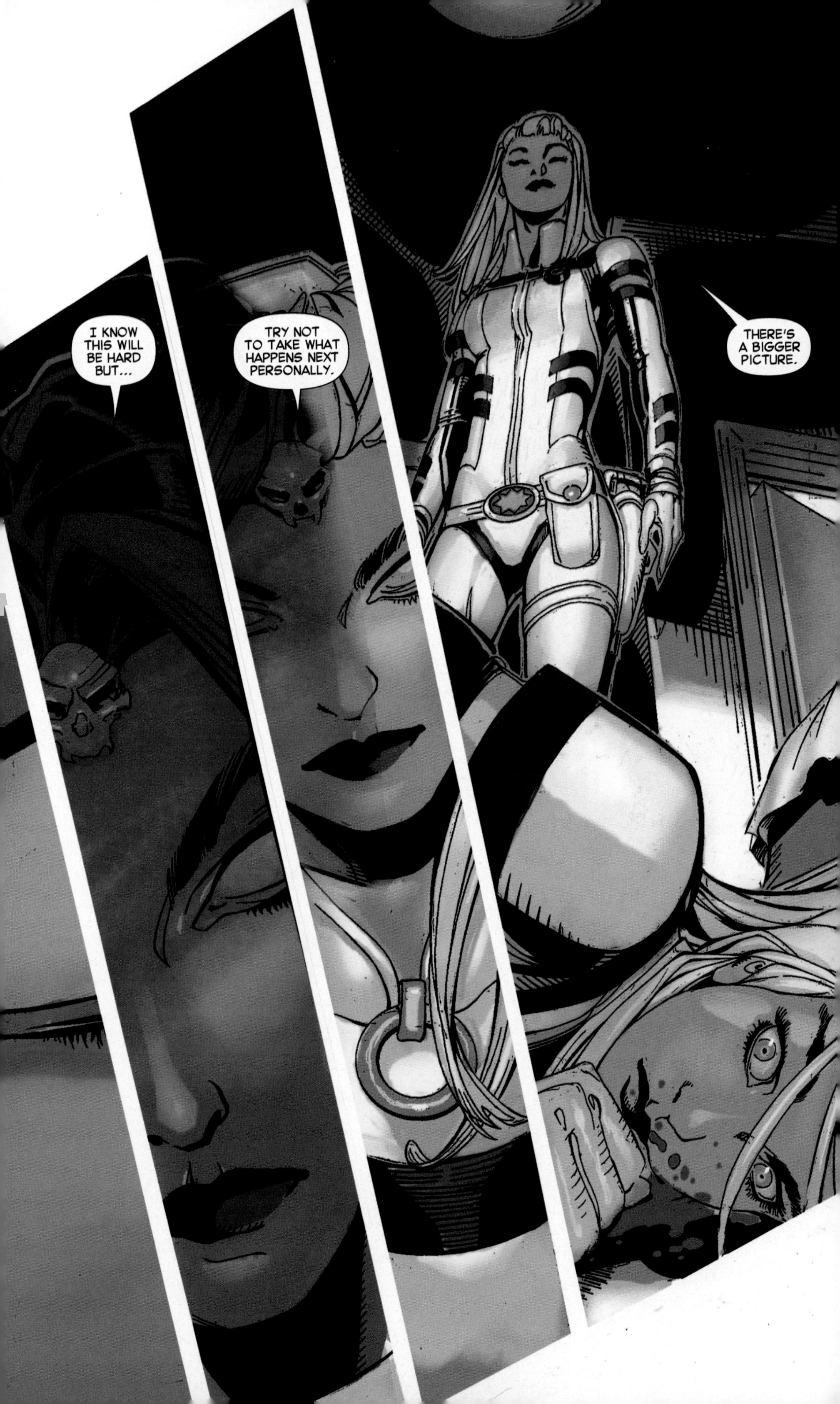

I KNOW THIS WILL BE HARD BUT...
TRY NOT TO TAKE WHAT HAPPENS NEXT PERSONALLY.
THERE'S A BIGGER PICTURE.

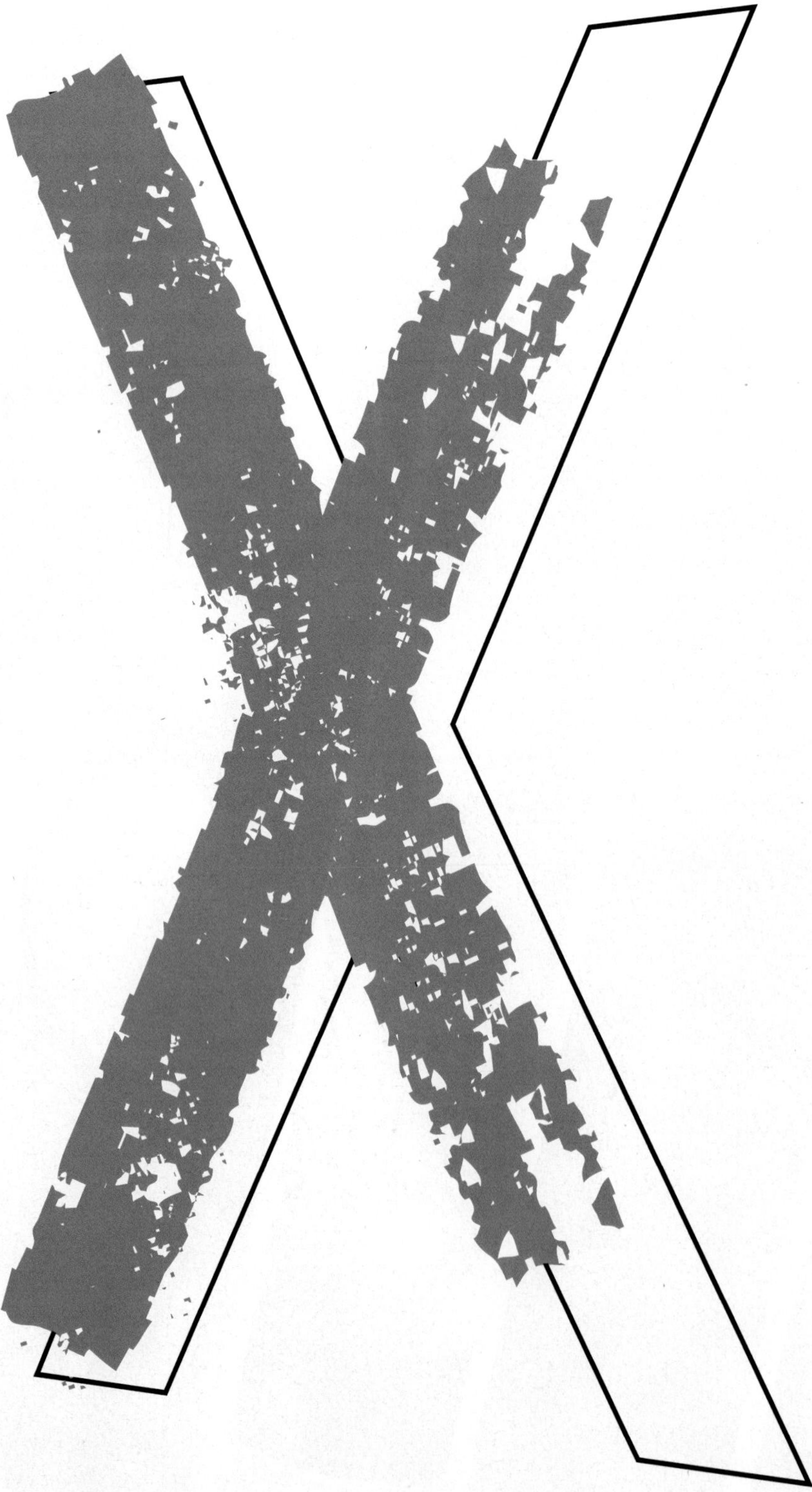

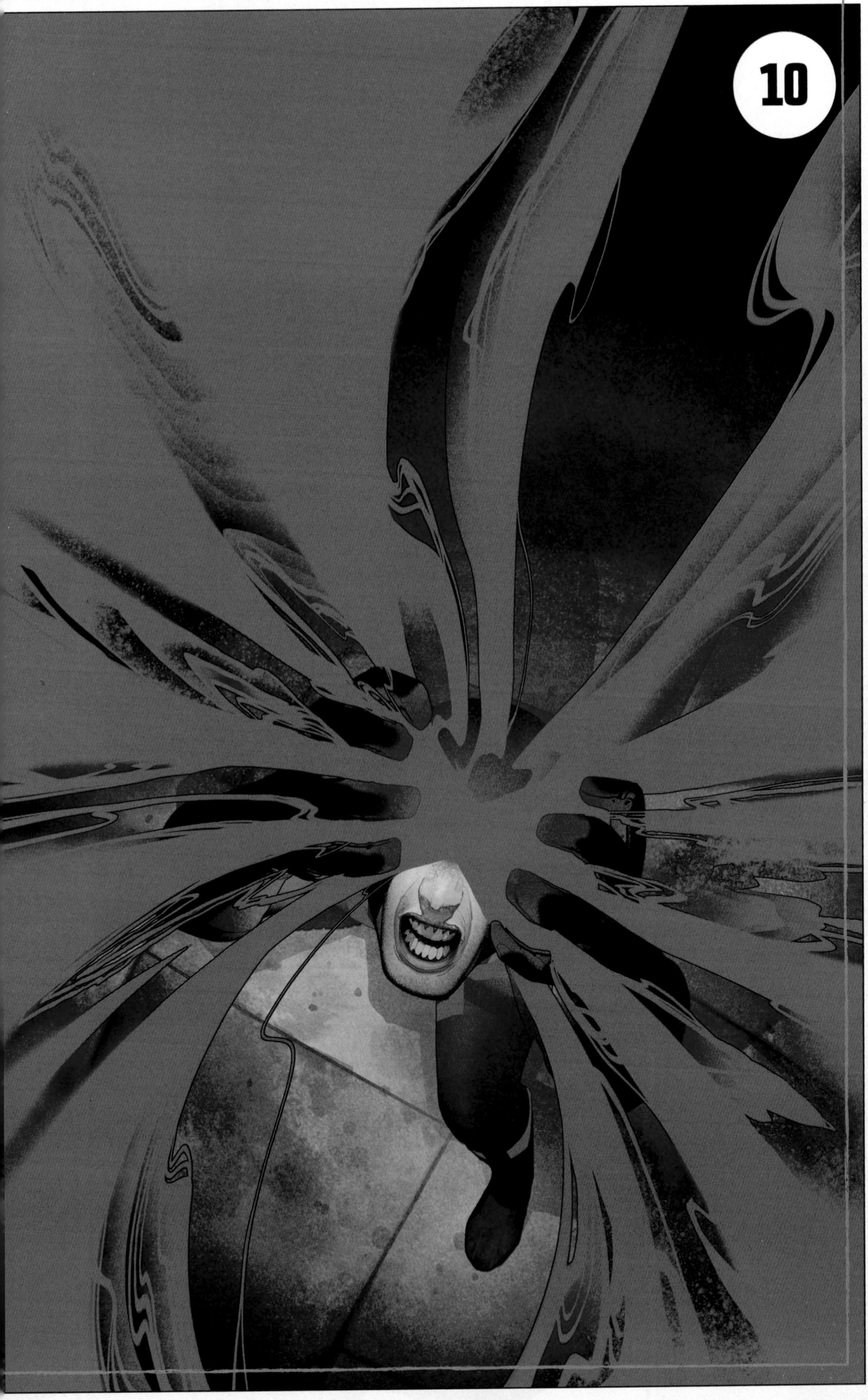
10

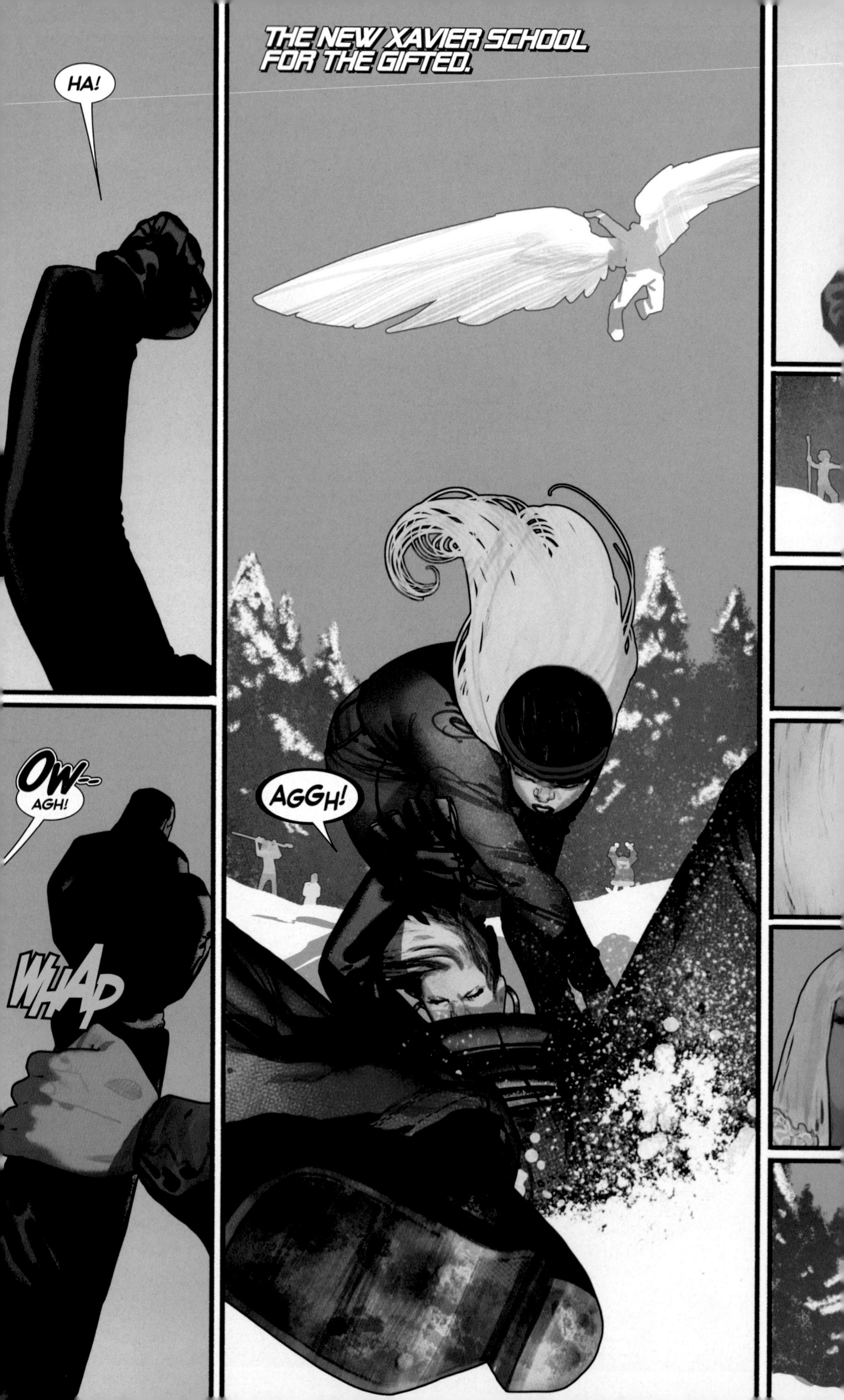
THE NEW XAVIER SCHOOL FOR THE GIFTED.
HA!
OW--AGH!
WHAP
AGGH!

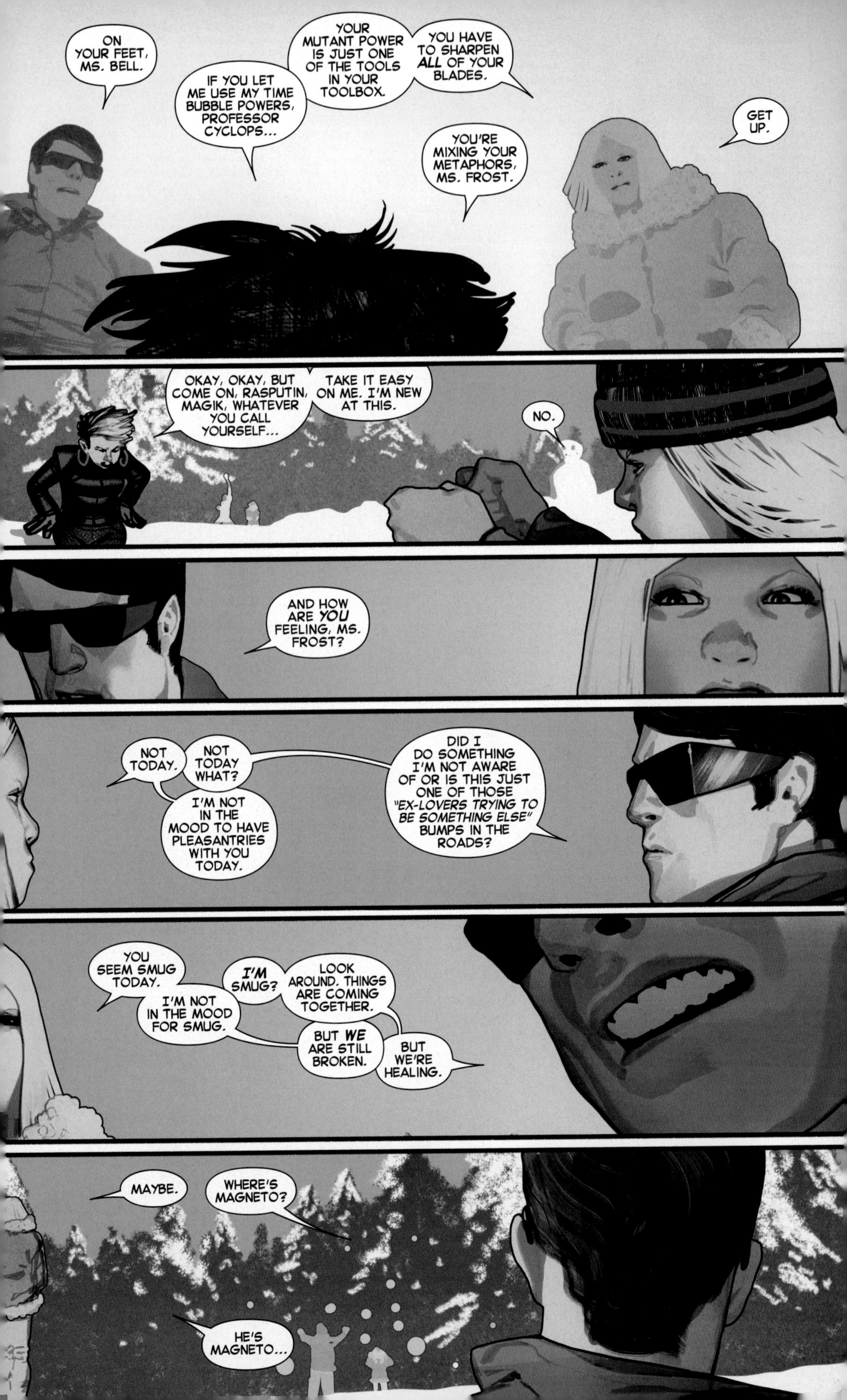

ON YOUR FEET, MS. BELL.
IF YOU LET ME USE MY TIME BUBBLE POWERS, PROFESSOR CYCLOPS...
YOUR MUTANT POWER IS JUST ONE OF THE TOOLS IN YOUR TOOLBOX.
YOU HAVE TO SHARPEN *ALL* OF YOUR BLADES.
YOU'RE MIXING YOUR METAPHORS, MS. FROST.
GET UP.
OKAY, OKAY, BUT COME ON, RASPUTIN, MAGIK, WHATEVER YOU CALL YOURSELF...
TAKE IT EASY ON ME. I'M NEW AT THIS.
NO.
AND HOW ARE *YOU* FEELING, MS. FROST?
NOT TODAY.
NOT TODAY WHAT?
I'M NOT IN THE MOOD TO HAVE PLEASANTRIES WITH YOU TODAY.
DID I DO SOMETHING I'M NOT AWARE OF OR IS THIS JUST ONE OF THOSE *"EX-LOVERS TRYING TO BE SOMETHING ELSE"* BUMPS IN THE ROADS?
YOU SEEM SMUG TODAY.
I'M SMUG?
LOOK AROUND. THINGS ARE COMING TOGETHER.
I'M NOT IN THE MOOD FOR SMUG.
BUT *WE* ARE STILL BROKEN.
BUT WE'RE HEALING.
MAYBE.
WHERE'S MAGNETO?
HE'S MAGNETO...

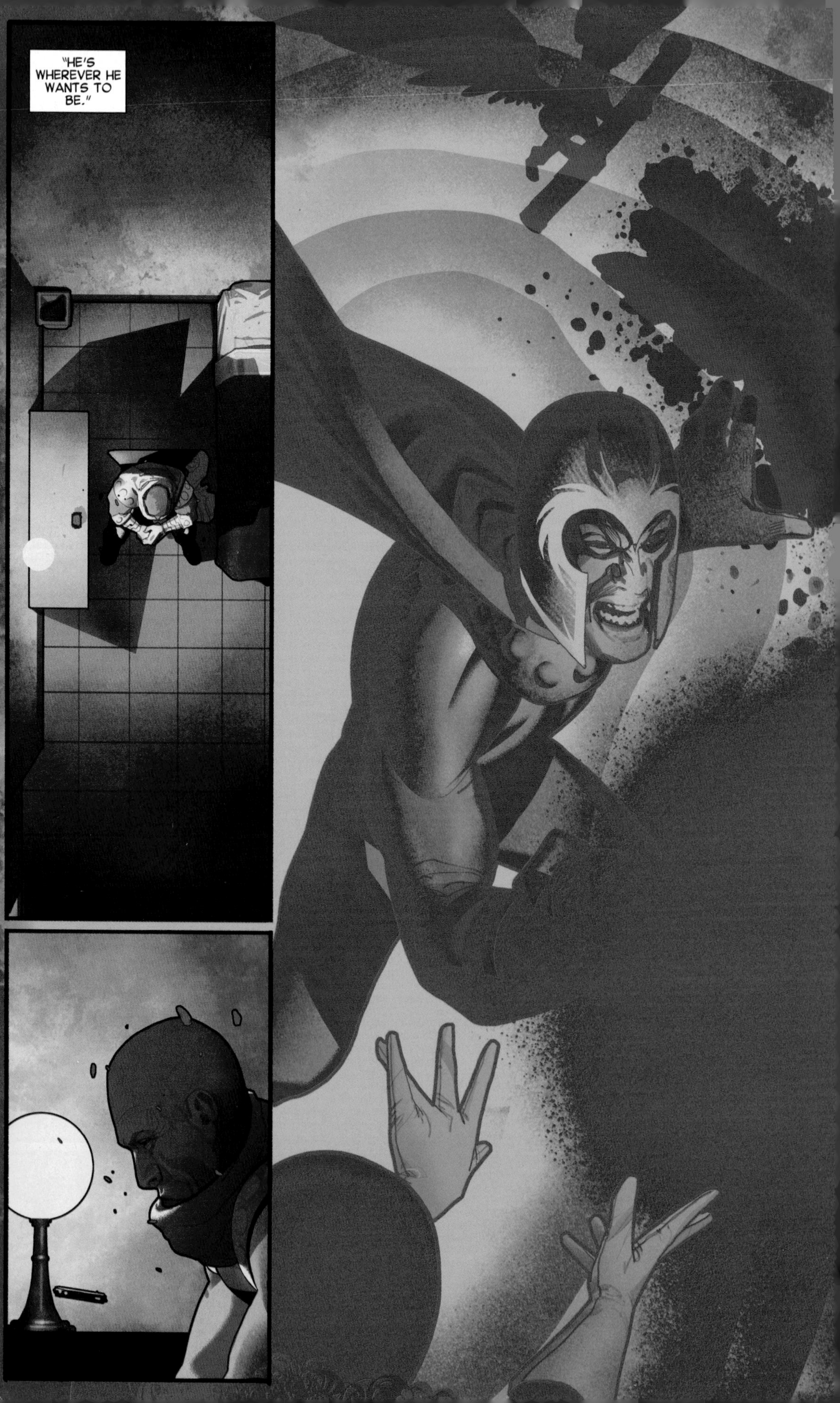
"HE'S WHEREVER HE WANTS TO BE."

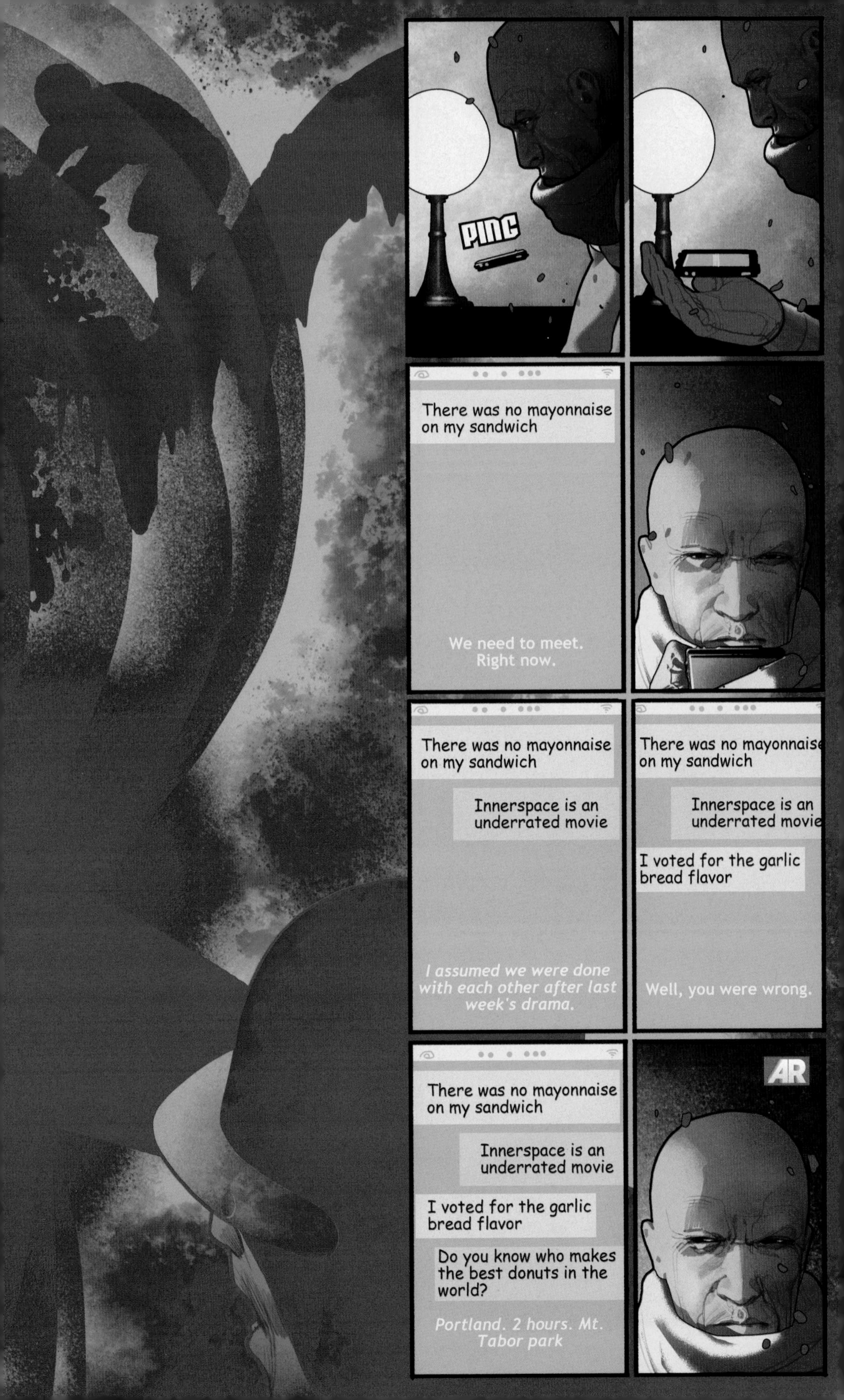

PING
There was no mayonnaise on my sandwich
We need to meet. Right now.
There was no mayonnaise on my sandwich
Innerspace is an underrated movie
I assumed we were done with each other after last week's drama.
There was no mayonnaise on my sandwich
Innerspace is an underrated movie
I voted for the garlic bread flavor
Well, you were wrong.
There was no mayonnaise on my sandwich
Innerspace is an underrated movie
I voted for the garlic bread flavor
Do you know who makes the best donuts in the world?
Portland. 2 hours. Mt. Tabor park

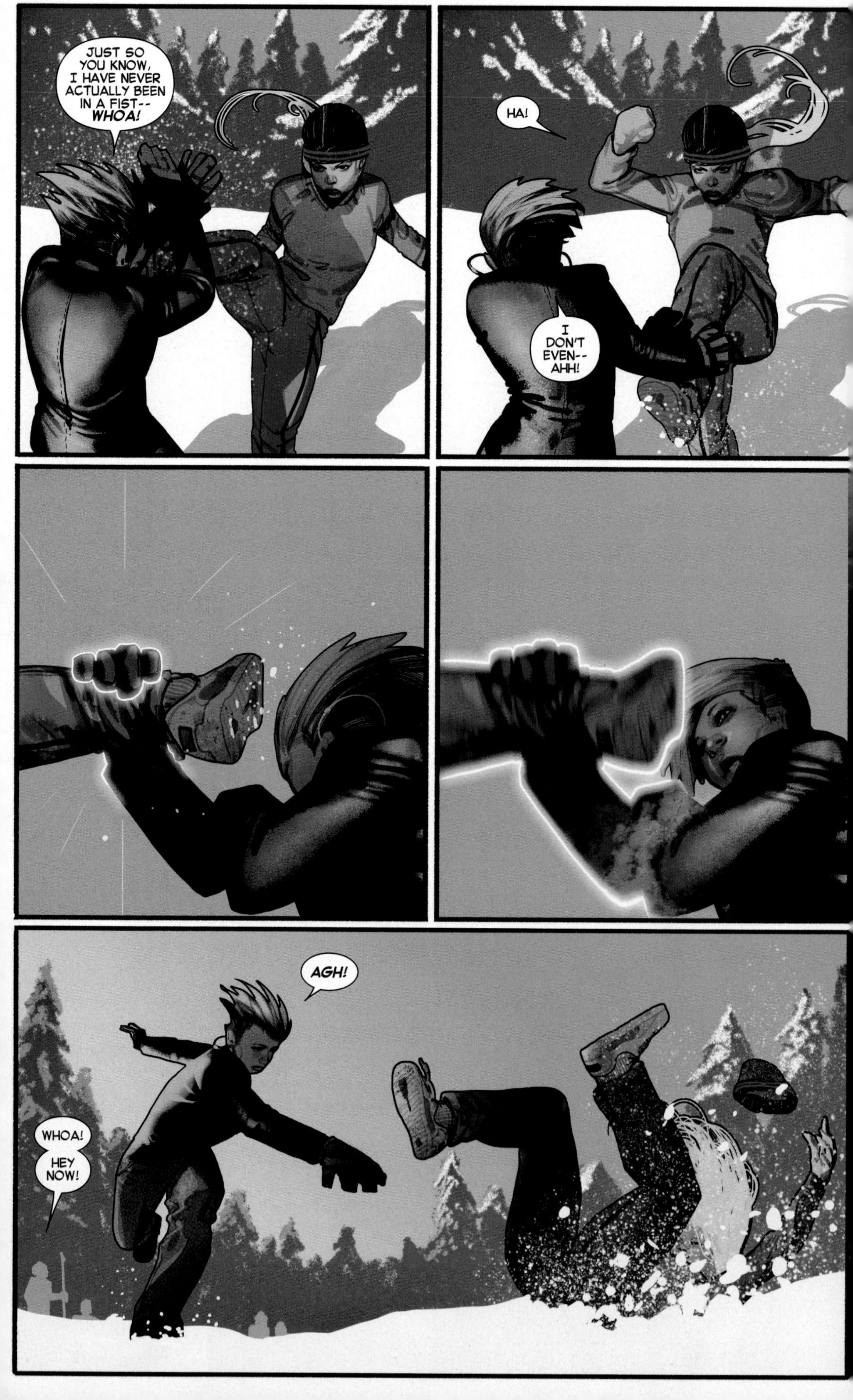
JUST SO YOU KNOW, I HAVE NEVER ACTUALLY BEEN IN A FIST-- WHOA!
HA!
I DON'T EVEN-- AHH!
AGH!
WHOA!
HEY NOW!

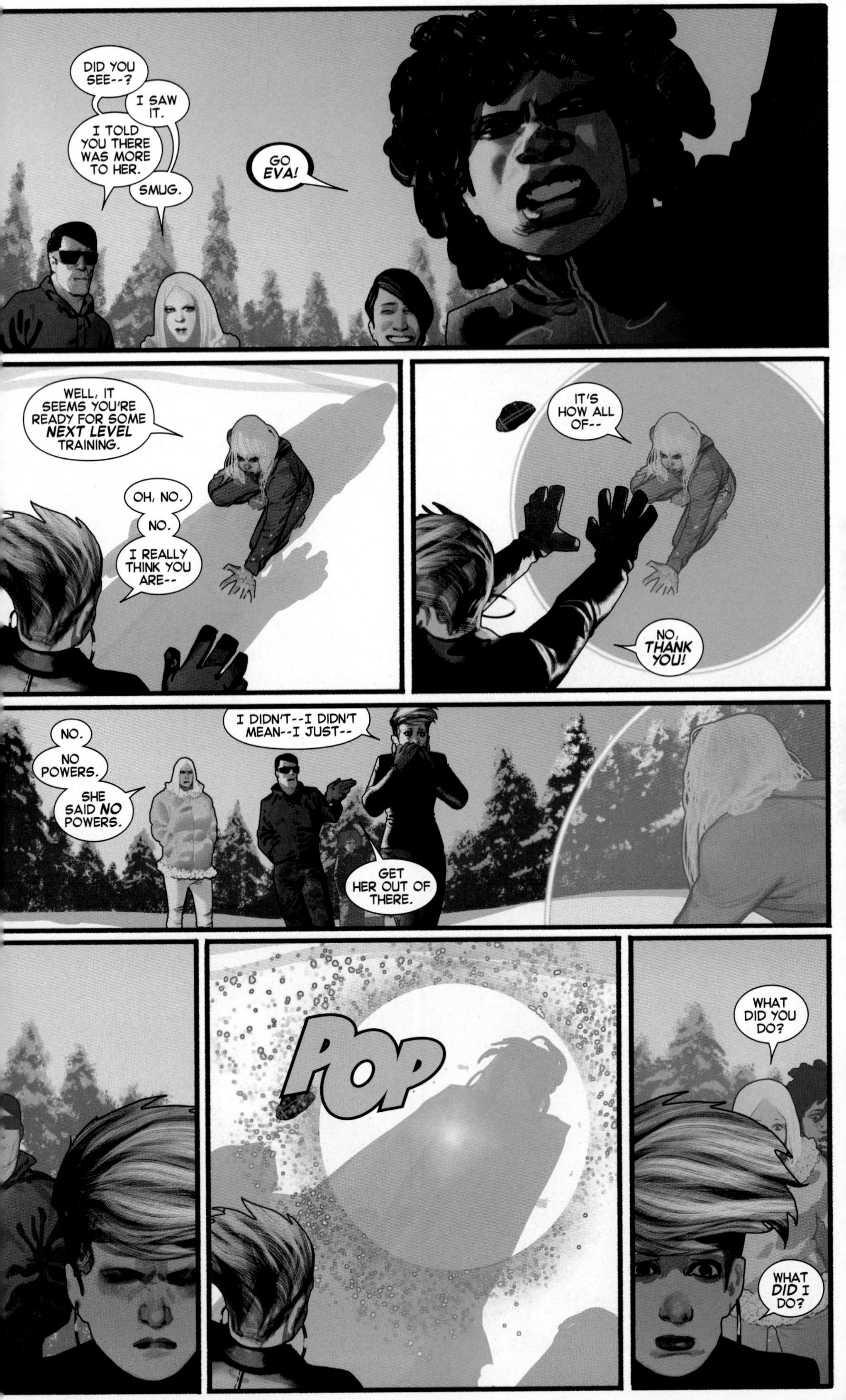
DID YOU SEE--?
I SAW IT.
I TOLD YOU THERE WAS MORE TO HER.
SMUG.
GO EVA!
WELL, IT SEEMS YOU'RE READY FOR SOME NEXT LEVEL TRAINING.
OH, NO.
NO.
I REALLY THINK YOU ARE--
IT'S HOW ALL OF--
NO, THANK YOU!
NO.
NO POWERS.
SHE SAID NO POWERS.
I DIDN'T--I DIDN'T MEAN--I JUST--
GET HER OUT OF THERE.
POP
WHAT DID YOU DO?
WHAT DID I DO?

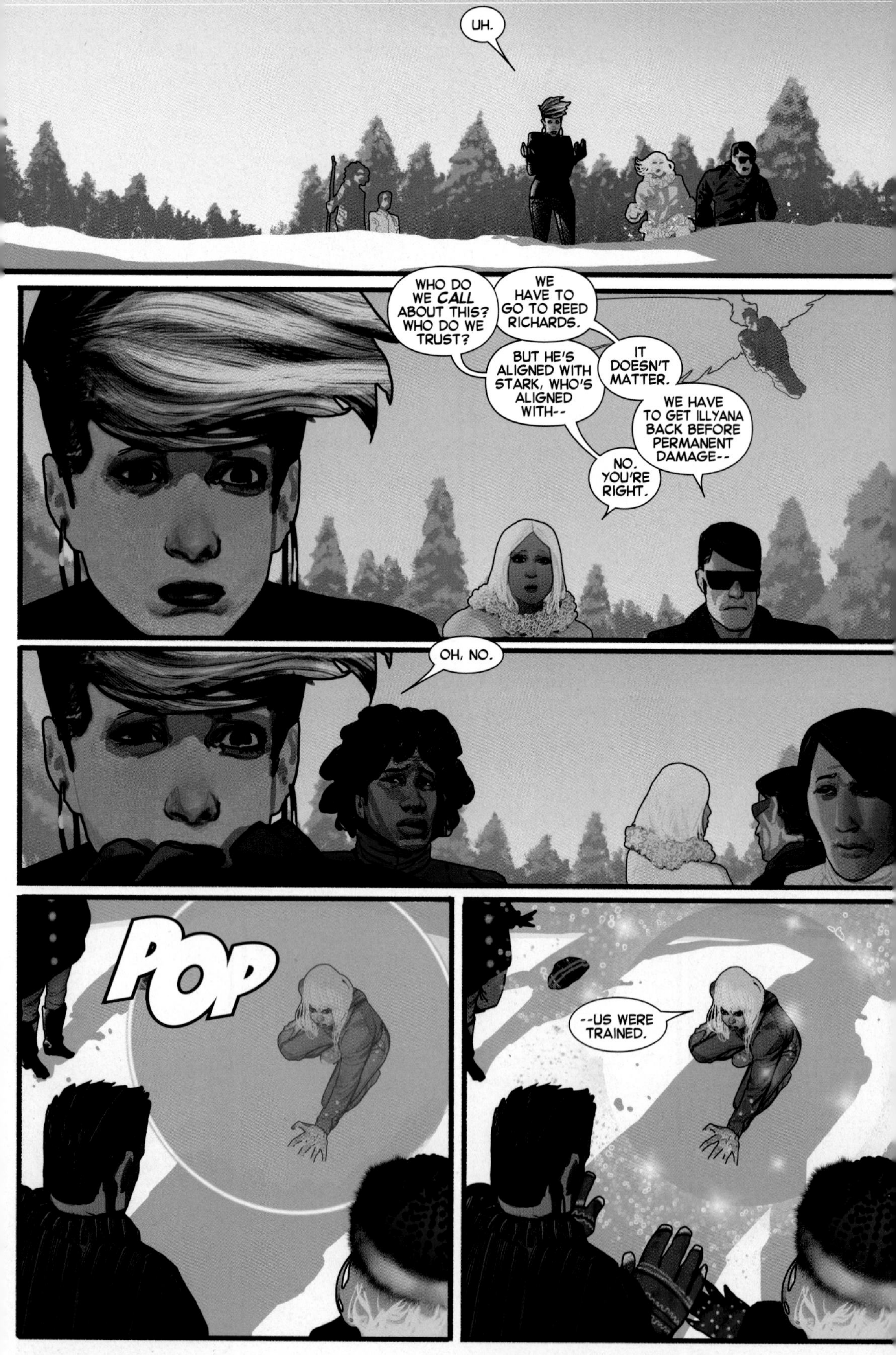
UH.
WHO DO WE CALL ABOUT THIS? WHO DO WE TRUST?
WE HAVE TO GO TO REED RICHARDS.
BUT HE'S ALIGNED WITH STARK, WHO'S ALIGNED WITH--
IT DOESN'T MATTER.
WE HAVE TO GET ILLYANA BACK BEFORE PERMANENT DAMAGE--
NO. YOU'RE RIGHT.
OH, NO.
POP
--US WERE TRAINED.

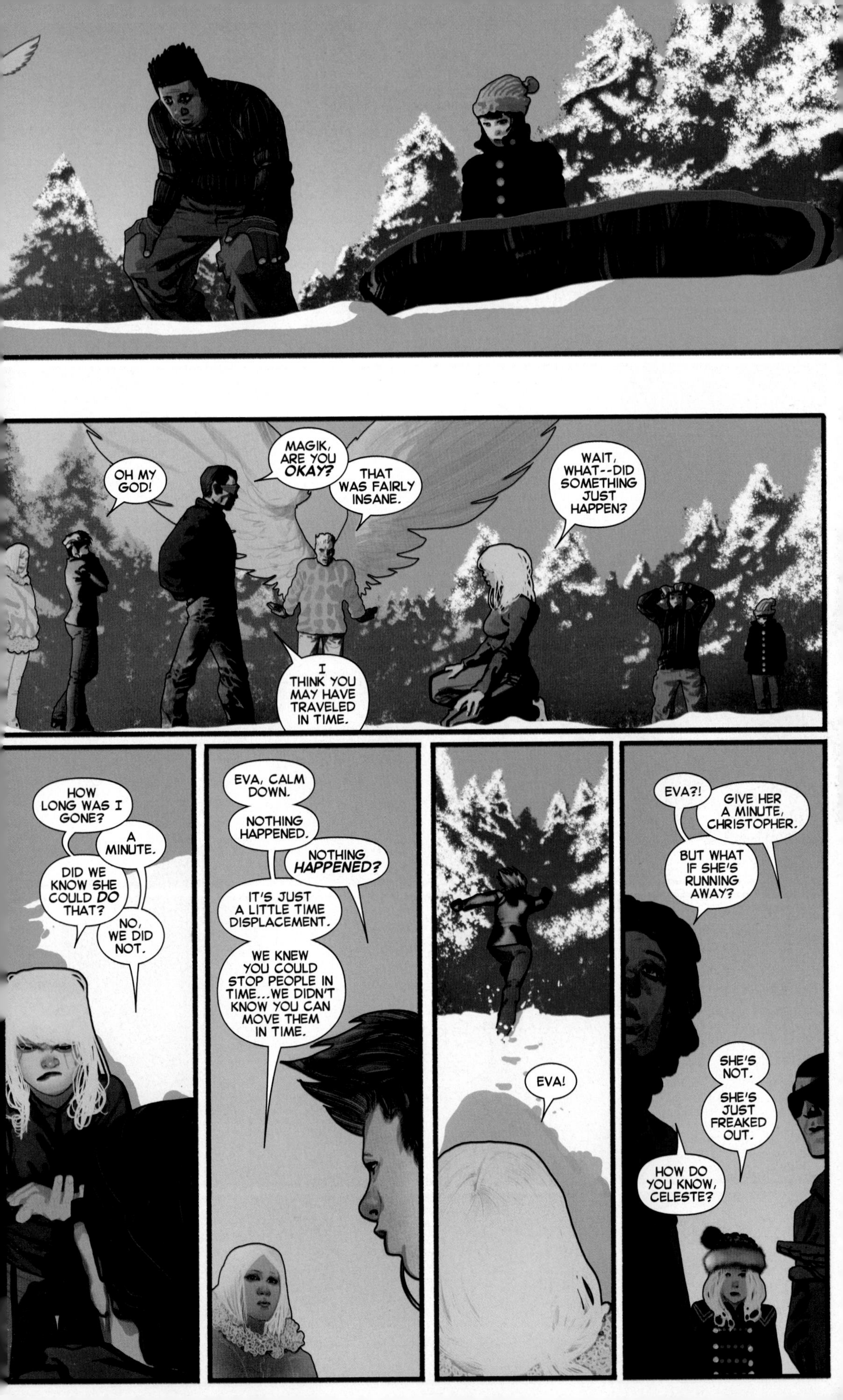
OH MY GOD!
MAGIK, ARE YOU OKAY?
THAT WAS FAIRLY INSANE.
WAIT, WHAT--DID SOMETHING JUST HAPPEN?
I THINK YOU MAY HAVE TRAVELED IN TIME.
HOW LONG WAS I GONE?
A MINUTE.
DID WE KNOW SHE COULD DO THAT?
NO, WE DID NOT.
EVA, CALM DOWN.
NOTHING HAPPENED.
NOTHING HAPPENED?
IT'S JUST A LITTLE TIME DISPLACEMENT.
WE KNEW YOU COULD STOP PEOPLE IN TIME...WE DIDN'T KNOW YOU CAN MOVE THEM IN TIME.
EVA!
EVA?!
GIVE HER A MINUTE, CHRISTOPHER.
BUT WHAT IF SHE'S RUNNING AWAY?
SHE'S NOT.
SHE'S JUST FREAKED OUT.
HOW DO YOU KNOW, CELESTE?

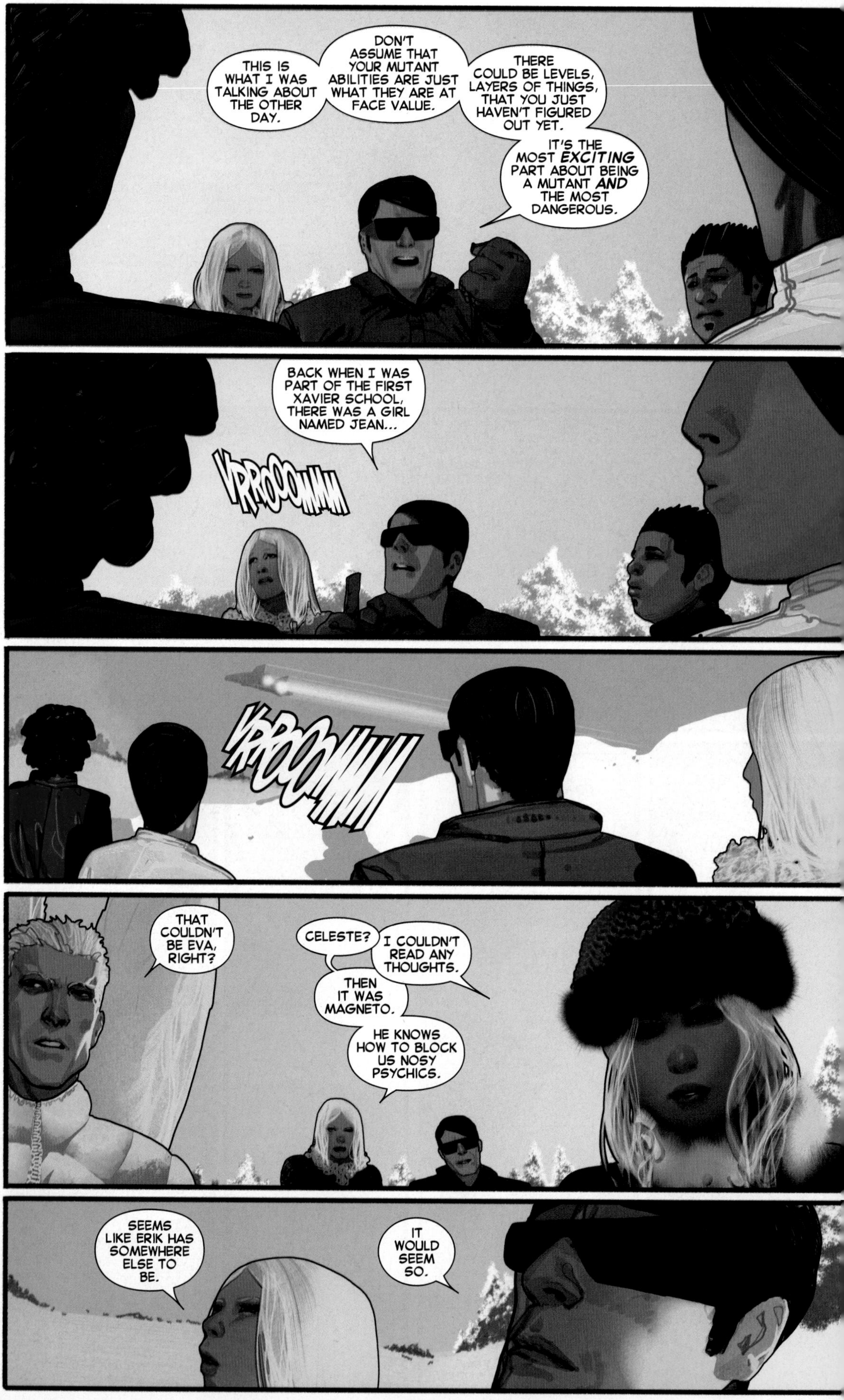
THIS IS WHAT I WAS TALKING ABOUT THE OTHER DAY.
DON'T ASSUME THAT YOUR MUTANT ABILITIES ARE JUST WHAT THEY ARE AT FACE VALUE.
THERE COULD BE LEVELS, LAYERS OF THINGS, THAT YOU JUST HAVEN'T FIGURED OUT YET.
IT'S THE MOST EXCITING PART ABOUT BEING A MUTANT AND THE MOST DANGEROUS.
BACK WHEN I WAS PART OF THE FIRST XAVIER SCHOOL, THERE WAS A GIRL NAMED JEAN...
VRROOOMMM
VRROOOMMM
THAT COULDN'T BE EVA, RIGHT?
CELESTE?
I COULDN'T READ ANY THOUGHTS.
THEN IT WAS MAGNETO.
HE KNOWS HOW TO BLOCK US NOSY PSYCHICS.
SEEMS LIKE ERIK HAS SOMEWHERE ELSE TO BE.
IT WOULD SEEM SO.

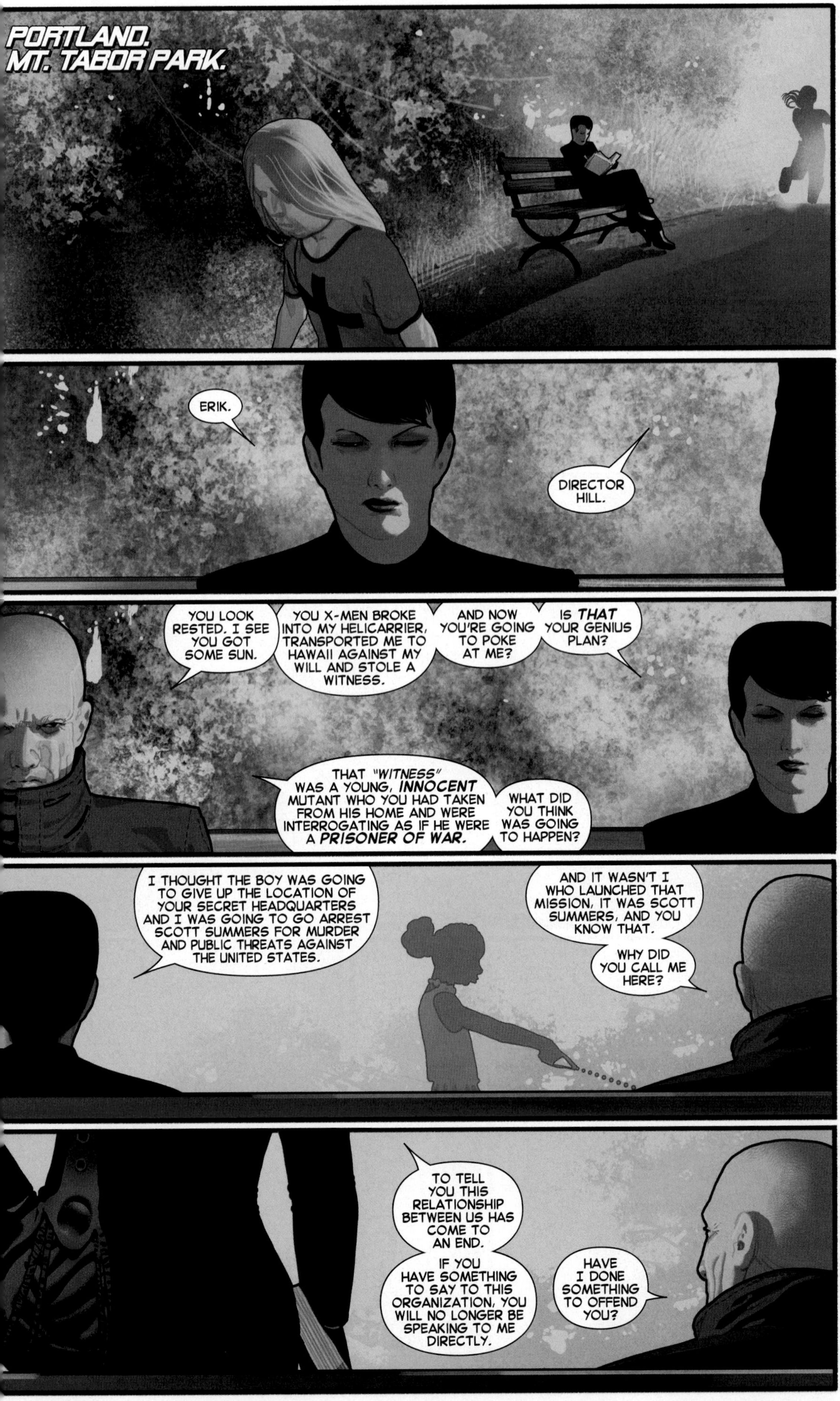
PORTLAND.
MT. TABOR PARK.
ERIK.
DIRECTOR HILL.
YOU LOOK RESTED. I SEE YOU GOT SOME SUN.
YOU X-MEN BROKE INTO MY HELICARRIER, TRANSPORTED ME TO HAWAII AGAINST MY WILL AND STOLE A WITNESS.
AND NOW YOU'RE GOING TO POKE AT ME?
IS THAT YOUR GENIUS PLAN?
THAT "WITNESS" WAS A YOUNG, INNOCENT MUTANT WHO YOU HAD TAKEN FROM HIS HOME AND WERE INTERROGATING AS IF HE WERE A PRISONER OF WAR.
WHAT DID YOU THINK WAS GOING TO HAPPEN?
I THOUGHT THE BOY WAS GOING TO GIVE UP THE LOCATION OF YOUR SECRET HEADQUARTERS AND I WAS GOING TO GO ARREST SCOTT SUMMERS FOR MURDER AND PUBLIC THREATS AGAINST THE UNITED STATES.
AND IT WASN'T I WHO LAUNCHED THAT MISSION, IT WAS SCOTT SUMMERS, AND YOU KNOW THAT.
WHY DID YOU CALL ME HERE?
TO TELL YOU THIS RELATIONSHIP BETWEEN US HAS COME TO AN END.
IF YOU HAVE SOMETHING TO SAY TO THIS ORGANIZATION, YOU WILL NO LONGER BE SPEAKING TO ME DIRECTLY.
HAVE I DONE SOMETHING TO OFFEND YOU?

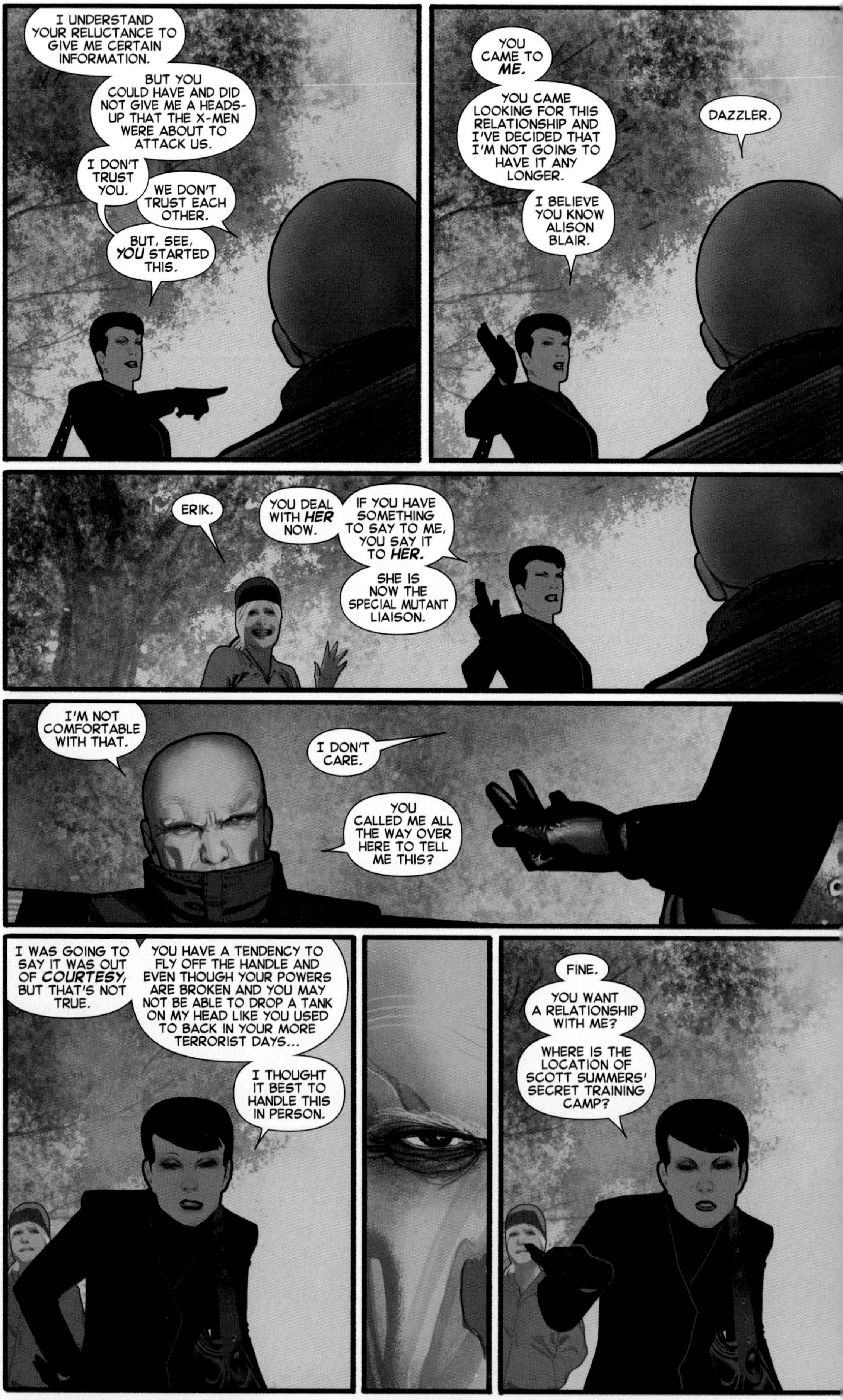
I UNDERSTAND YOUR RELUCTANCE TO GIVE ME CERTAIN INFORMATION.
BUT YOU COULD HAVE AND DID NOT GIVE ME A HEADS-UP THAT THE X-MEN WERE ABOUT TO ATTACK US.
I DON'T TRUST YOU.
WE DON'T TRUST EACH OTHER.
BUT, SEE, *YOU* STARTED THIS.
YOU CAME TO *ME.*
YOU CAME LOOKING FOR THIS RELATIONSHIP AND I'VE DECIDED THAT I'M NOT GOING TO HAVE IT ANY LONGER.
I BELIEVE YOU KNOW ALISON BLAIR.
DAZZLER.
ERIK.
YOU DEAL WITH *HER* NOW.
IF YOU HAVE SOMETHING TO SAY TO ME, YOU SAY IT TO *HER.*
SHE IS NOW THE SPECIAL MUTANT LIAISON.
I'M NOT COMFORTABLE WITH THAT.
I DON'T CARE.
YOU CALLED ME ALL THE WAY OVER HERE TO TELL ME THIS?
I WAS GOING TO SAY IT WAS OUT OF *COURTESY,* BUT THAT'S NOT TRUE.
YOU HAVE A TENDENCY TO FLY OFF THE HANDLE AND EVEN THOUGH YOUR POWERS ARE BROKEN AND YOU MAY NOT BE ABLE TO DROP A TANK ON MY HEAD LIKE YOU USED TO BACK IN YOUR MORE TERRORIST DAYS...
I THOUGHT IT BEST TO HANDLE THIS IN PERSON.
FINE.
YOU WANT A RELATIONSHIP WITH ME?
WHERE IS THE LOCATION OF SCOTT SUMMERS' SECRET TRAINING CAMP?

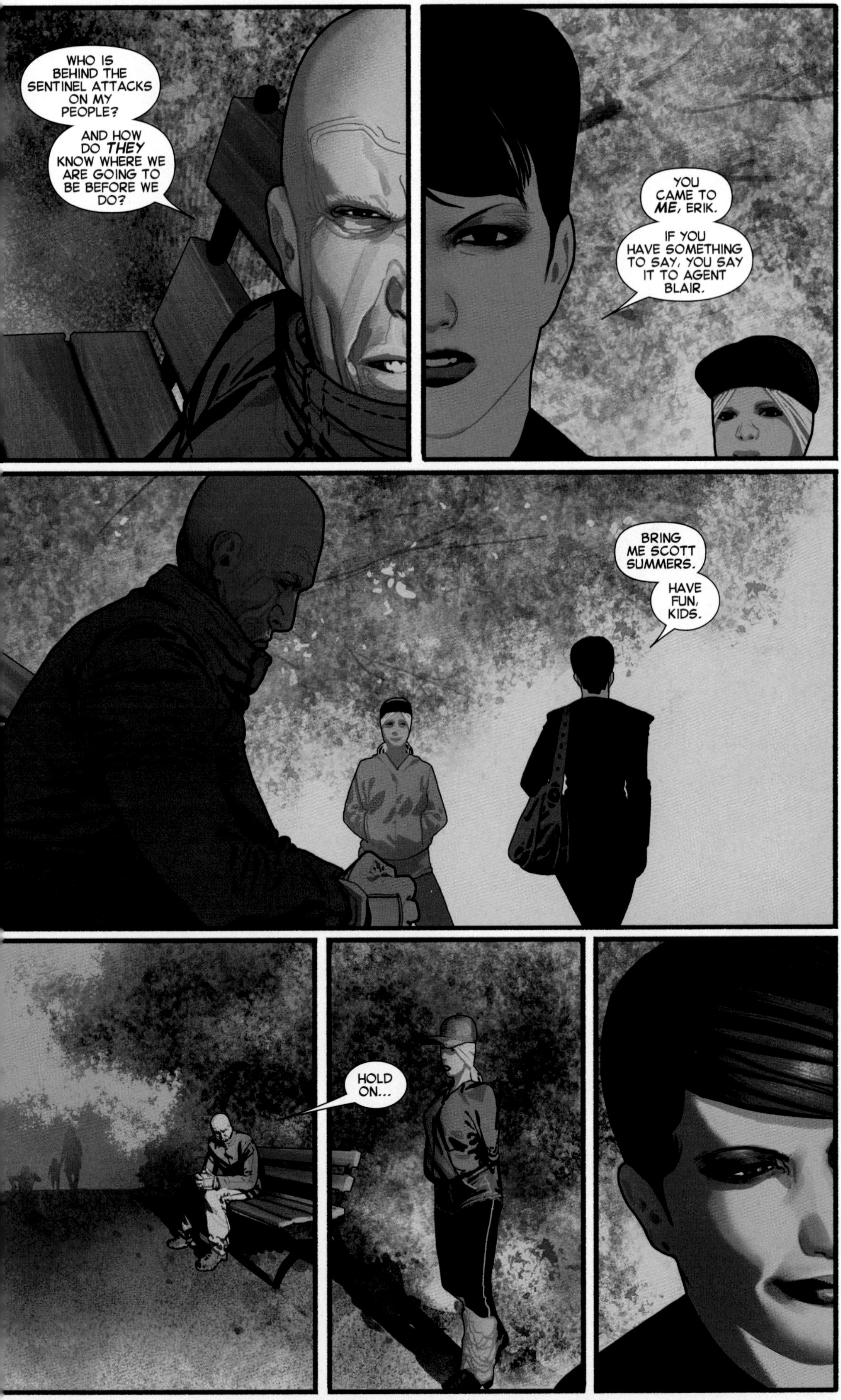
WHO IS BEHIND THE SENTINEL ATTACKS ON MY PEOPLE?
AND HOW DO THEY KNOW WHERE WE ARE GOING TO BE BEFORE WE DO?
YOU CAME TO ME, ERIK.
IF YOU HAVE SOMETHING TO SAY, YOU SAY IT TO AGENT BLAIR.
BRING ME SCOTT SUMMERS.
HAVE FUN, KIDS.
HOLD ON...

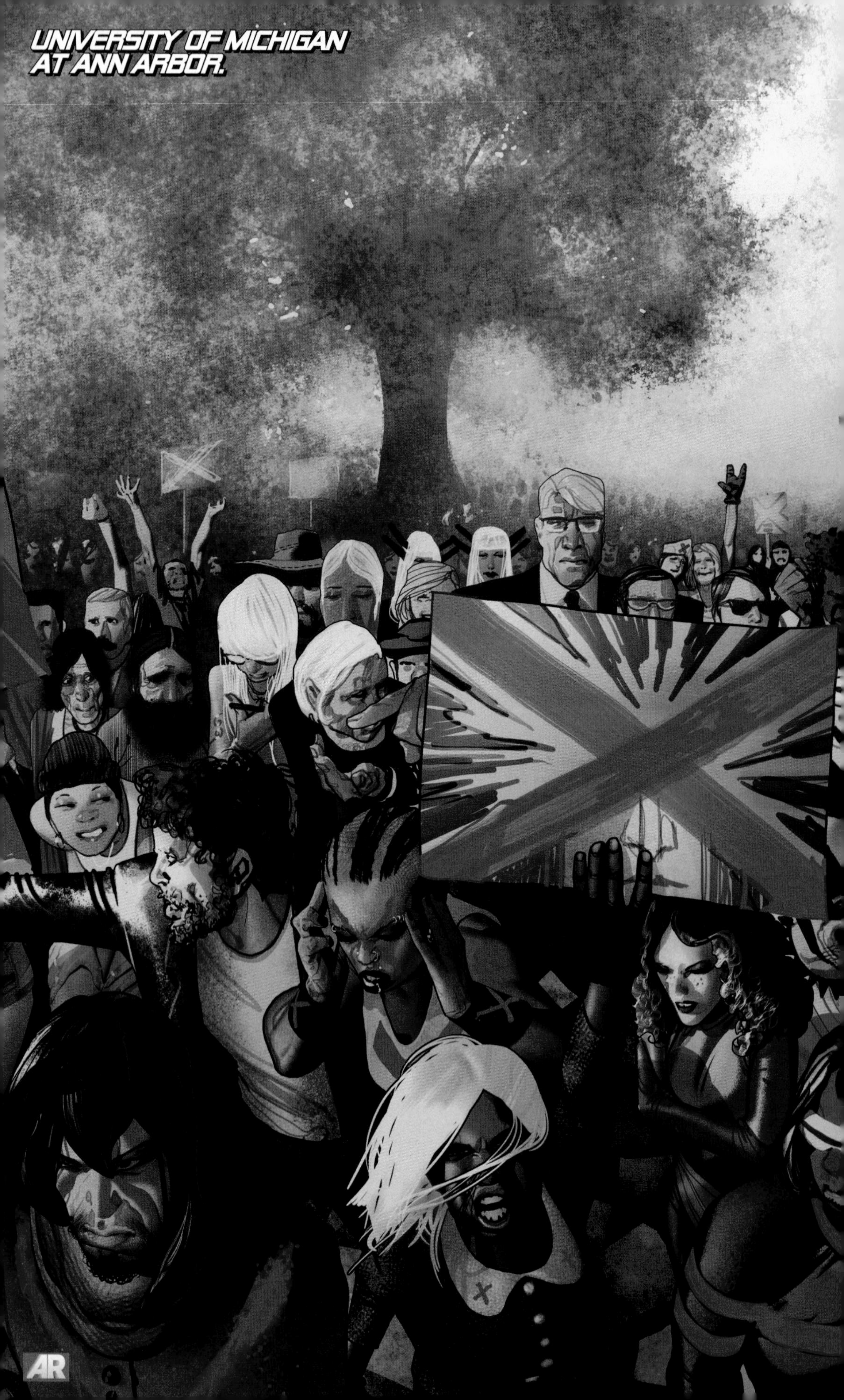
UNIVERSITY OF MICHIGAN
AT ANN ARBOR.

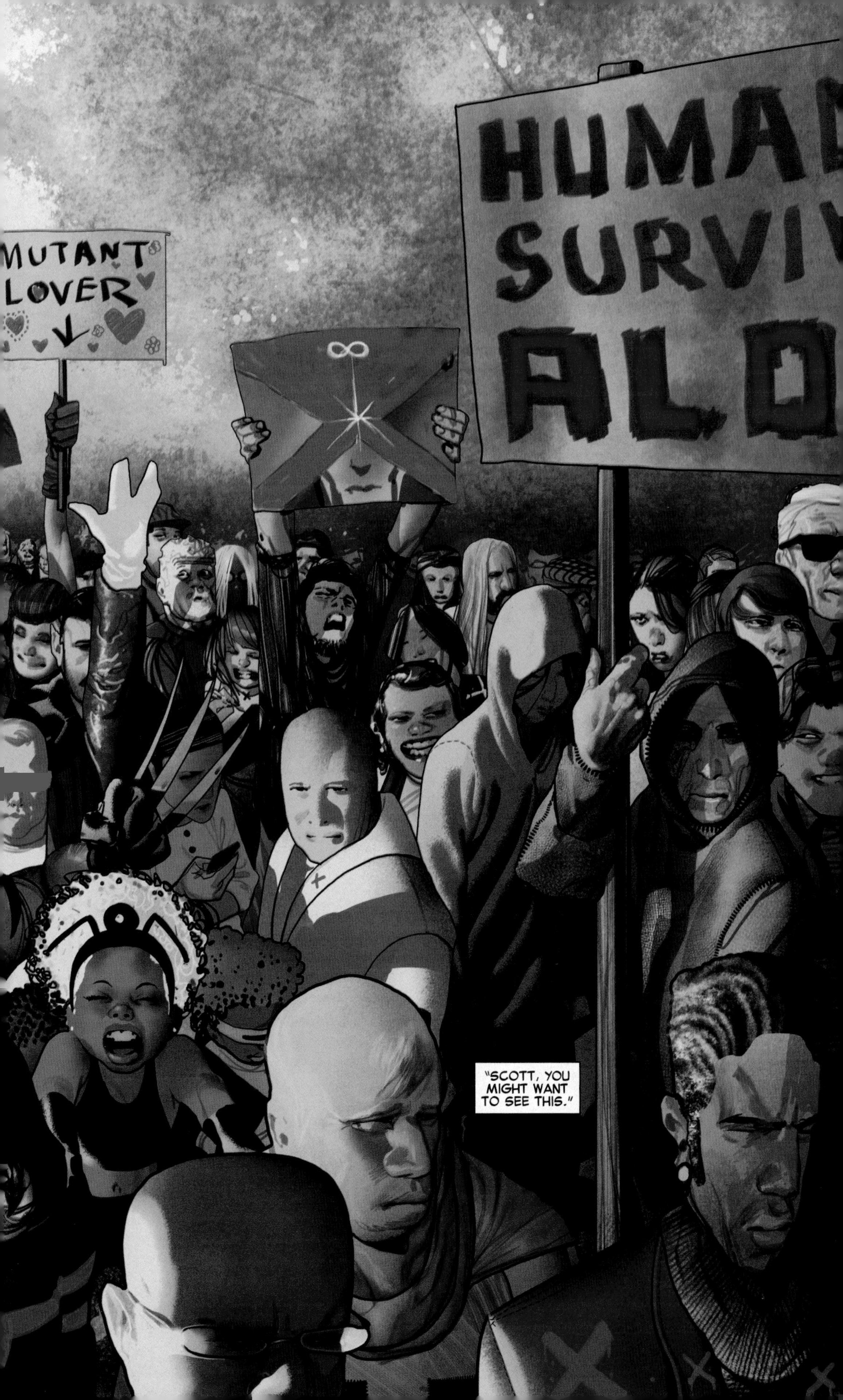

MUTANT LOVER
HUMA
SURVIV
ALO
"SCOTT, YOU MIGHT WANT TO SEE THIS."

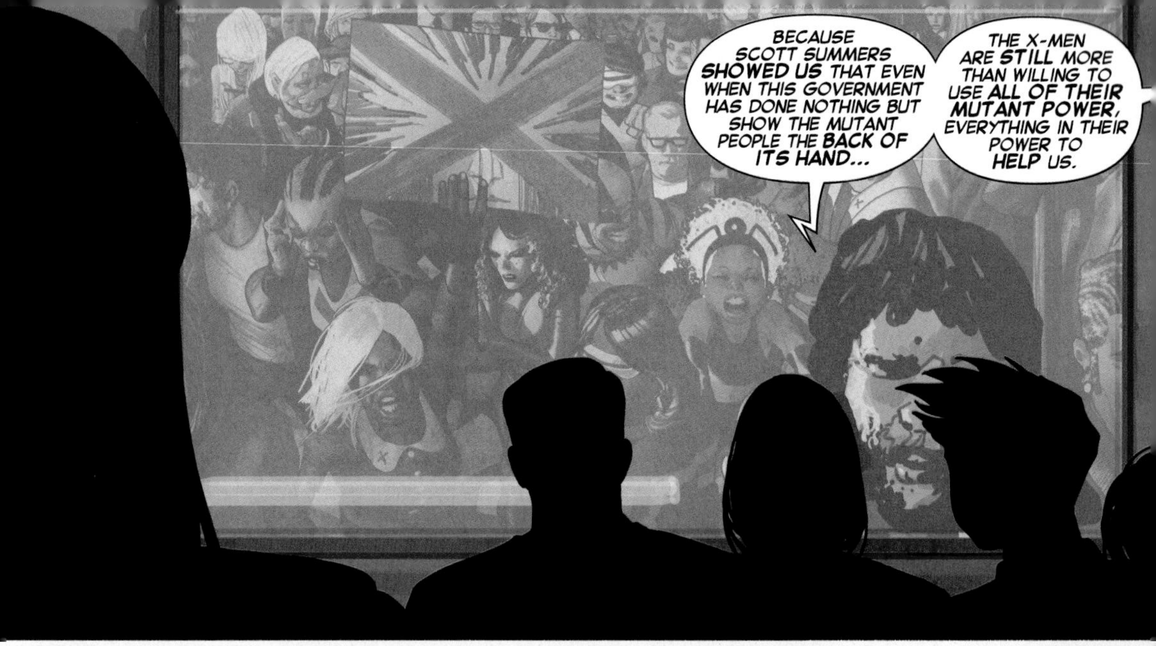
BECAUSE SCOTT SUMMERS SHOWED US THAT EVEN WHEN THIS GOVERNMENT HAS DONE NOTHING BUT SHOW THE MUTANT PEOPLE THE BACK OF ITS HAND...
THE X-MEN ARE STILL MORE THAN WILLING TO USE ALL OF THEIR MUTANT POWER, EVERYTHING IN THEIR POWER TO HELP US.

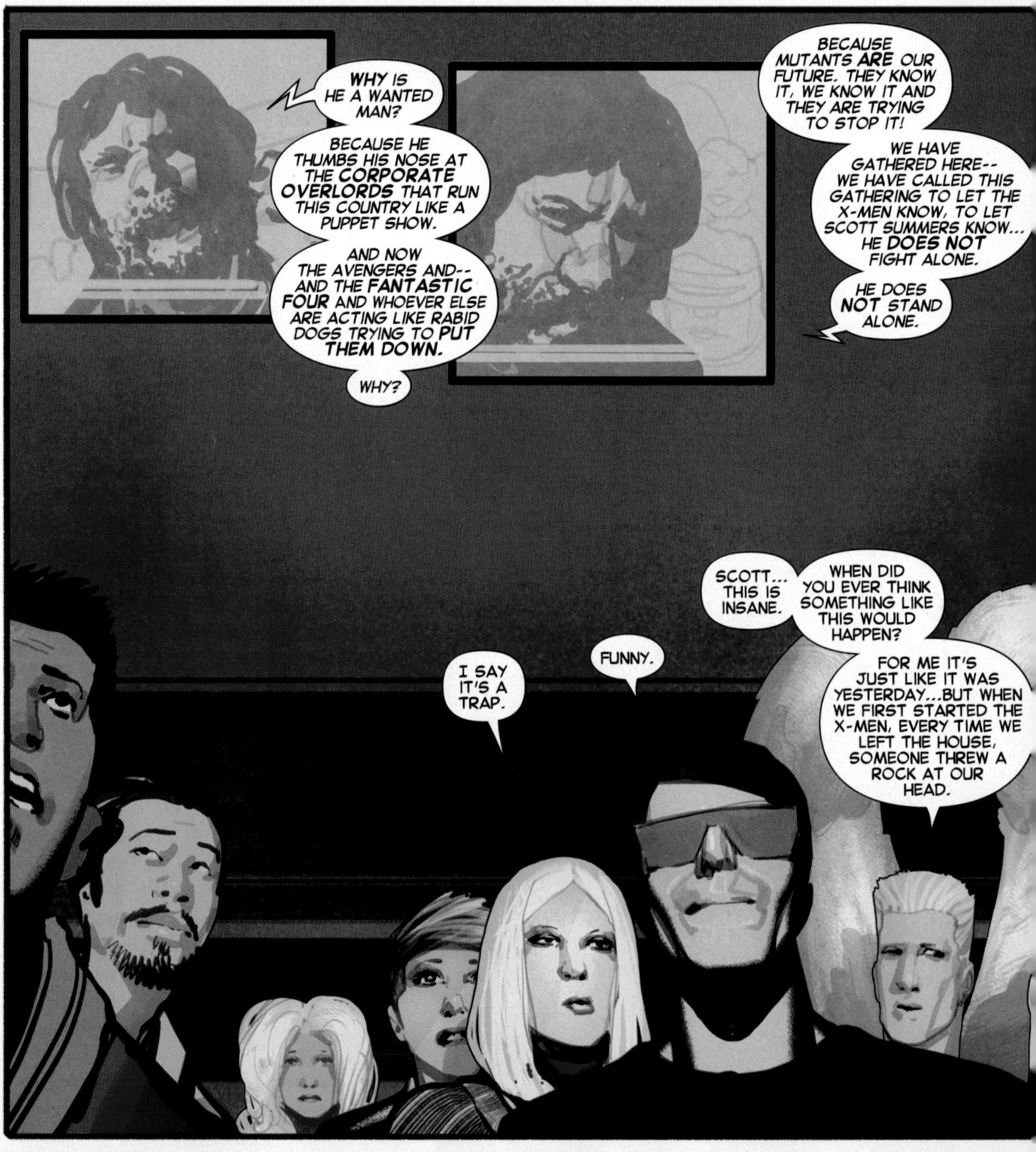
WHY IS HE A WANTED MAN?
BECAUSE HE THUMBS HIS NOSE AT THE CORPORATE OVERLORDS THAT RUN THIS COUNTRY LIKE A PUPPET SHOW.
AND NOW THE AVENGERS AND-- AND THE FANTASTIC FOUR AND WHOEVER ELSE ARE ACTING LIKE RABID DOGS TRYING TO PUT THEM DOWN.
WHY?
BECAUSE MUTANTS ARE OUR FUTURE. THEY KNOW IT, WE KNOW IT AND THEY ARE TRYING TO STOP IT!
WE HAVE GATHERED HERE-- WE HAVE CALLED THIS GATHERING TO LET THE X-MEN KNOW, TO LET SCOTT SUMMERS KNOW... HE DOES NOT FIGHT ALONE.
HE DOES NOT STAND ALONE.
I SAY IT'S A TRAP.
FUNNY.
SCOTT... THIS IS INSANE.
WHEN DID YOU EVER THINK SOMETHING LIKE THIS WOULD HAPPEN?
FOR ME IT'S JUST LIKE IT WAS YESTERDAY...BUT WHEN WE FIRST STARTED THE X-MEN, EVERY TIME WE LEFT THE HOUSE, SOMEONE THREW A ROCK AT OUR HEAD.

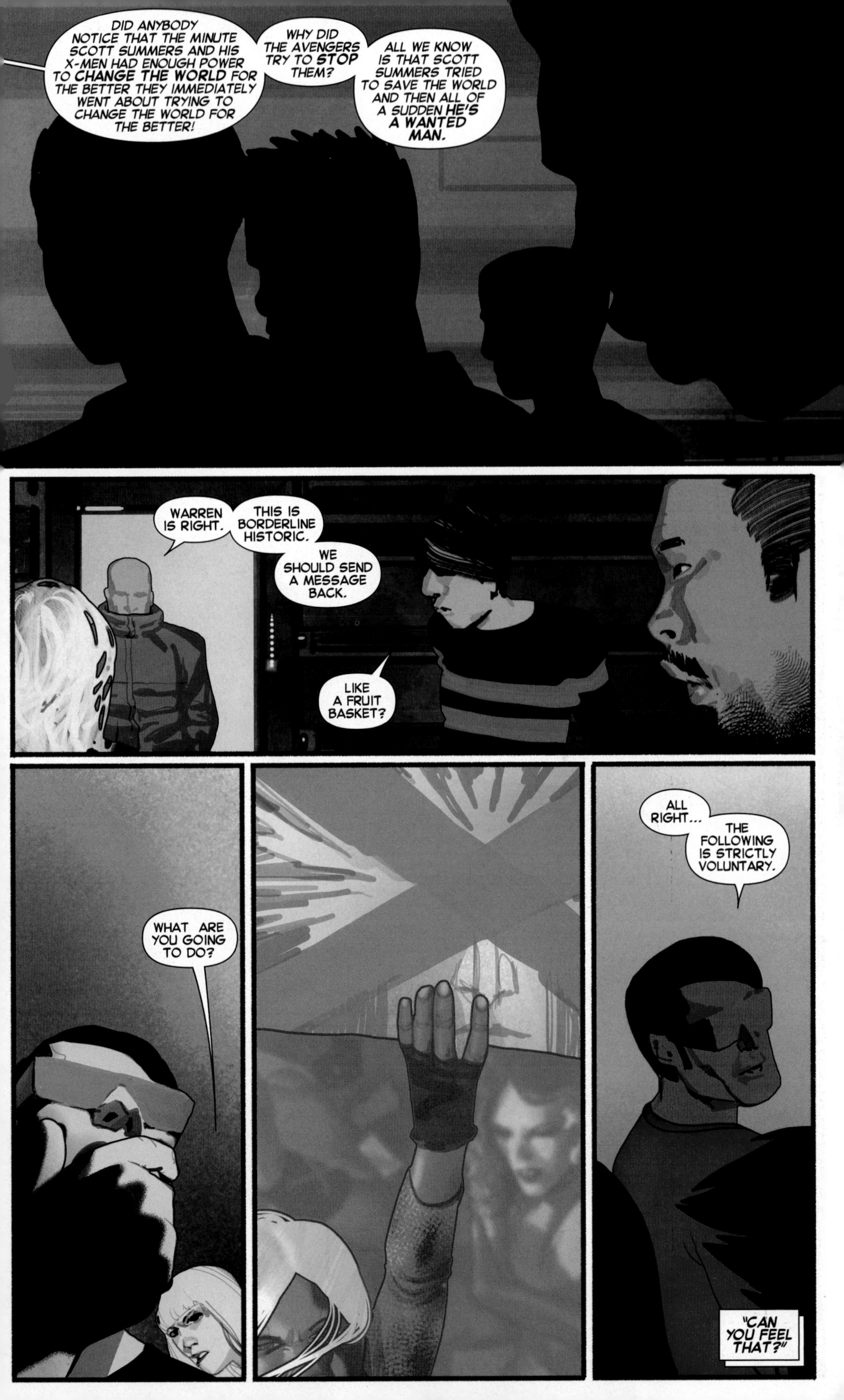
DID ANYBODY NOTICE THAT THE MINUTE SCOTT SUMMERS AND HIS X-MEN HAD ENOUGH POWER TO CHANGE THE WORLD FOR THE BETTER THEY IMMEDIATELY WENT ABOUT TRYING TO CHANGE THE WORLD FOR THE BETTER!
WHY DID THE AVENGERS TRY TO STOP THEM?
ALL WE KNOW IS THAT SCOTT SUMMERS TRIED TO SAVE THE WORLD AND THEN ALL OF A SUDDEN HE'S A WANTED MAN.
WARREN IS RIGHT.
THIS IS BORDERLINE HISTORIC.
WE SHOULD SEND A MESSAGE BACK.
LIKE A FRUIT BASKET?
WHAT ARE YOU GOING TO DO?
ALL RIGHT...
THE FOLLOWING IS STRICTLY VOLUNTARY.
"CAN YOU FEEL THAT?"

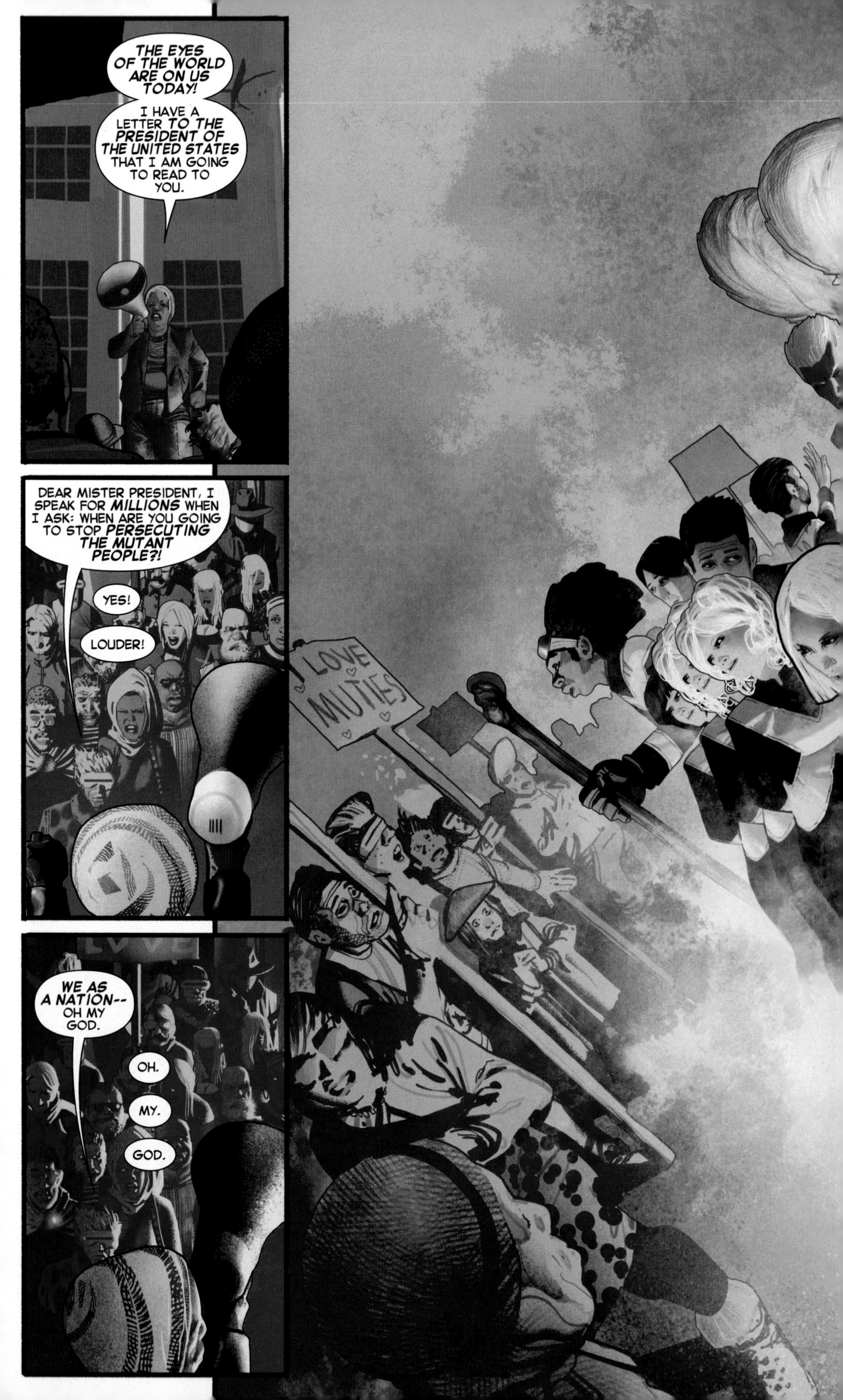
THE EYES OF THE WORLD ARE ON US TODAY!
I HAVE A LETTER TO THE PRESIDENT OF THE UNITED STATES THAT I AM GOING TO READ TO YOU.
DEAR MISTER PRESIDENT, I SPEAK FOR MILLIONS WHEN I ASK: WHEN ARE YOU GOING TO STOP PERSECUTING THE MUTANT PEOPLE?!
YES!
LOUDER!
LOVE MUTIES
WE AS A NATION-- OH MY GOD.
OH.
MY.
GOD.

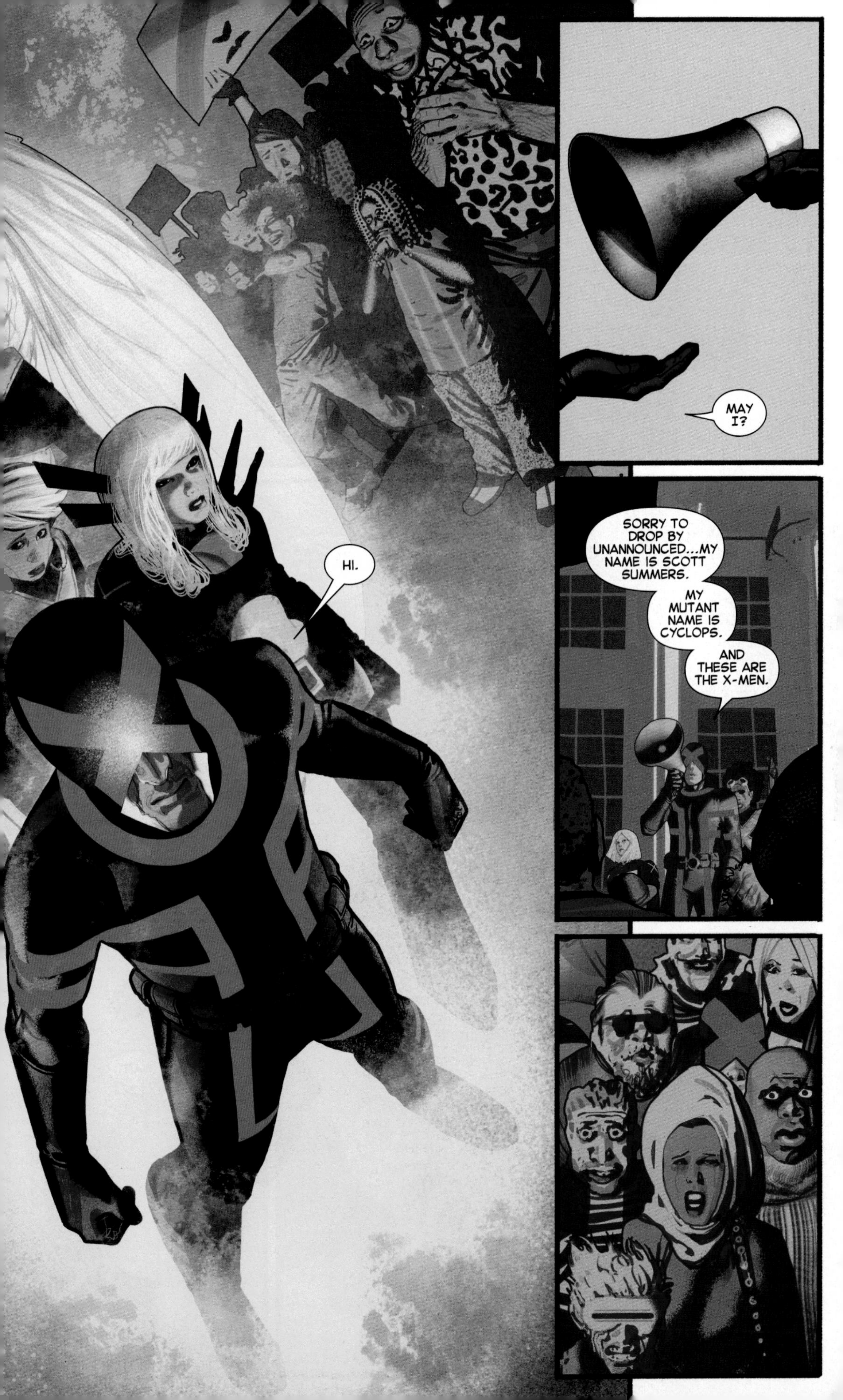
HI.
MAY I?
SORRY TO DROP BY UNANNOUNCED...MY NAME IS SCOTT SUMMERS.
MY MUTANT NAME IS CYCLOPS.
AND THESE ARE THE X-MEN.

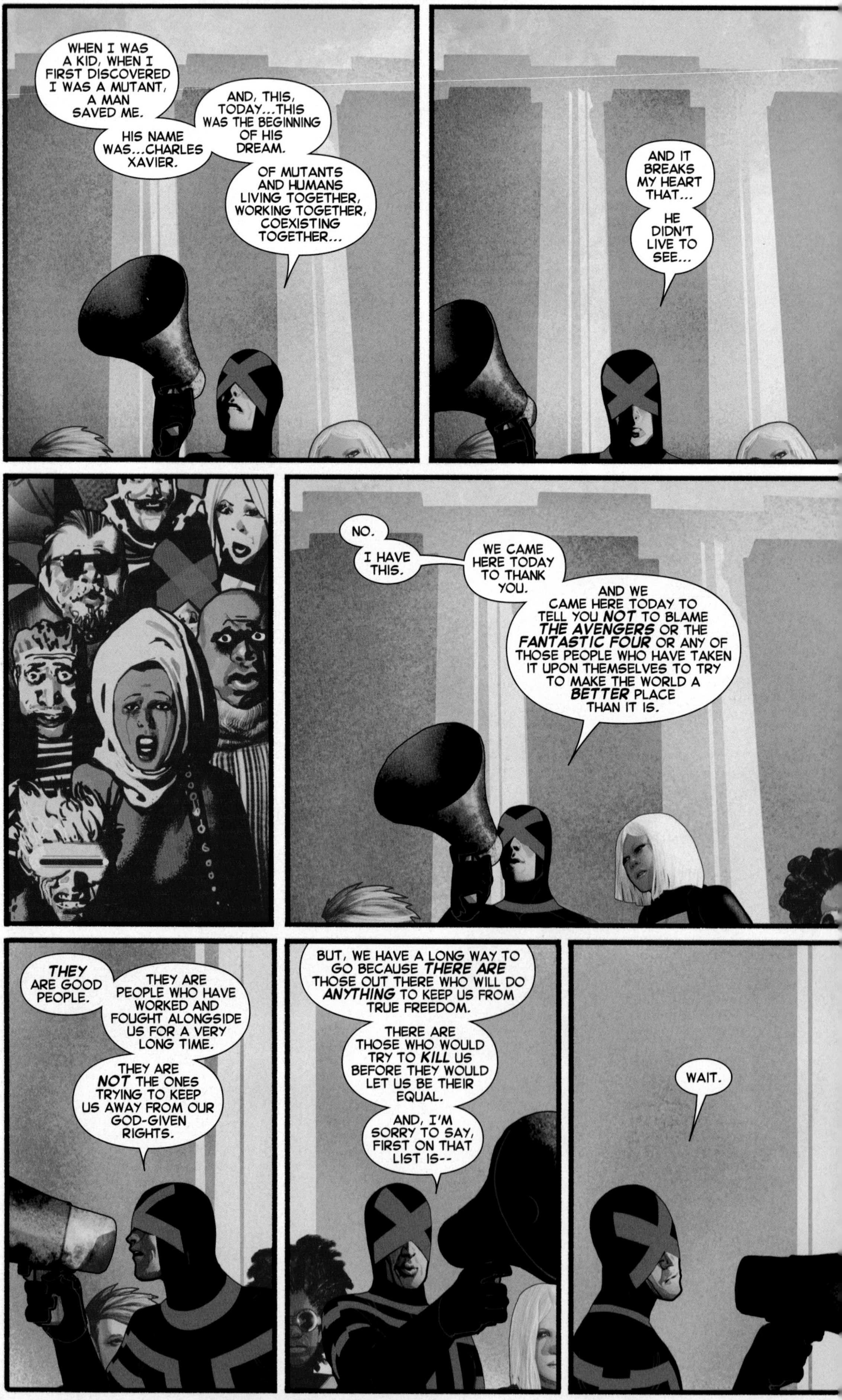

WHEN I WAS A KID, WHEN I FIRST DISCOVERED I WAS A MUTANT, A MAN SAVED ME.
HIS NAME WAS...CHARLES XAVIER.
AND, THIS, TODAY...THIS WAS THE BEGINNING OF HIS DREAM.
OF MUTANTS AND HUMANS LIVING TOGETHER, WORKING TOGETHER, COEXISTING TOGETHER...
AND IT BREAKS MY HEART THAT...
HE DIDN'T LIVE TO SEE...
NO.
I HAVE THIS.
WE CAME HERE TODAY TO THANK YOU.
AND WE CAME HERE TODAY TO TELL YOU *NOT* TO BLAME *THE AVENGERS* OR THE *FANTASTIC FOUR* OR ANY OF THOSE PEOPLE WHO HAVE TAKEN IT UPON THEMSELVES TO TRY TO MAKE THE WORLD A *BETTER* PLACE THAN IT IS.
THEY ARE GOOD PEOPLE.
THEY ARE PEOPLE WHO HAVE WORKED AND FOUGHT ALONGSIDE US FOR A VERY LONG TIME.
THEY ARE *NOT* THE ONES TRYING TO KEEP US AWAY FROM OUR GOD-GIVEN RIGHTS.
BUT, WE HAVE A LONG WAY TO GO BECAUSE *THERE ARE* THOSE OUT THERE WHO WILL DO *ANYTHING* TO KEEP US FROM TRUE FREEDOM.
THERE ARE THOSE WHO WOULD TRY TO *KILL* US BEFORE THEY WOULD LET US BE THEIR EQUAL.
AND, I'M SORRY TO SAY, FIRST ON THAT LIST IS--
WAIT.

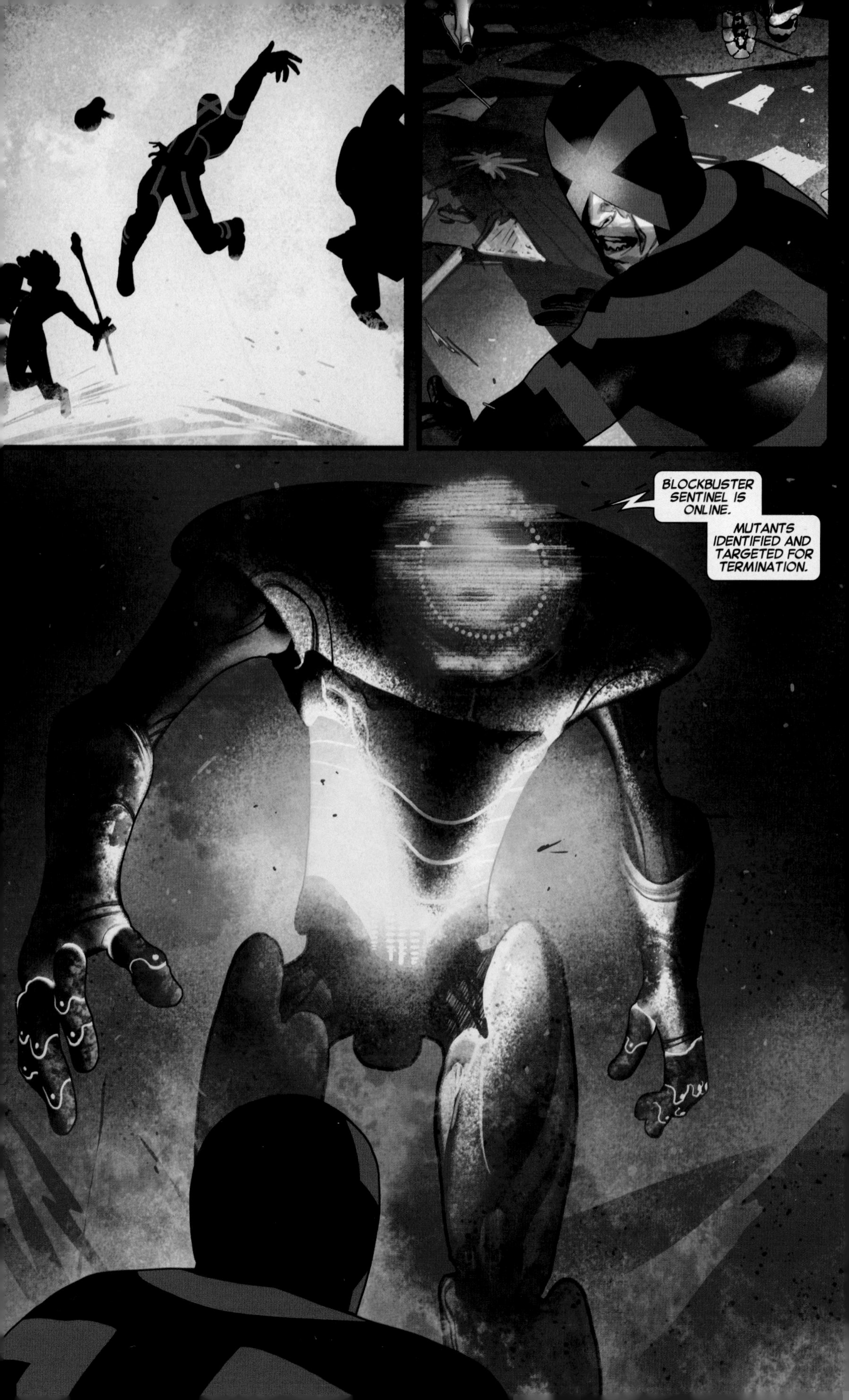
BLOCKBUSTER SENTINEL IS ONLINE.
MUTANTS IDENTIFIED AND TARGETED FOR TERMINATION.

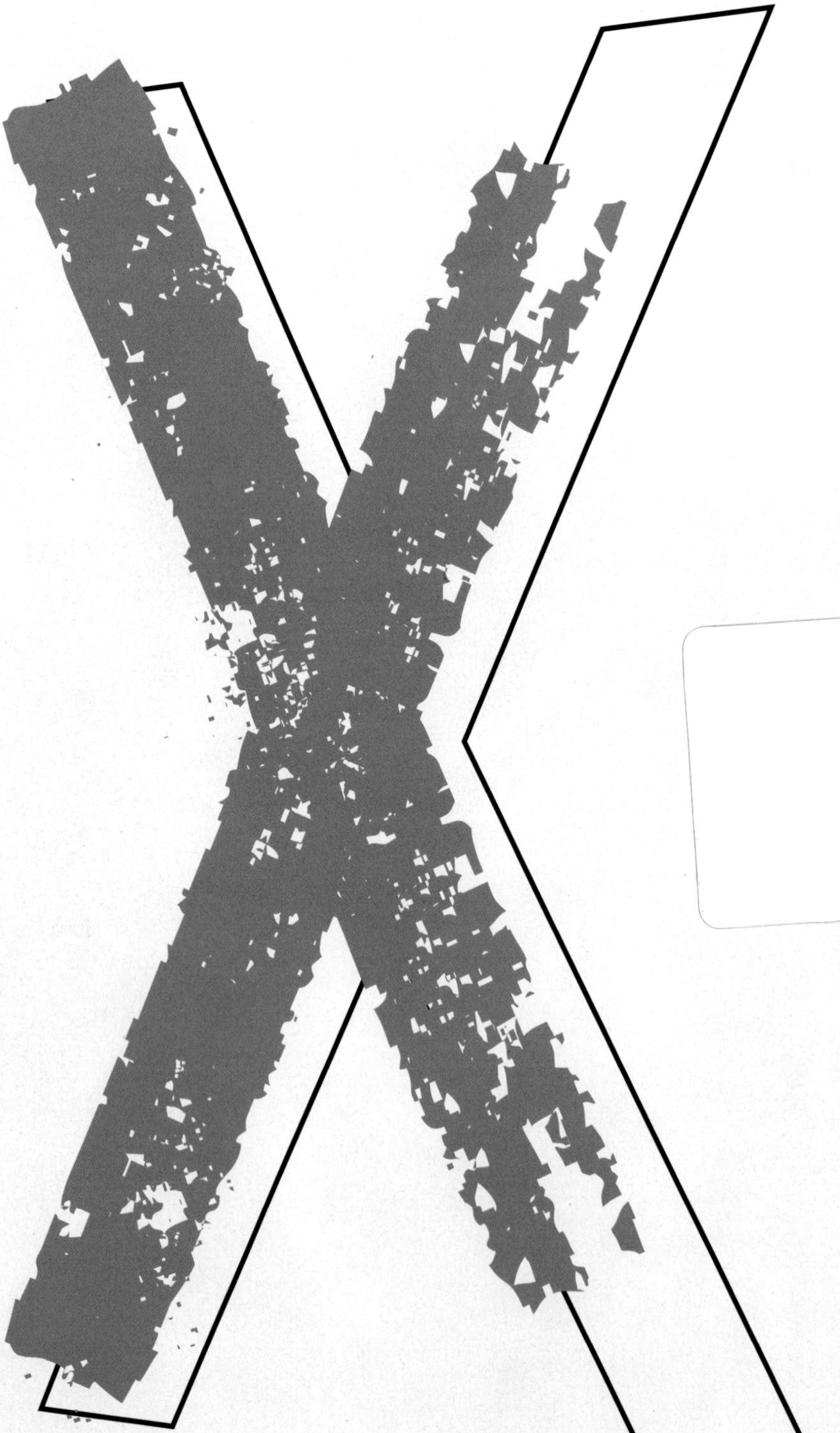

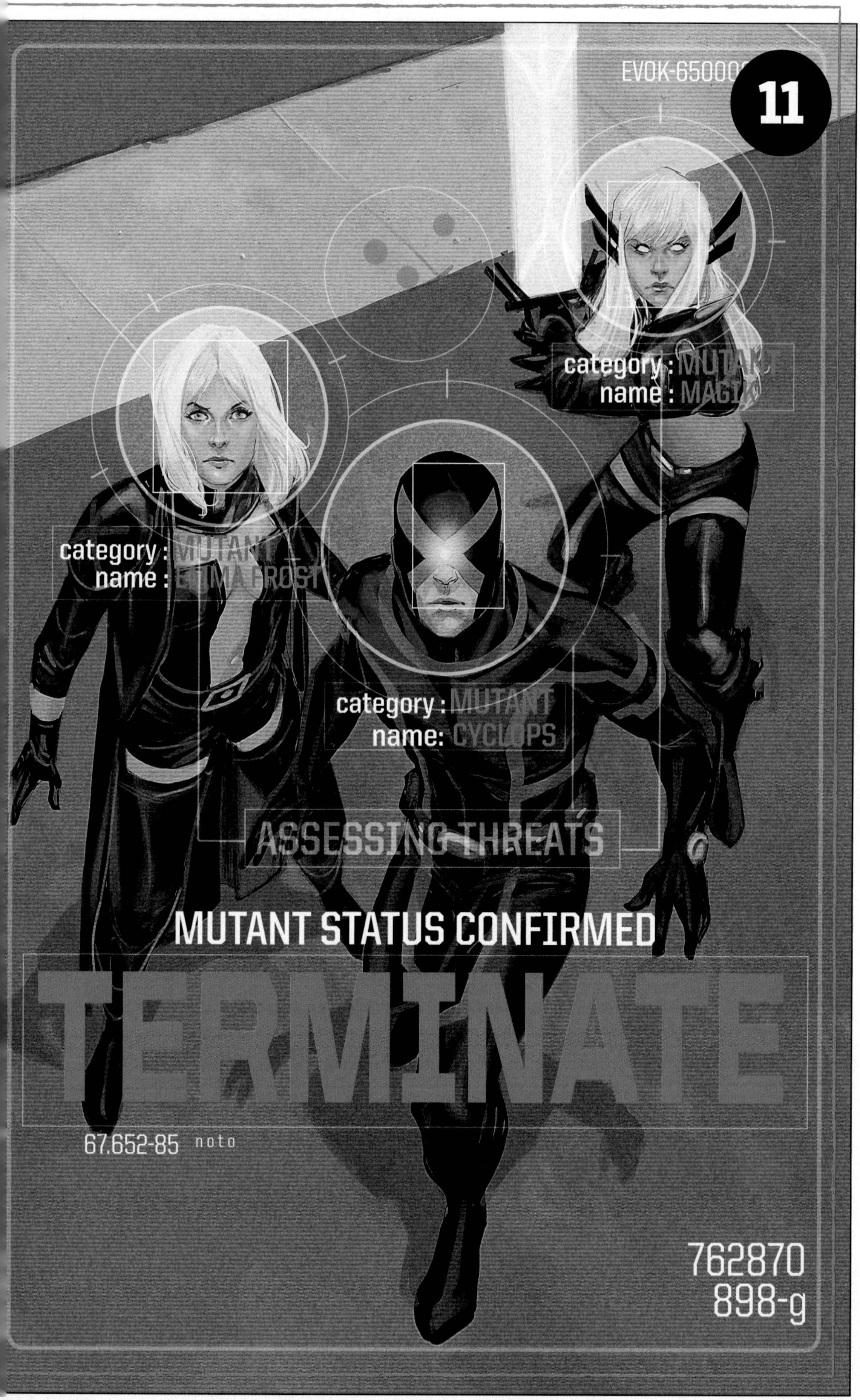

11
category :
name :
category :
name :
category : MUTANT
name: CYCLOPS
ASSESSING THREATS
MUTANT STATUS CONFIRMED
TERMINATE
67.652-85 noto
762870
898-g

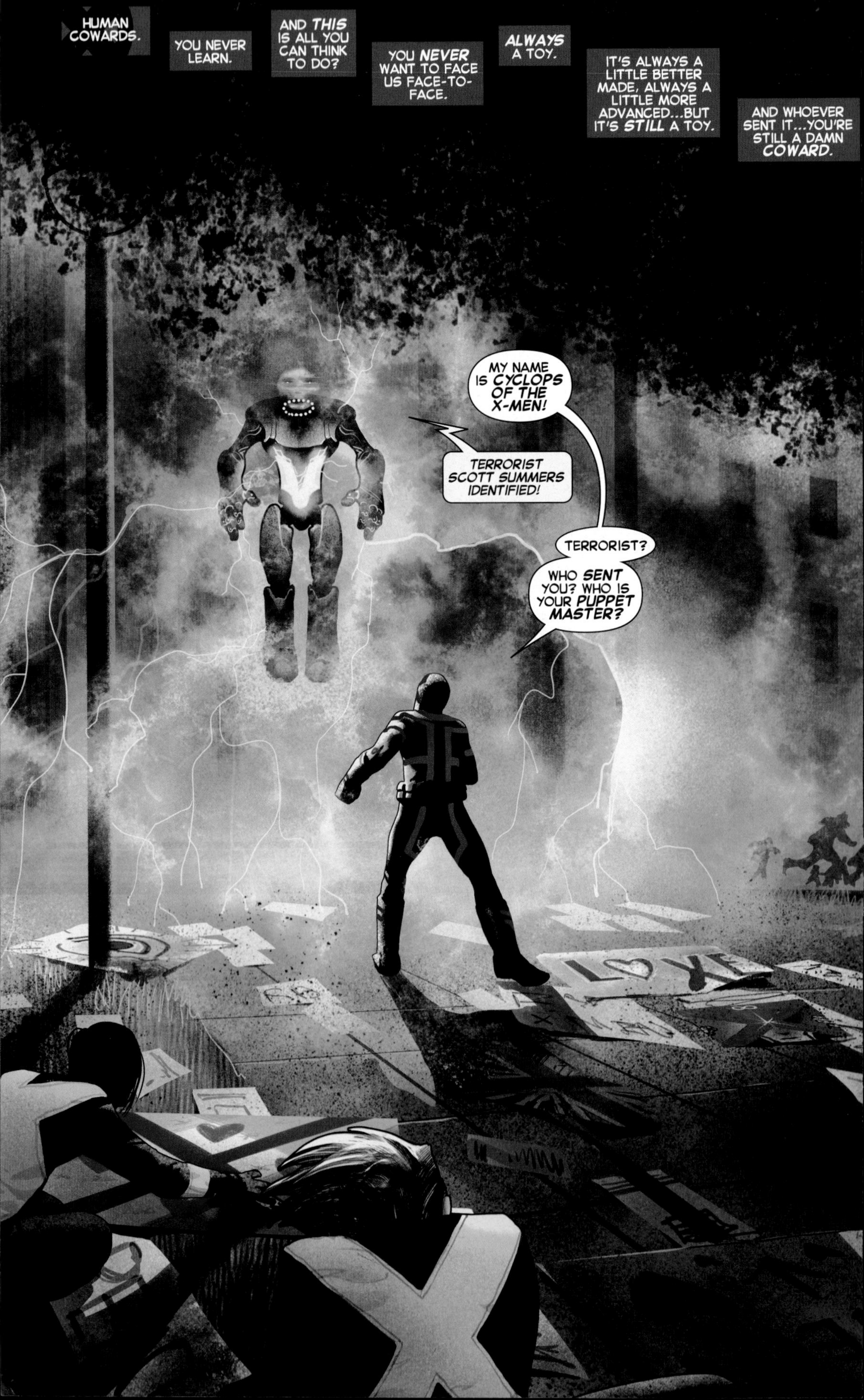

HUMAN COWARDS.
YOU NEVER LEARN.
AND THIS IS ALL YOU CAN THINK TO DO?
YOU NEVER WANT TO FACE US FACE-TO-FACE.
ALWAYS A TOY.
IT'S ALWAYS A LITTLE BETTER MADE, ALWAYS A LITTLE MORE ADVANCED...BUT IT'S STILL A TOY.
AND WHOEVER SENT IT...YOU'RE STILL A DAMN COWARD.
MY NAME IS CYCLOPS OF THE X-MEN!
TERRORIST SCOTT SUMMERS IDENTIFIED!
TERRORIST?
WHO SENT YOU? WHO IS YOUR PUPPET MASTER?
LOVE

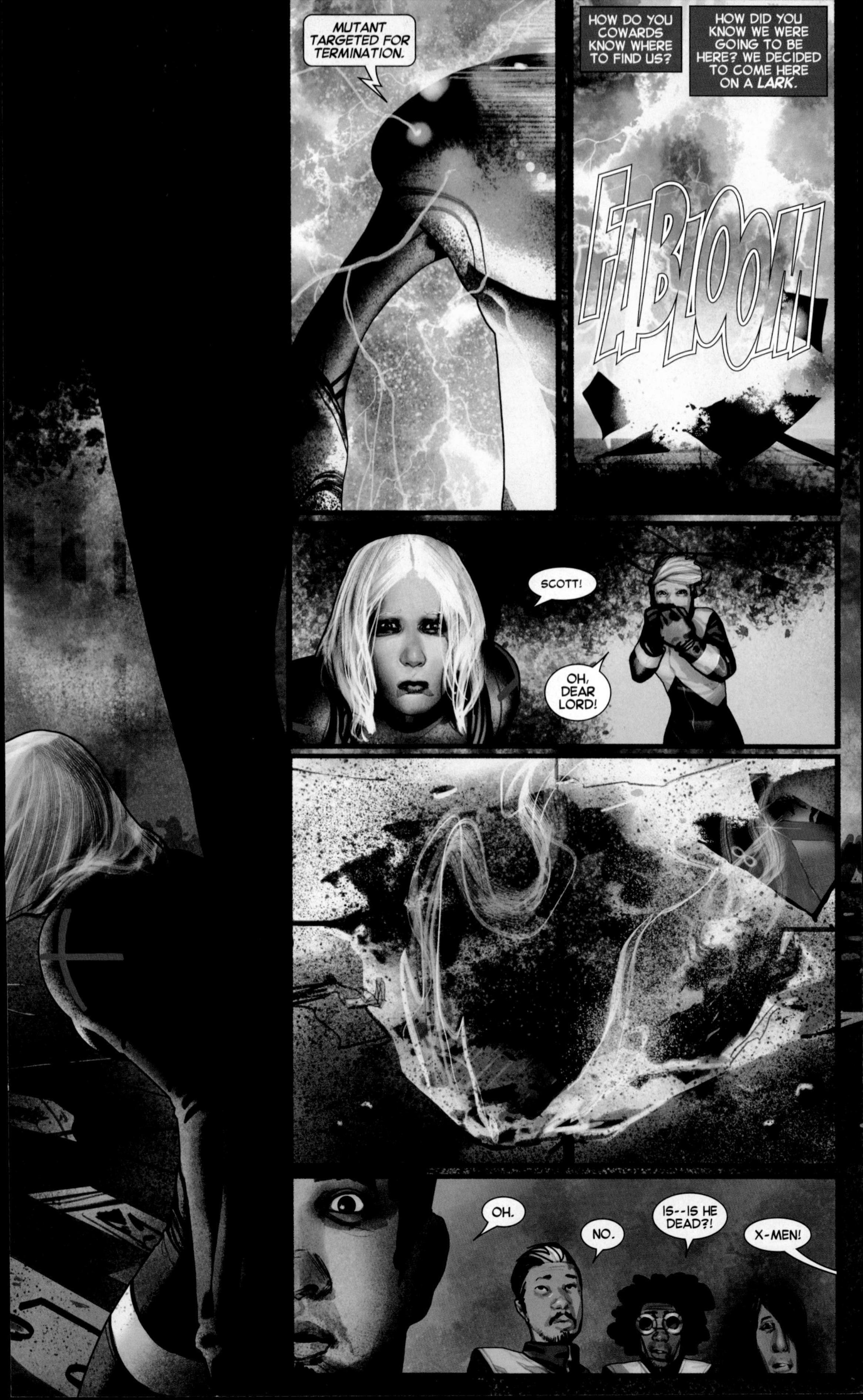
MUTANT TARGETED FOR TERMINATION.
HOW DO YOU COWARDS KNOW WHERE TO FIND US?
HOW DID YOU KNOW WE WERE GOING TO BE HERE? WE DECIDED TO COME HERE ON A LARK.
FZBLOOOM
SCOTT!
OH, DEAR LORD!
OH.
NO.
IS--IS HE DEAD?!
X-MEN!

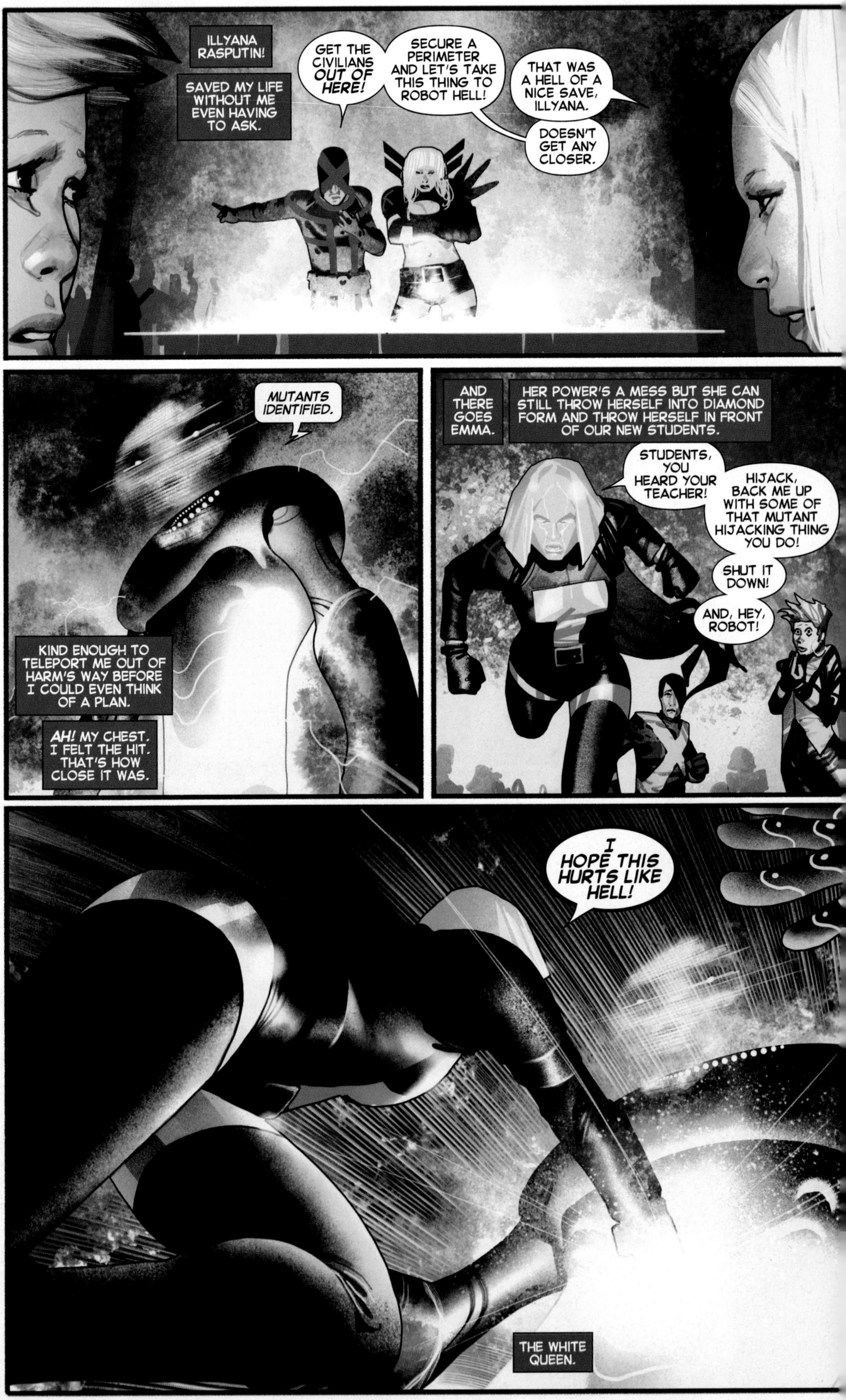
ILLYANA RASPUTIN!
SAVED MY LIFE WITHOUT ME EVEN HAVING TO ASK.
GET THE CIVILIANS *OUT OF HERE!*
SECURE A PERIMETER AND LET'S TAKE THIS THING TO ROBOT HELL!
THAT WAS A HELL OF A NICE SAVE, ILLYANA.
DOESN'T GET ANY CLOSER.
MUTANTS IDENTIFIED.
KIND ENOUGH TO TELEPORT ME OUT OF HARM'S WAY BEFORE I COULD EVEN THINK OF A PLAN.
AH! MY CHEST. I FELT THE HIT. THAT'S HOW CLOSE IT WAS.
AND THERE GOES EMMA.
HER POWER'S A MESS BUT SHE CAN STILL THROW HERSELF INTO DIAMOND FORM AND THROW HERSELF IN FRONT OF OUR NEW STUDENTS.
STUDENTS, YOU HEARD YOUR TEACHER!
HIJACK, BACK ME UP WITH SOME OF THAT MUTANT HIJACKING THING YOU DO!
SHUT IT DOWN!
AND, HEY, ROBOT!
I HOPE THIS HURTS LIKE HELL!
THE WHITE QUEEN.

AGH!

ALL I CAN THINK ABOUT IS *THESE* AMAZING HUMANS WHO HAVE COME HERE TO RALLY IN SUPPORT OF US...

AND HOW THEY ARE BEING PUNISHED FOR DOING SO.

IN MY LIFETIME, I NEVER THOUGHT I WOULD SEE THE DAY THAT HUMANS WOULD STAND UP FOR US...FOR ME.

JUST LIKE I NEVER THOUGHT I WOULD BE FIGHTING ALONGSIDE ANGEL AGAIN.

TWO ORIGINAL X-MEN STILL ON THE SAME TEAM AFTER ALL THESE YEARS.

I DON'T THINK WARREN KNOWS HOW MUCH IT MEANS TO ME THAT HE IS HERE.

AND HERE COMES DAVID BOND/HIJACK.

HE HASN'T BEEN AN X-MEN TWO DAYS, HASN'T BEEN A MUTANT FOR MORE THAN THREE, AND LOOK AT HIM.

UH... ROBOT GUY.

SHUT DOWN.

UNIDENTIFIED MUTANT.

UH-OH.

UH...POWER OFF.

UH, SHUT DOWN. GO TO SLEEP. FREEZE. TIME OUT. YOU'RE DONE. NIGHT-NIGHT. ROBOT OUT!

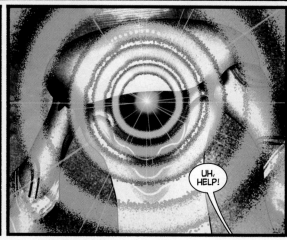

UH, HELP!

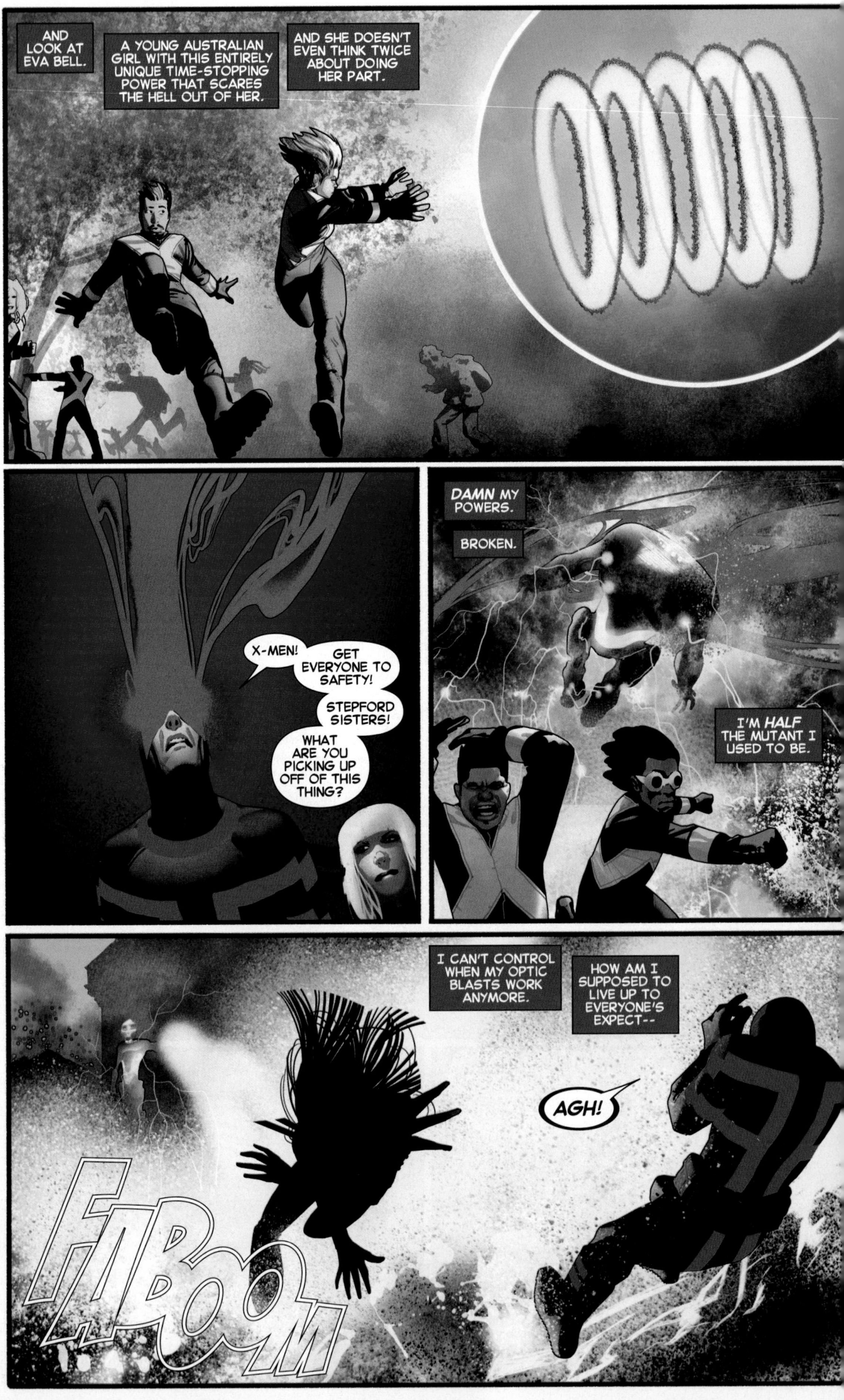
AND LOOK AT EVA BELL.
A YOUNG AUSTRALIAN GIRL WITH THIS ENTIRELY UNIQUE TIME-STOPPING POWER THAT SCARES THE HELL OUT OF HER.
AND SHE DOESN'T EVEN THINK TWICE ABOUT DOING HER PART.
X-MEN!
GET EVERYONE TO SAFETY!
STEPFORD SISTERS!
WHAT ARE YOU PICKING UP OFF OF THIS THING?
DAMN MY POWERS.
BROKEN.
I'M HALF THE MUTANT I USED TO BE.
I CAN'T CONTROL WHEN MY OPTIC BLASTS WORK ANYMORE.
HOW AM I SUPPOSED TO LIVE UP TO EVERYONE'S EXPECT--
AGH!
FFBOOM

THIS THING IS NOT BIOLOGICAL.

THERE'S NO BRAIN IN THERE FOR US TO MANIPULATE WITH OUR HIVE-MIND.

BUT IT'S, HUH...IT'S NOT REALLY A MACHINE EITHER.

MINDEE'S RIGHT--IT'S SOMETHING IN BETWEEN.

WHAT DOES *THAT* MEAN?

AAGGH!

HEY, YOU GUYS NEED TO GET *OUT* OF HERE!

MY LEG!

LET'S SEE WHAT I CAN DO!

WHAT-- WHAT?!

JUST--

WHAT ARE YOU DOING?!

I'M CHRISTOPHER. JUST--JUST STAY STILL!

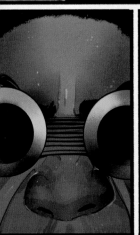

OH-OH MY GOD. YOU-- YOU HEALED HER.

HOW DID YOU DO THAT?

IF ONLY I KNEW.

YOU REALLY HAVE TO GET OUT OF HERE.

I-I THINK I CAN *DO* THIS!

FABIO, CYCLOPS TOLD US TO--

NO, FABIO. YOU'RE NOT READY.

IF I THOUGHT FOR A *SECOND* THAT THIS WOULD TURN INTO A HOSTILE SITUATION I WOULD HAVE NEVER ALLOWED YOU TO--

I HAVE THIS!

POINK!

GOLD BALLS!

YEAH, I SAID IT.

POINK! POINK! POINK! POINK!

POINK! POINK!

POINK!

POINK! POINK!

POINK! POINK!

WELL, HOW ABOUT THAT.

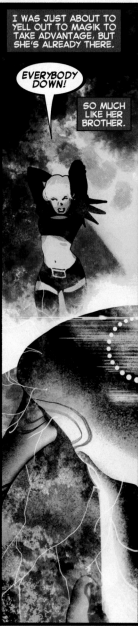

I WAS JUST ABOUT TO YELL OUT TO MAGIK TO TAKE ADVANTAGE, BUT SHE'S ALREADY THERE.

EVERYBODY DOWN!

SO MUCH LIKE HER BROTHER.

FABIO!

POINK!

AGH!

SFXH!

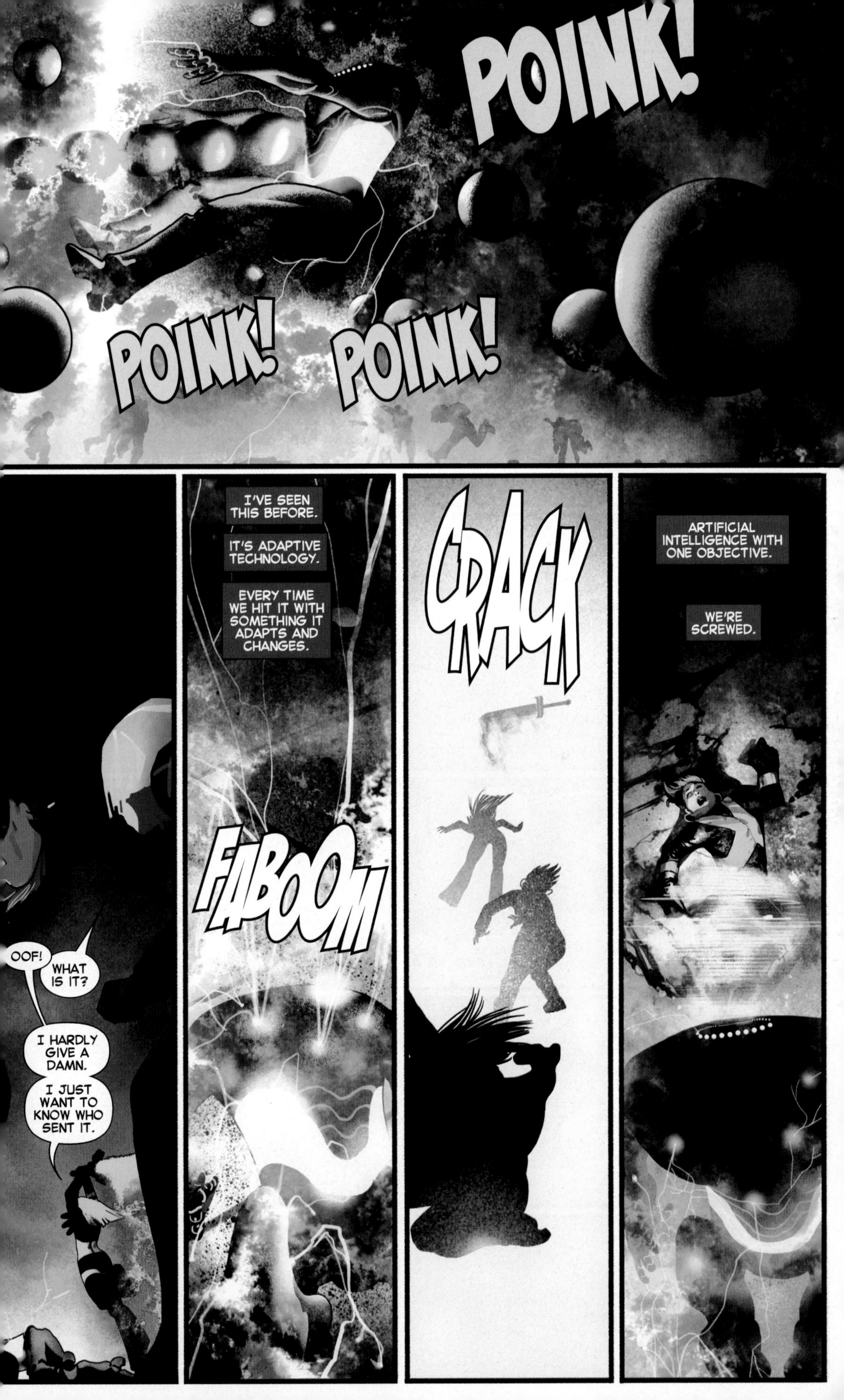
POINK!
POINK!
POINK!
OOF!
WHAT IS IT?
I HARDLY GIVE A DAMN.
I JUST WANT TO KNOW WHO SENT IT.
I'VE SEEN THIS BEFORE.
IT'S ADAPTIVE TECHNOLOGY.
EVERY TIME WE HIT IT WITH SOMETHING IT ADAPTS AND CHANGES.
FABOOM
CRACK
ARTIFICIAL INTELLIGENCE WITH ONE OBJECTIVE.
WE'RE SCREWED.

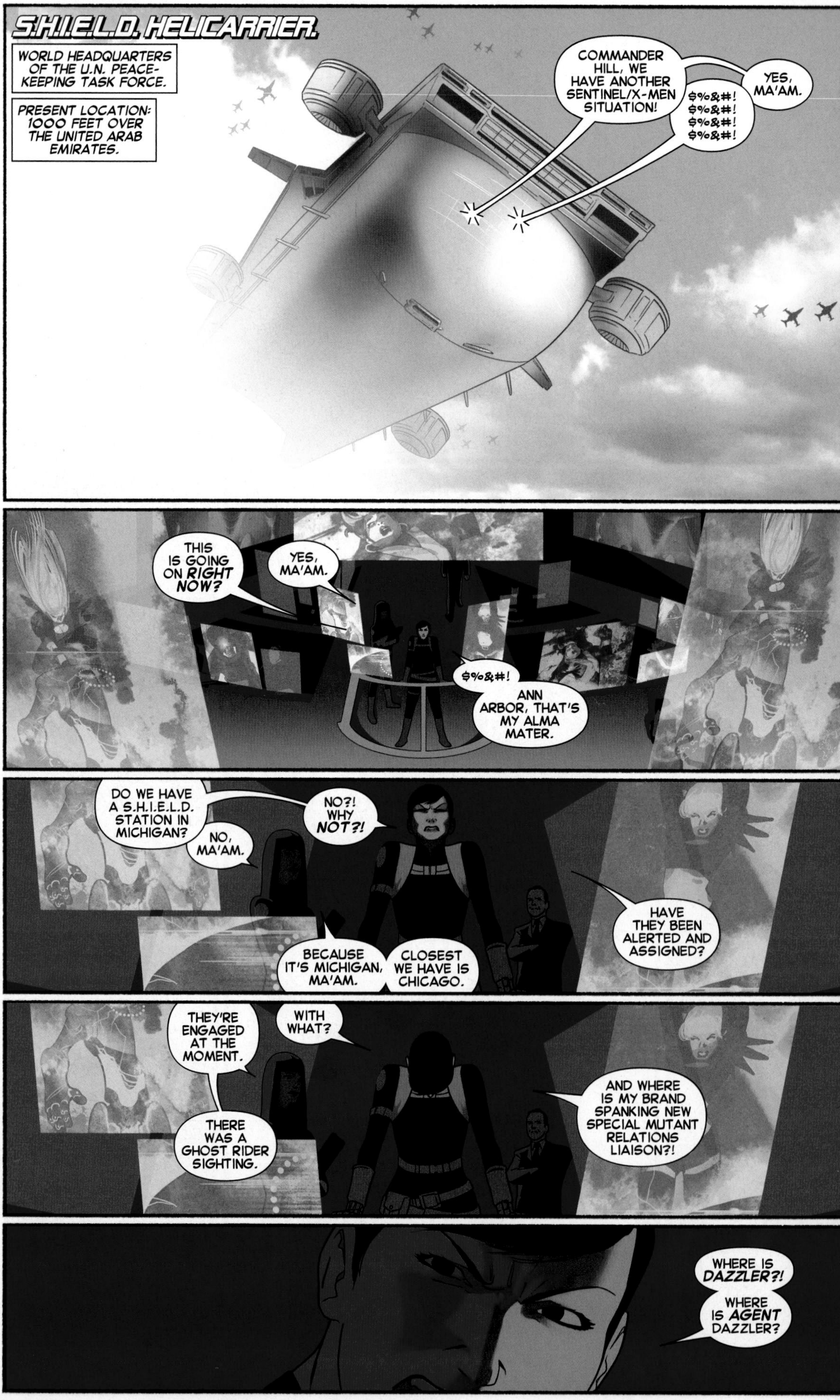
S.H.I.E.L.D. HELICARRIER.
WORLD HEADQUARTERS OF THE U.N. PEACE-KEEPING TASK FORCE.
PRESENT LOCATION: 1000 FEET OVER THE UNITED ARAB EMIRATES.
COMMANDER HILL, WE HAVE ANOTHER SENTINEL/X-MEN SITUATION!
$%&#! $%&#! $%&#! $%&#!
YES, MA'AM.
THIS IS GOING ON RIGHT NOW?
YES, MA'AM.
$%&#!
ANN ARBOR, THAT'S MY ALMA MATER.
DO WE HAVE A S.H.I.E.L.D. STATION IN MICHIGAN?
NO, MA'AM.
NO?! WHY NOT?!
BECAUSE IT'S MICHIGAN, MA'AM.
CLOSEST WE HAVE IS CHICAGO.
HAVE THEY BEEN ALERTED AND ASSIGNED?
THEY'RE ENGAGED AT THE MOMENT.
WITH WHAT?
THERE WAS A GHOST RIDER SIGHTING.
AND WHERE IS MY BRAND SPANKING NEW SPECIAL MUTANT RELATIONS LIAISON?!
WHERE IS DAZZLER?!
WHERE IS AGENT DAZZLER?

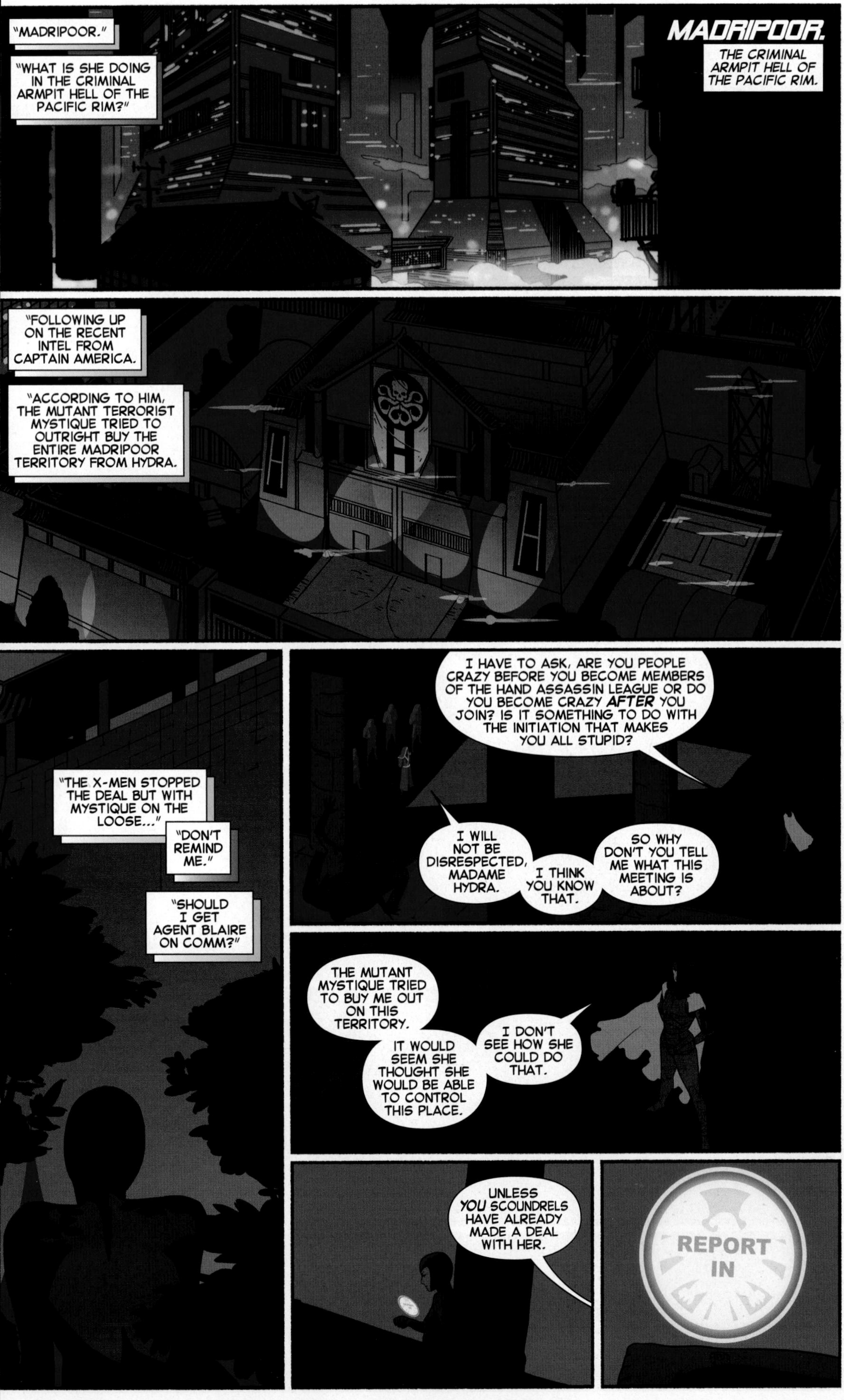
"MADRIPOOR."
"WHAT IS SHE DOING IN THE CRIMINAL ARMPIT HELL OF THE PACIFIC RIM?"
MADRIPOOR.
THE CRIMINAL ARMPIT HELL OF THE PACIFIC RIM.
"FOLLOWING UP ON THE RECENT INTEL FROM CAPTAIN AMERICA.
"ACCORDING TO HIM, THE MUTANT TERRORIST MYSTIQUE TRIED TO OUTRIGHT BUY THE ENTIRE MADRIPOOR TERRITORY FROM HYDRA.
"THE X-MEN STOPPED THE DEAL BUT WITH MYSTIQUE ON THE LOOSE..."
"DON'T REMIND ME."
"SHOULD I GET AGENT BLAIRE ON COMM?"
I HAVE TO ASK, ARE YOU PEOPLE CRAZY BEFORE YOU BECOME MEMBERS OF THE HAND ASSASSIN LEAGUE OR DO YOU BECOME CRAZY AFTER YOU JOIN? IS IT SOMETHING TO DO WITH THE INITIATION THAT MAKES YOU ALL STUPID?
I WILL NOT BE DISRESPECTED, MADAME HYDRA.
I THINK YOU KNOW THAT.
SO WHY DON'T YOU TELL ME WHAT THIS MEETING IS ABOUT?
THE MUTANT MYSTIQUE TRIED TO BUY ME OUT ON THIS TERRITORY.
IT WOULD SEEM SHE THOUGHT SHE WOULD BE ABLE TO CONTROL THIS PLACE.
I DON'T SEE HOW SHE COULD DO THAT.
UNLESS YOU SCOUNDRELS HAVE ALREADY MADE A DEAL WITH HER.
REPORT IN

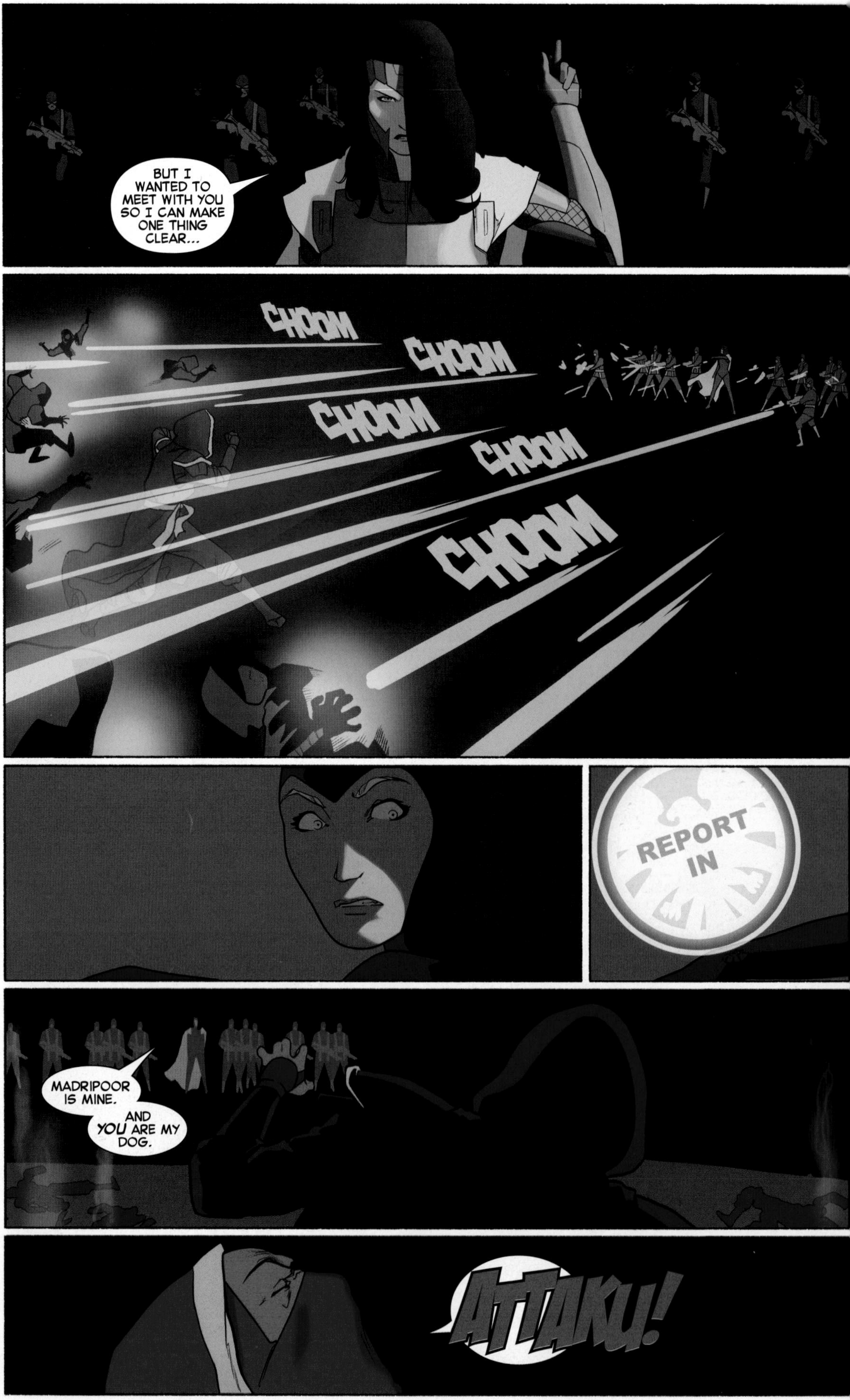
BUT I WANTED TO MEET WITH YOU SO I CAN MAKE ONE THING CLEAR...
CHOOM
CHOOM
CHOOM
CHOOM
CHOOM
REPORT IN
MADRIPOOR IS MINE.
AND YOU ARE MY DOG.
ATTAKU!

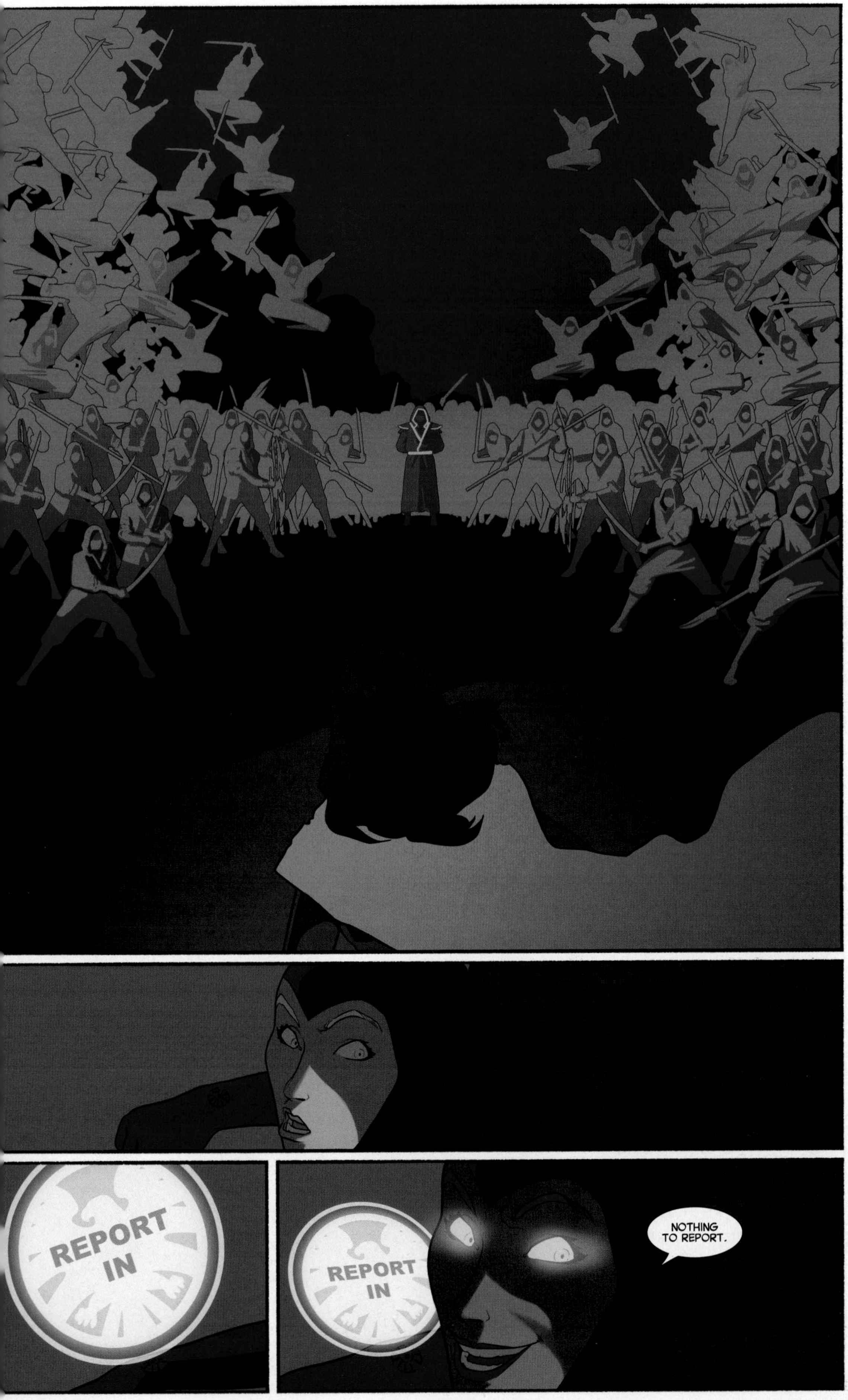
REPORT
IN
REPORT
IN
NOTHING
TO REPORT.

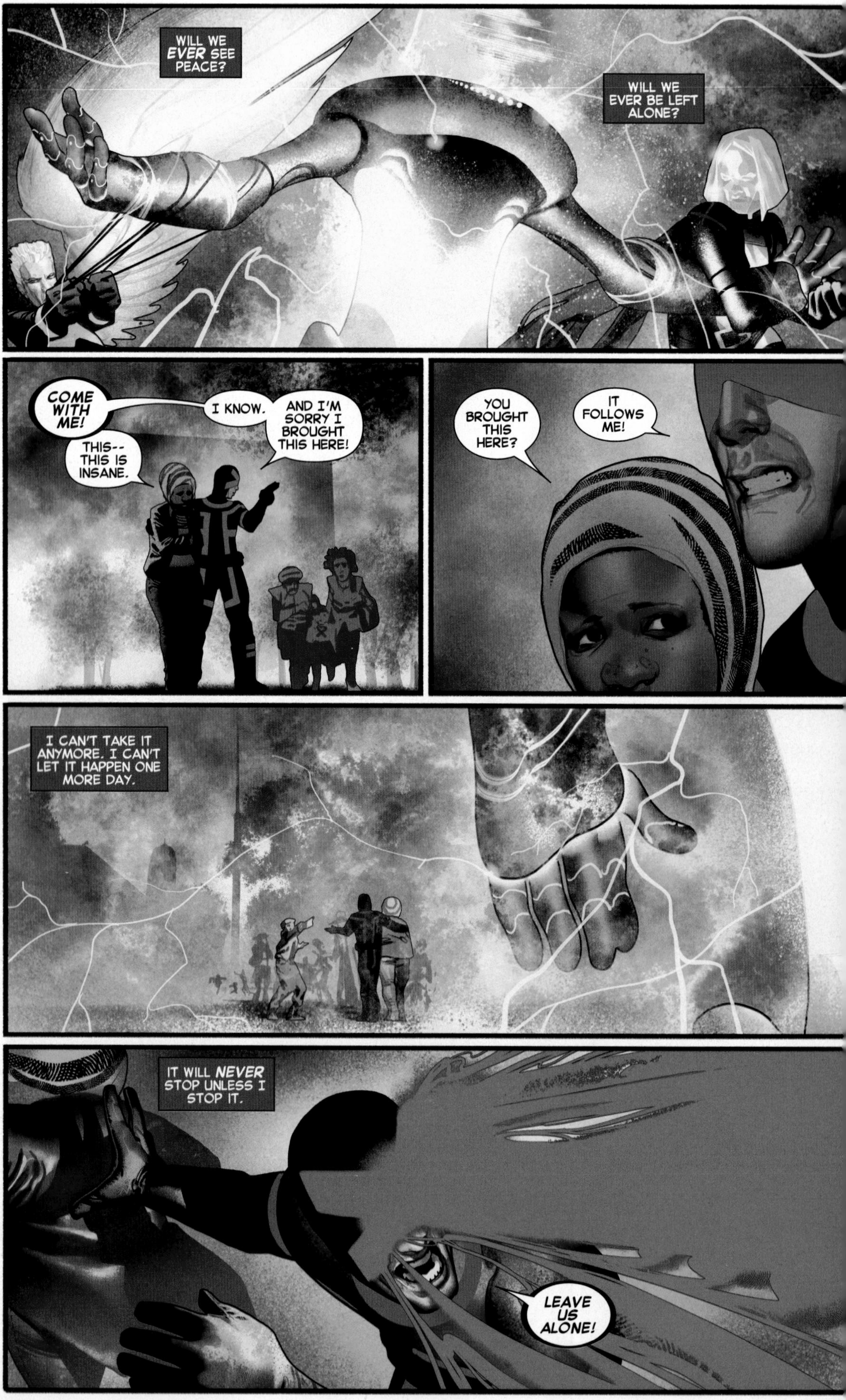

WILL WE *EVER* SEE PEACE?
WILL WE EVER BE LEFT ALONE?
COME WITH ME!
THIS-- THIS IS INSANE.
I KNOW.
AND I'M SORRY I BROUGHT THIS HERE!
YOU BROUGHT THIS HERE?
IT FOLLOWS ME!
I CAN'T TAKE IT ANYMORE. I CAN'T LET IT HAPPEN ONE MORE DAY.
IT WILL *NEVER* STOP UNLESS I STOP IT.
LEAVE US ALONE!

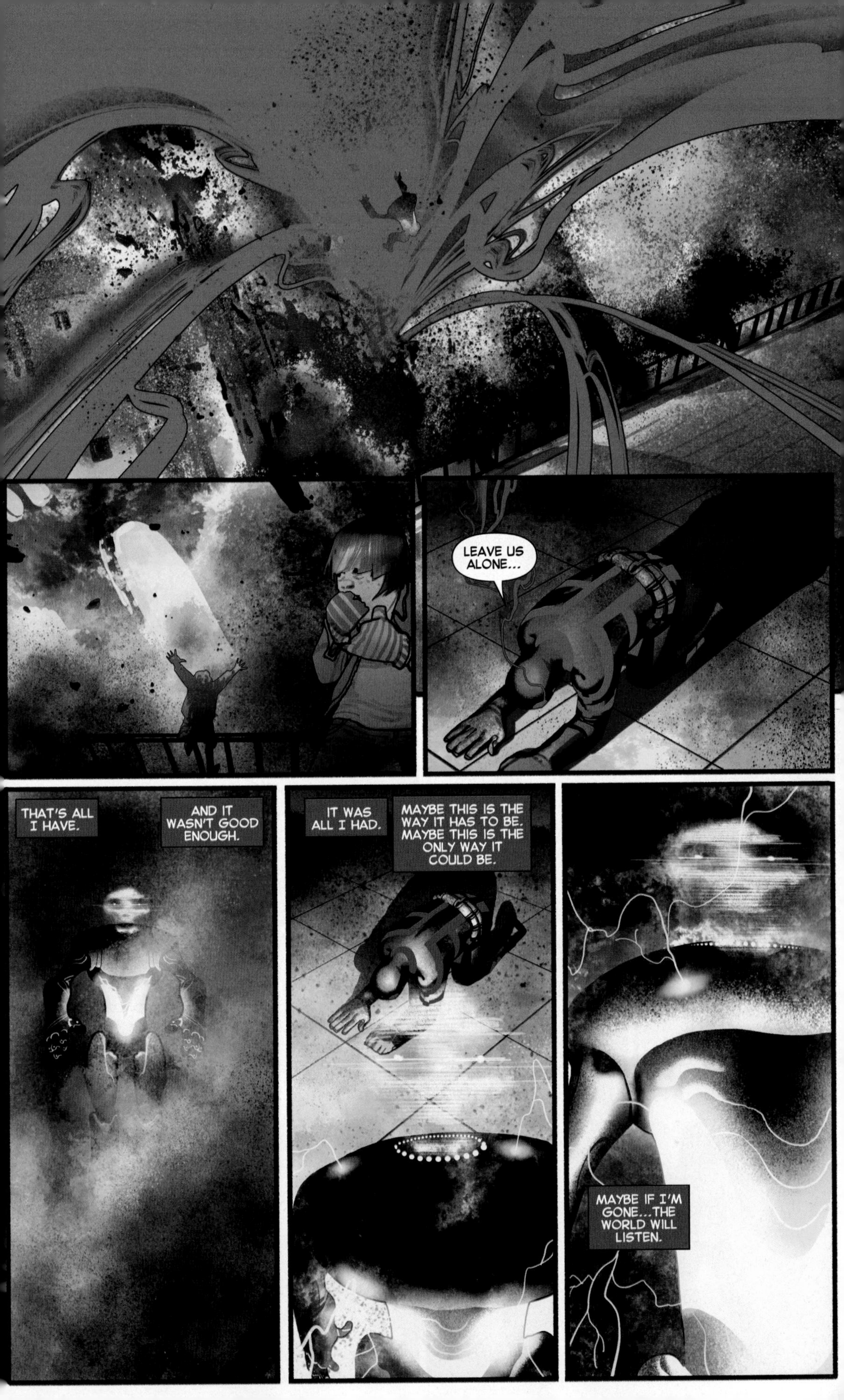
LEAVE US ALONE...
THAT'S ALL I HAVE.
AND IT WASN'T GOOD ENOUGH.
IT WAS ALL I HAD.
MAYBE THIS IS THE WAY IT HAS TO BE. MAYBE THIS IS THE ONLY WAY IT COULD BE.
MAYBE IF I'M GONE...THE WORLD WILL LISTEN.

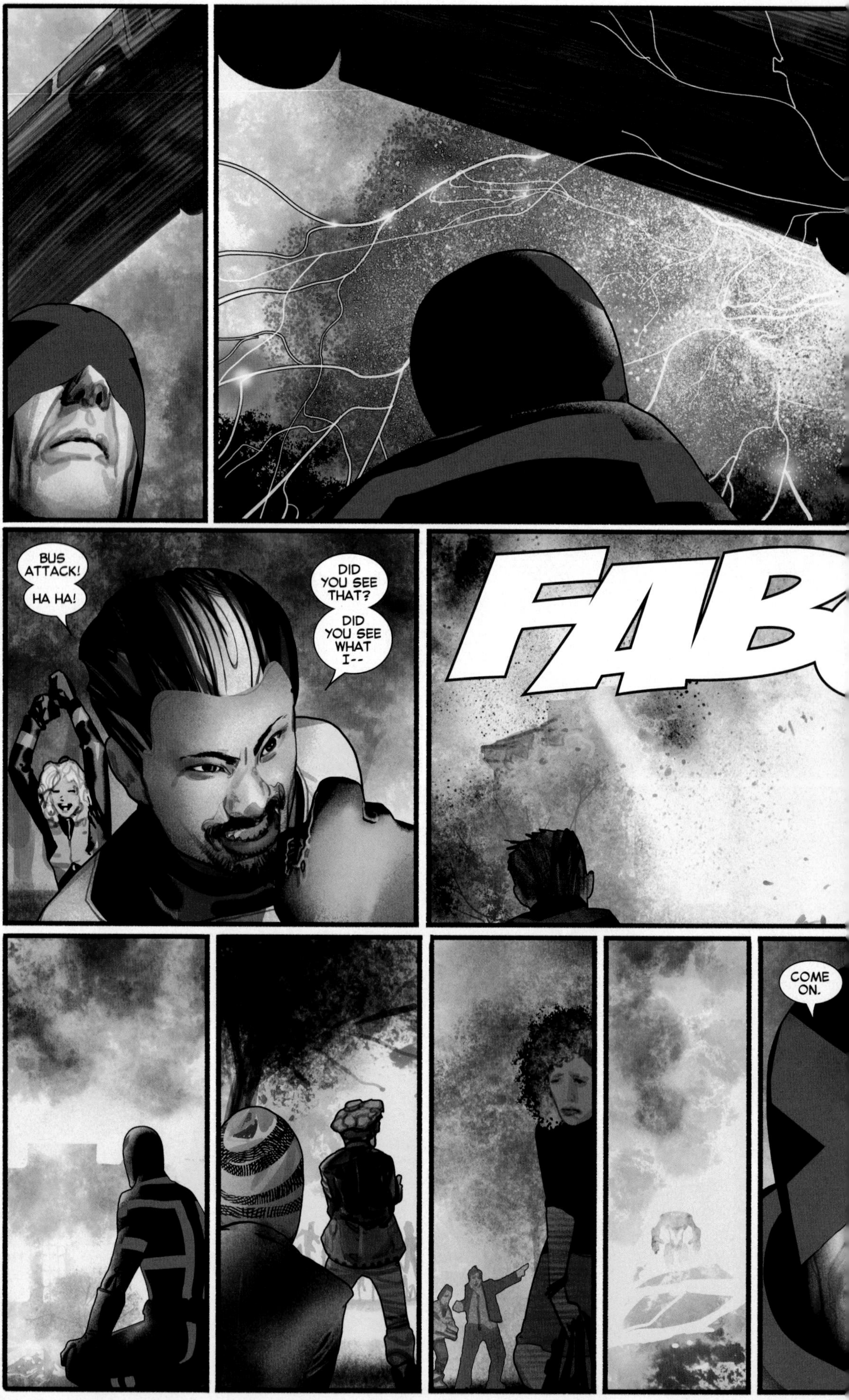
BUS ATTACK!
HA HA!
DID YOU SEE THAT?
DID YOU SEE WHAT I--
FAB
COME ON.

THIS IS NOT THE DREAM.

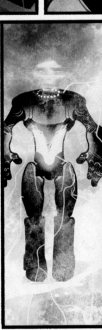

COME ON!

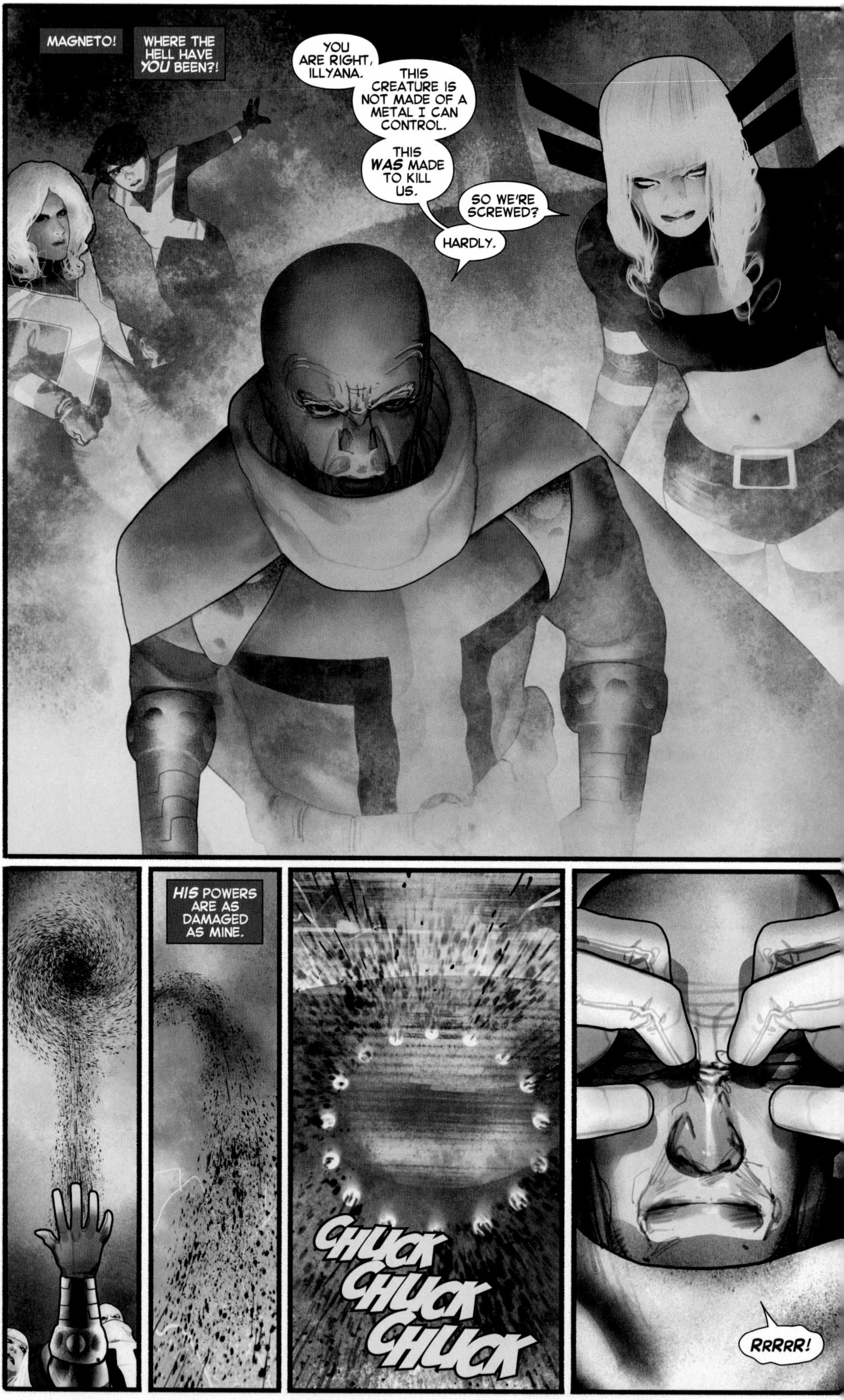
MAGNETO!
WHERE THE HELL HAVE YOU BEEN?!
YOU ARE RIGHT, ILLYANA.
THIS CREATURE IS NOT MADE OF A METAL I CAN CONTROL.
THIS WAS MADE TO KILL US.
SO WE'RE SCREWED?
HARDLY.
HIS POWERS ARE AS DAMAGED AS MINE.
CHUCK CHUCK CHUCK
RRRRR!

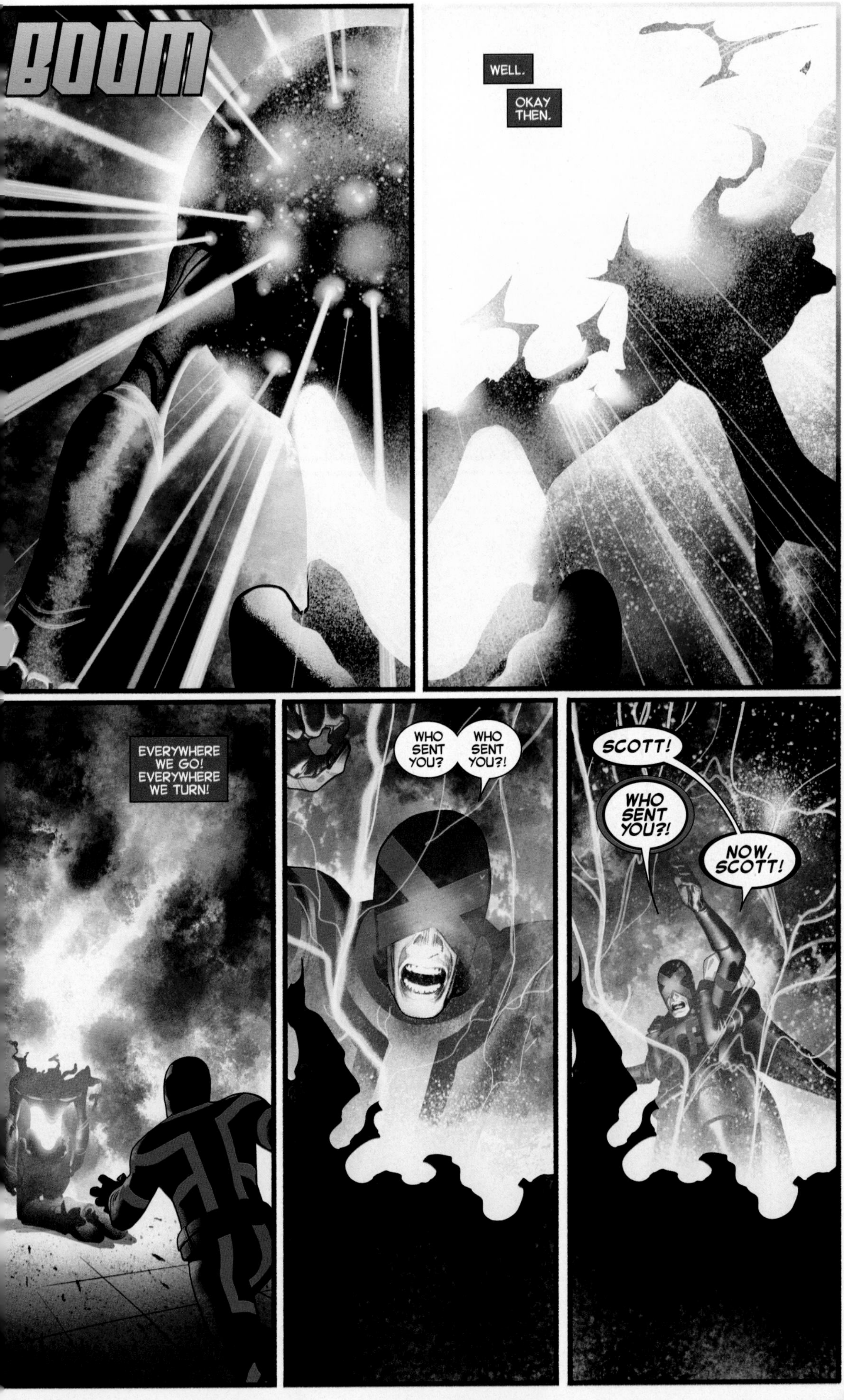
BOOM
WELL.
OKAY THEN.
EVERYWHERE WE GO! EVERYWHERE WE TURN!
WHO SENT YOU?
WHO SENT YOU?!
SCOTT!
WHO SENT YOU?!
NOW, SCOTT!

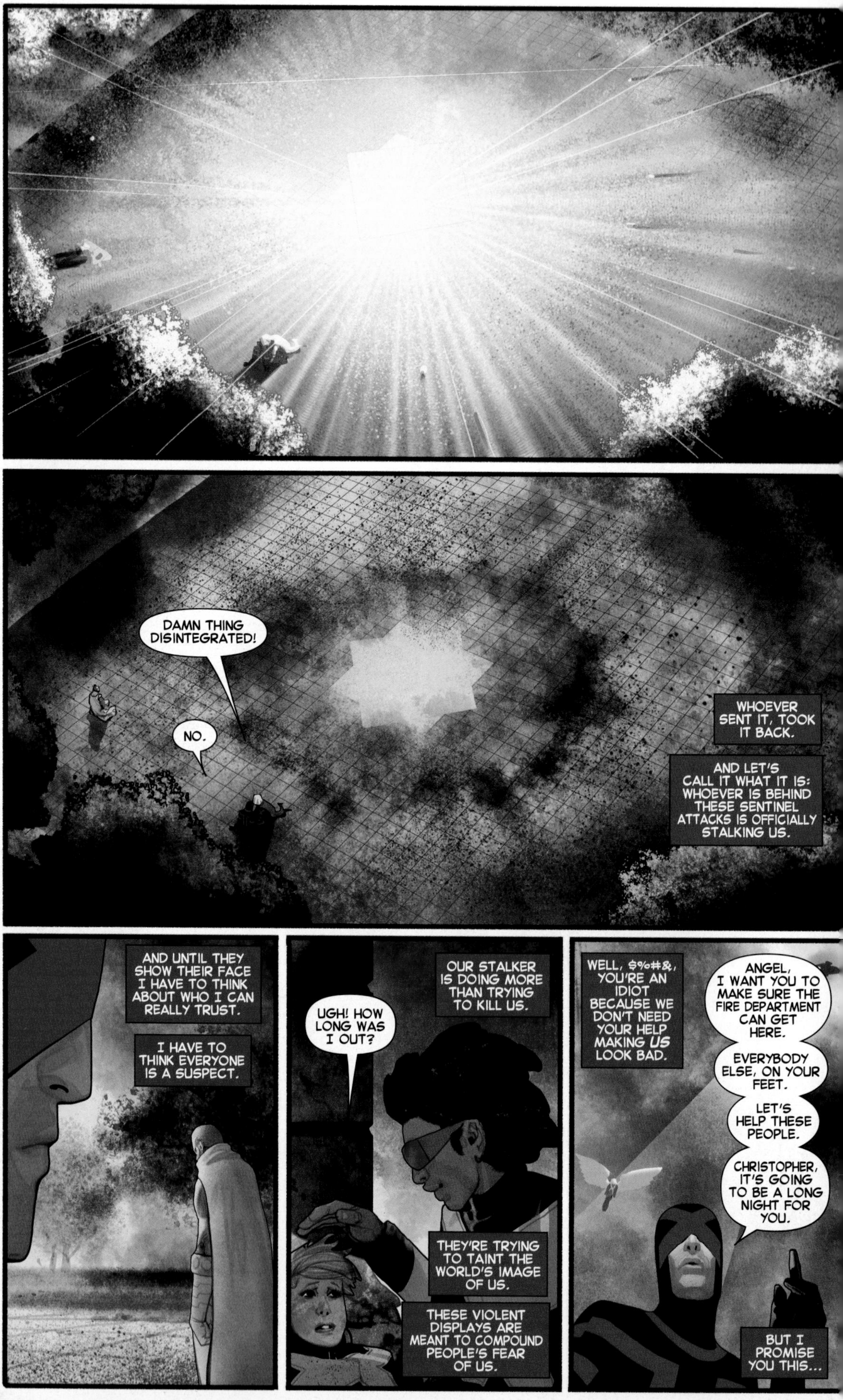

DAMN THING DISINTEGRATED!
NO.
WHOEVER SENT IT, TOOK IT BACK.
AND LET'S CALL IT WHAT IT IS: WHOEVER IS BEHIND THESE SENTINEL ATTACKS IS OFFICIALLY STALKING US.
AND UNTIL THEY SHOW THEIR FACE I HAVE TO THINK ABOUT WHO I CAN REALLY TRUST.
I HAVE TO THINK EVERYONE IS A SUSPECT.
OUR STALKER IS DOING MORE THAN TRYING TO KILL US.
UGH! HOW LONG WAS I OUT?
THEY'RE TRYING TO TAINT THE WORLD'S IMAGE OF US.
THESE VIOLENT DISPLAYS ARE MEANT TO COMPOUND PEOPLE'S FEAR OF US.
WELL, $%#&, YOU'RE AN IDIOT BECAUSE WE DON'T NEED YOUR HELP MAKING US LOOK BAD.
ANGEL, I WANT YOU TO MAKE SURE THE FIRE DEPARTMENT CAN GET HERE.
EVERYBODY ELSE, ON YOUR FEET.
LET'S HELP THESE PEOPLE.
CHRISTOPHER, IT'S GOING TO BE A LONG NIGHT FOR YOU.
BUT I PROMISE YOU THIS...

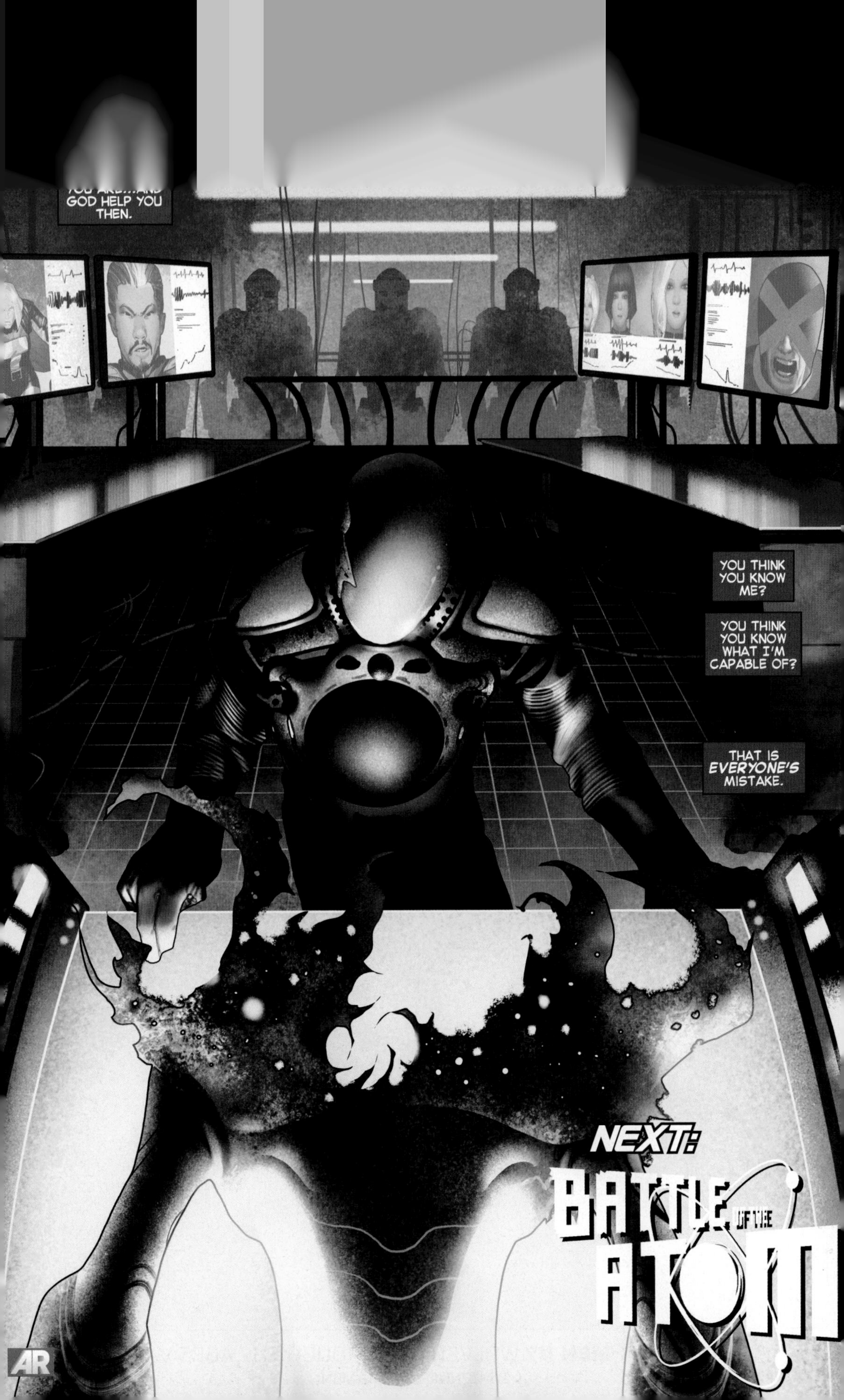
GOD HELP YOU THEN.
YOU THINK YOU KNOW ME?
YOU THINK YOU KNOW WHAT I'M CAPABLE OF?
THAT IS EVERYONE'S MISTAKE.
NEXT:
BATTLE OF THE ATOM

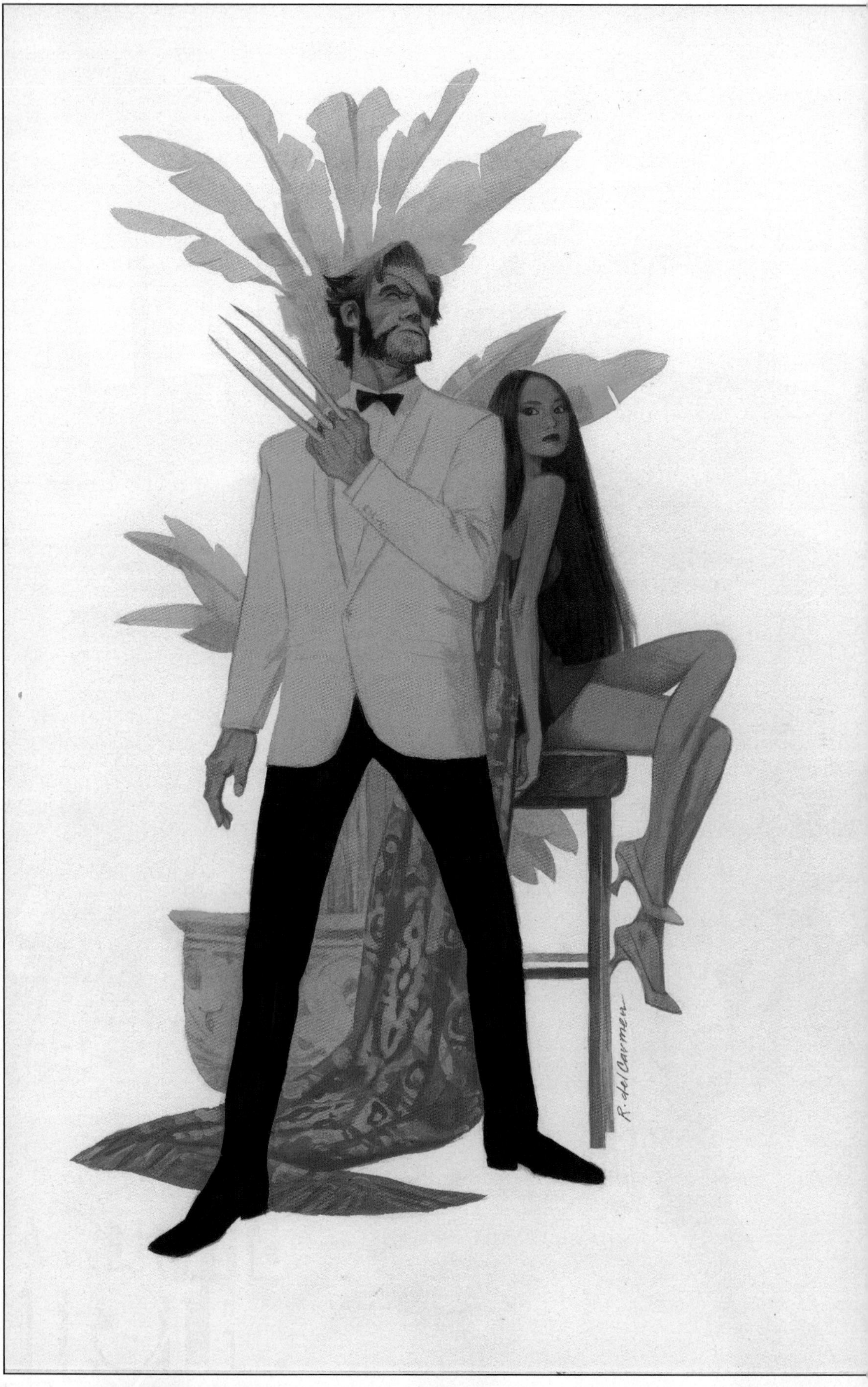
R. del Carmen

UNCANNY X-MEN #7 WOLVERINE THROUGH THE AGES VARIANT
BY RONNIE DEL CARMEN

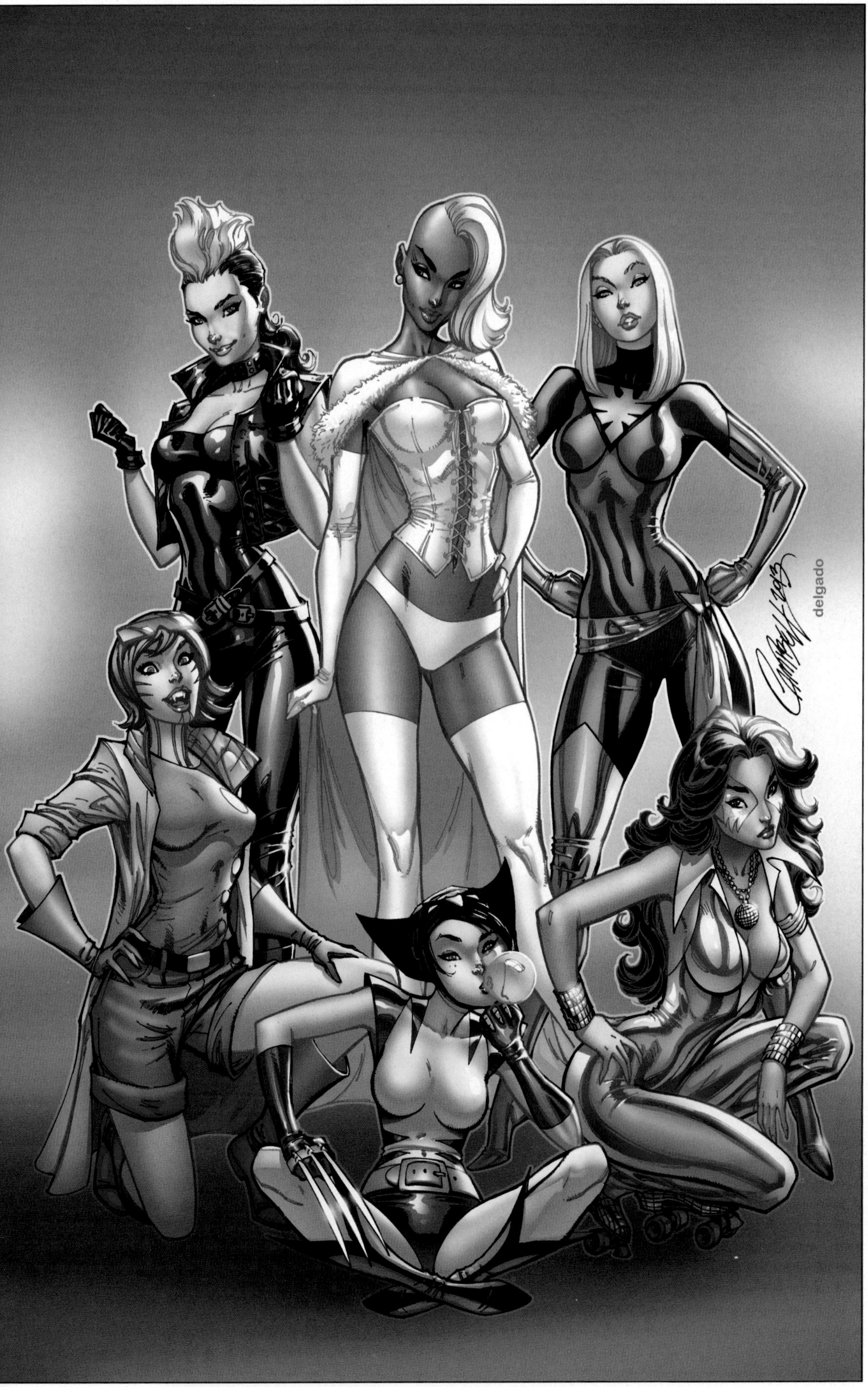
delgado

UNCANNY X-MEN #8 SDCC COSPLAY VARIANT
BY J. SCOTT CAMPBELL & EDGAR DELGADO

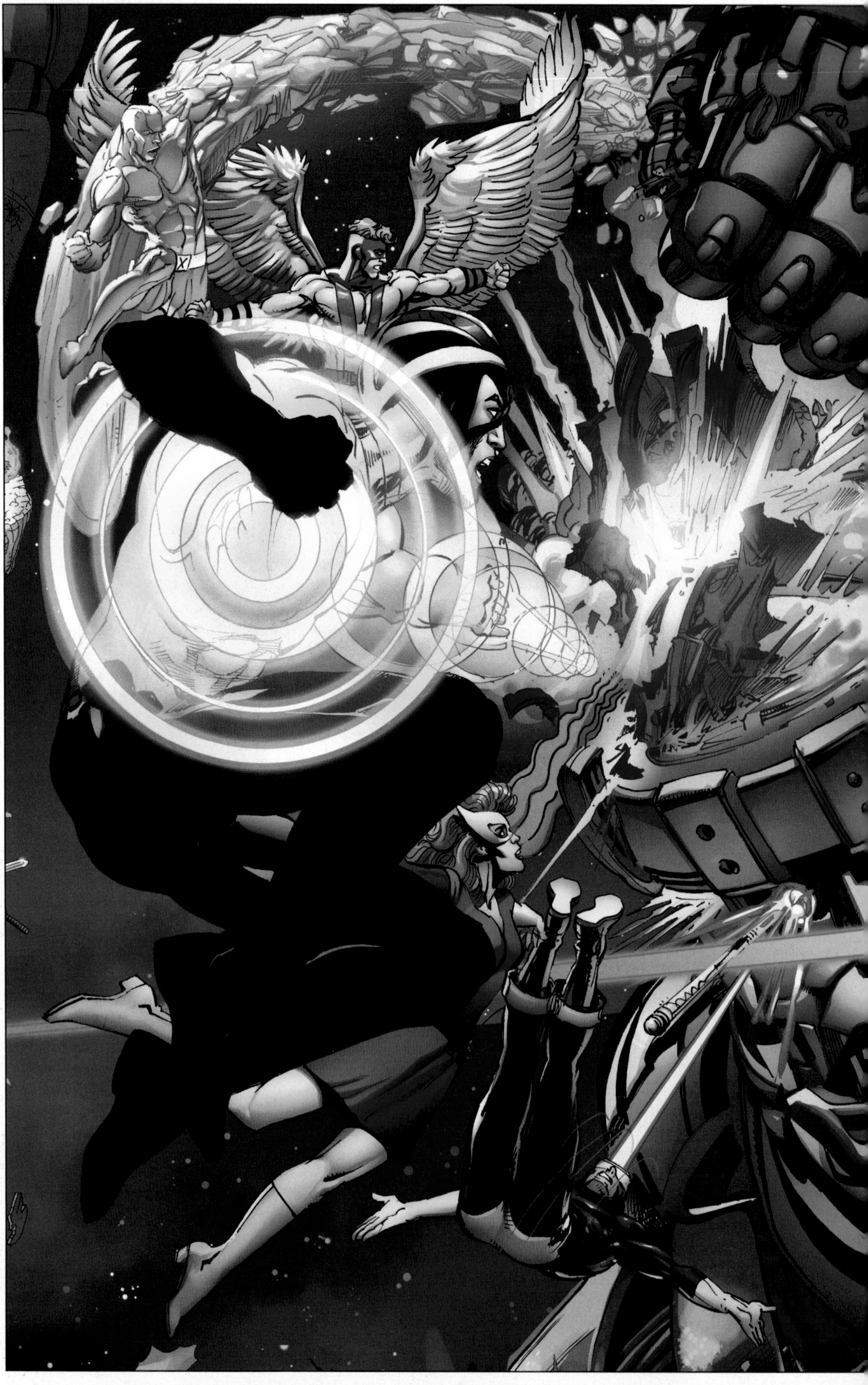

UNCANNY X-MEN #10 X-MEN 50TH ANNIVERSARY VARIANT
BY NEAL ADAMS & DAVID CURIEL

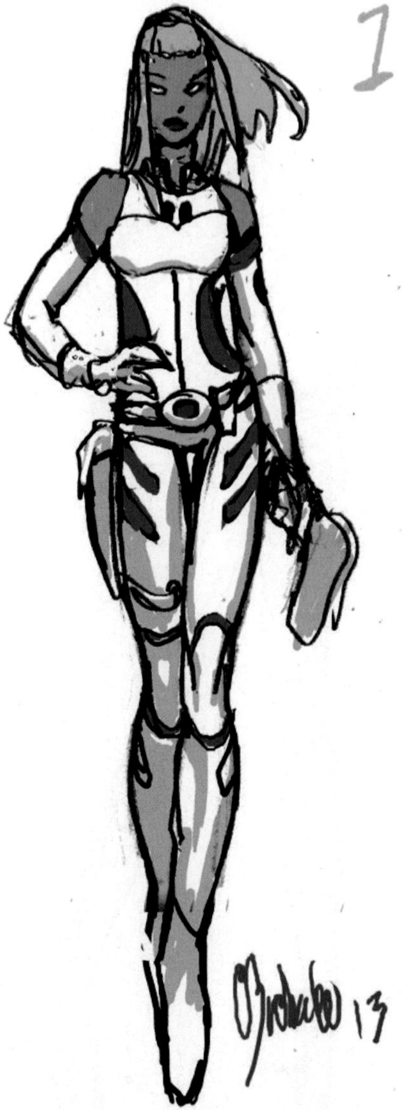
1
13

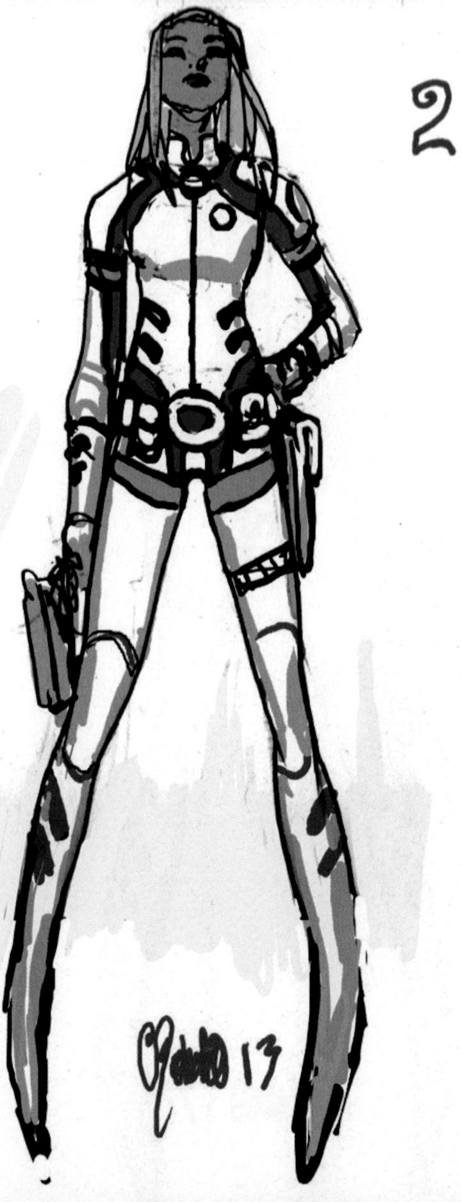
2
13

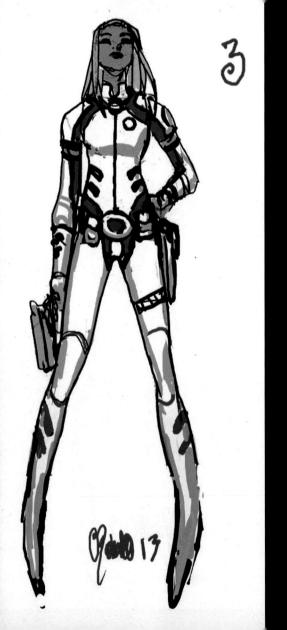

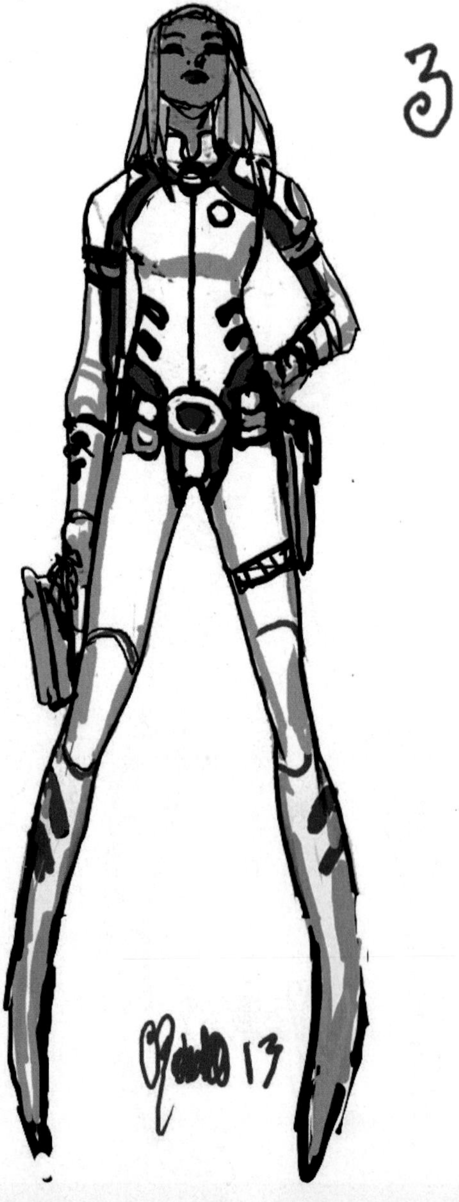
3

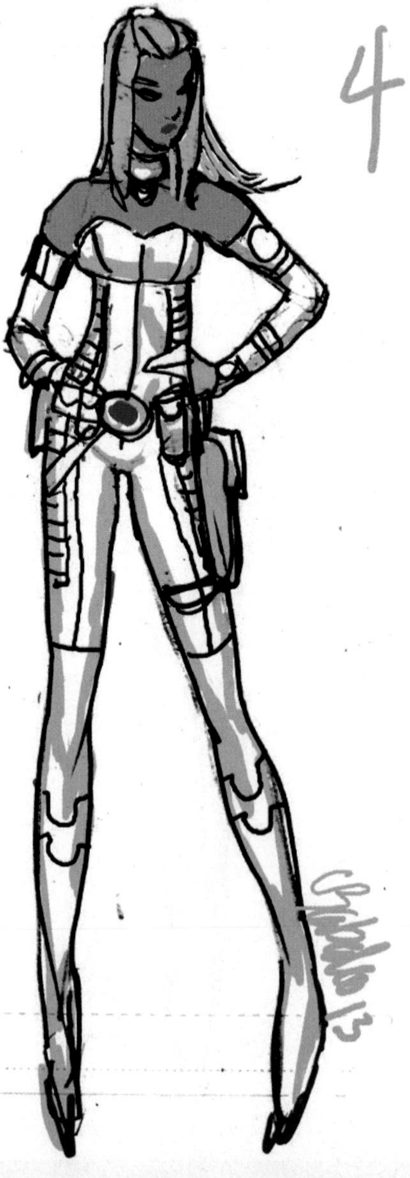
4

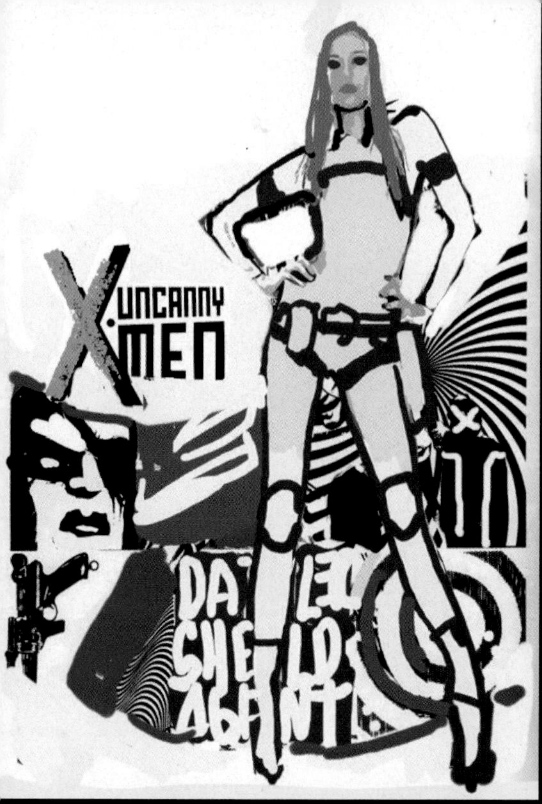
UNCANNY
X-MEN

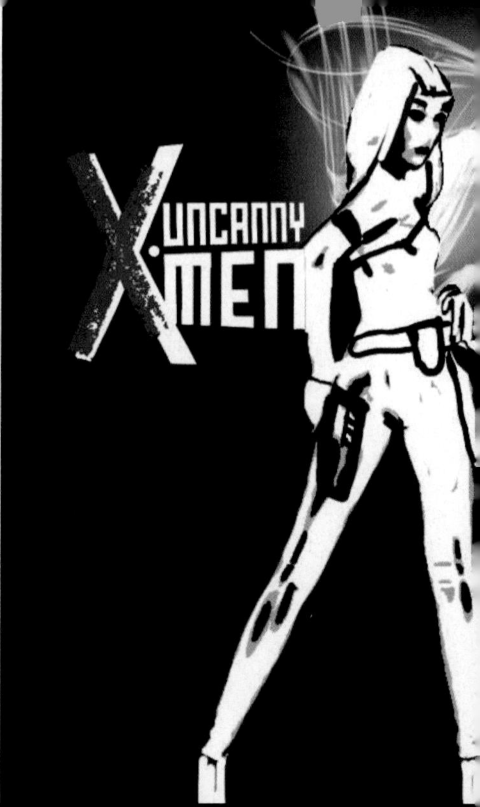
UNCANNY
X-MEN

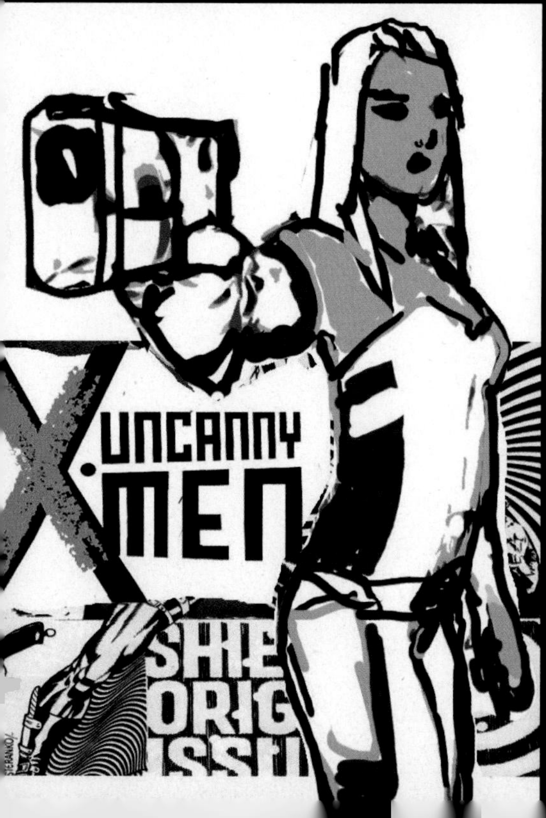
UNCANNY
X-MEN

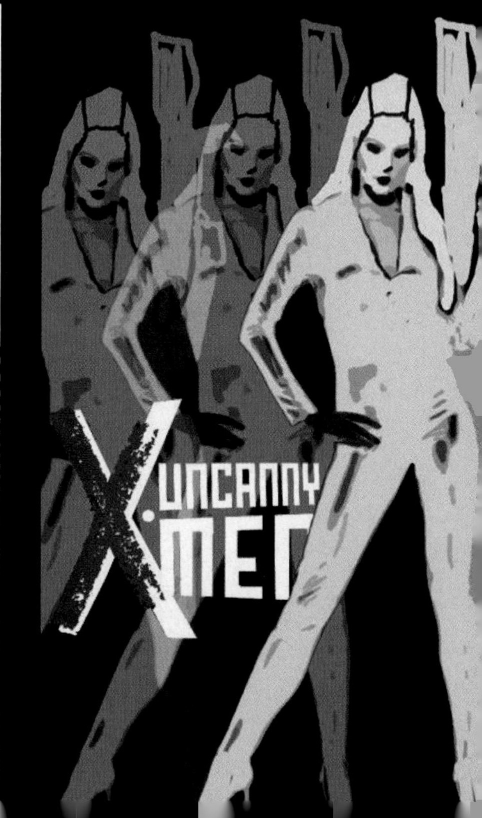
UNCANNY
X-MEN

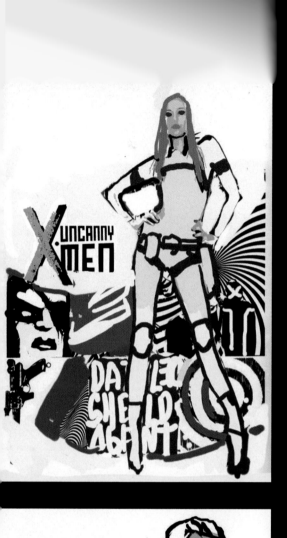

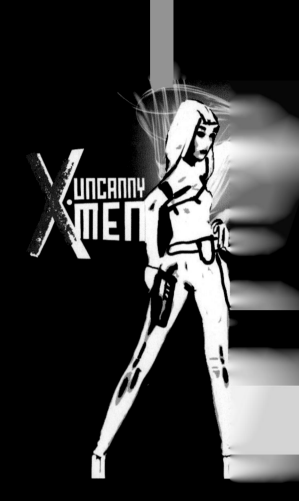

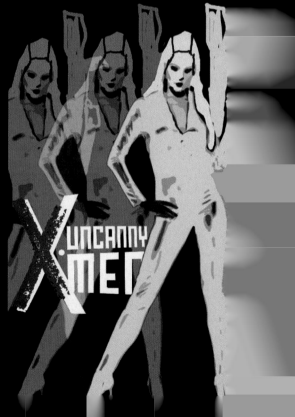

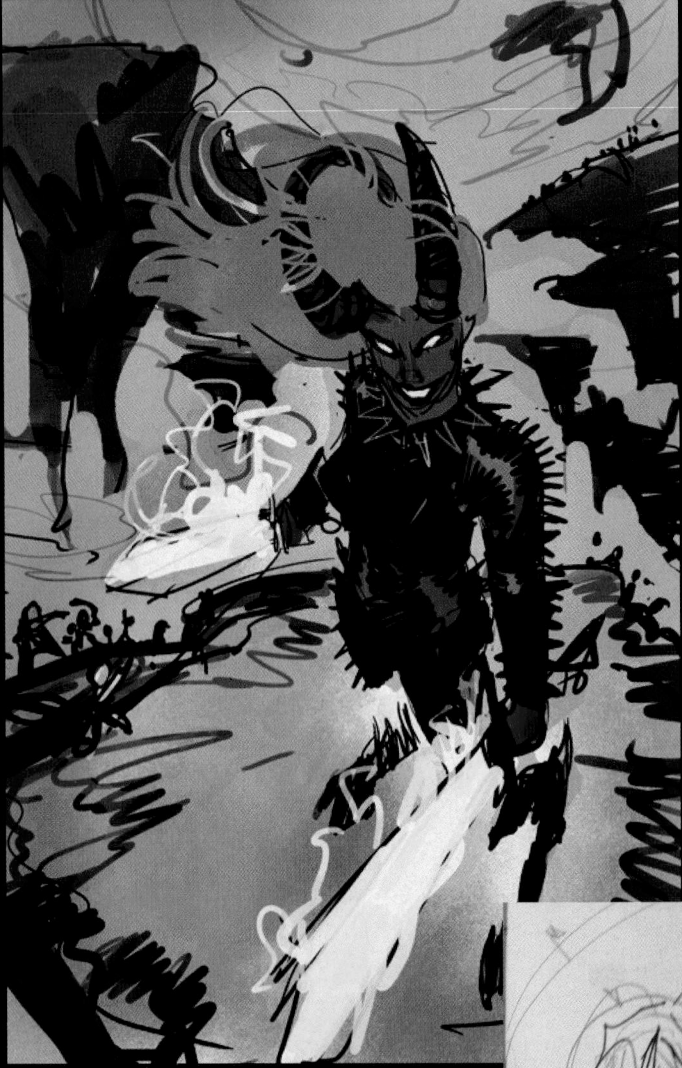

#7 COVER SKETCH BY
FRAZER IRVING

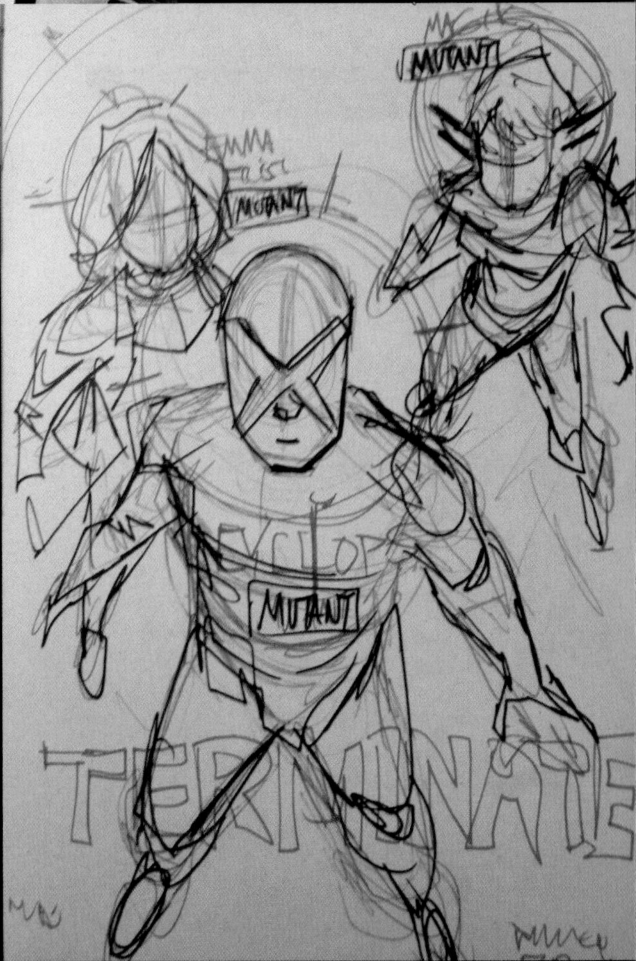
MUTANT
MUTANT
MUTANT
TERMINATE

#11 COVER SKETCH BY
PHIL NOTO

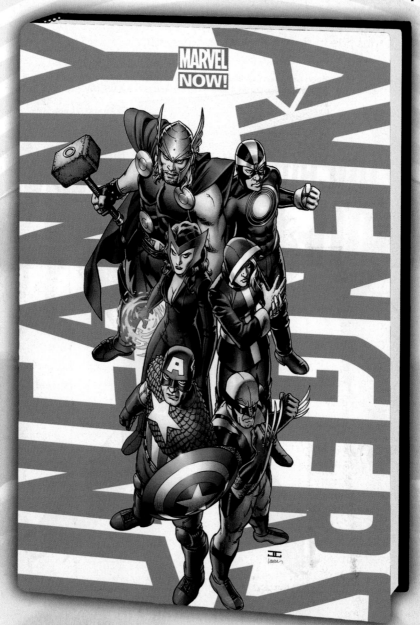

MARVEL AUGMENTED REALITY (AR) ENHANCES AND CHANGES THE WAY YOU EXPERIENCE COMICS!

TO ACCESS THE FREE MARVEL AR CONTENT IN THIS BOOK*:

1. Locate the **AR** logo within the comic.
2. Go to Marvel.com/AR in your web browser.
3. Search by series title to find the corresponding AR.
4. Enjoy Marvel AR!

*All AR content that appears in this book has been archived and will be available only at Marvel.com/AR – no longer in the Marvel AR App. Content subject to change and availability.